Creative
Campaigning

TRANSFORMING AMERICAN POLITICS
Lawrence C. Dodd, Series Editor

Dramatic changes in political institutions and behavior over the past two decades have underscored the dynamic nature of American politics, confronting political scientists with a new and pressing intellectual agenda. The pioneering work of early postwar scholars, while laying a firm empirical foundation for contemporary scholarship, failed to consider how American politics might change or to recognize the forces that would make fundamental change inevitable. In reassessing the static interpretations fostered by these classic studies, political scientists are now examining the underlying dynamics that generate transformational change.

Transforming American Politics will bring together texts and monographs that address four closely related aspects of change. A first concern is documenting and explaining recent changes in American politics—in institutions, processes, behavior, and policymaking. A second is reinterpreting classic studies and theories to provide a more accurate perspective on postwar politics. The series will look at historical change to identify recurring patterns of political transformation within and across the distinctive eras of American politics. Last and perhaps most importantly, the series will present new theories and interpretations that explain the dynamic processes at work and thus clarify the direction of contemporary politics. All of the books will focus on the central theme of transformation—transformation in both the conduct of American politics and in the way we study and understand its many aspects.

TITLES IN THIS SERIES

Creative Campaigning

PACs AND THE PRESIDENTIAL SELECTION PROCESS

Anthony Corrado

Westview Press

BOULDER • SAN FRANCISCO • OXFORD

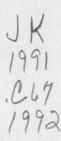

Transforming American Politics

Copyright © 1992 by Westview Press, Inc.

Published in 1992 in the United States of America by Westview Press, Inc., 5500 Central Avenue, Boulder, Colorado 80301-2847, and in the United Kingdom by Westview Press, 36 Lonsdale Road, Summertown, Oxford OX2 7EW

Library of Congress Cataloging-in-Publication Data
Corrado, Anthony, 1957–
    Creative campaigning : PACs and the presidential selection process
/ Anthony Corrado.
        p.   cm. — (Transforming American politics)
    Includes bibliographical references and index.
    ISBN 0-8133-1450-X
    1. Campaign funds—United States.   2. Political action committees—
United States.   3. Presidents—United States—Election.   I. Title.
II. Series: Transforming American politics series.
JK1991.C67   1992
324.7'8'0973—dc20   91-43588
                                                                                          CIP

Printed and bound in the United States of America

The paper used in this publication meets the requirements
of the American National Standard for Permanence of Paper
for Printed Library Materials Z39.48-1984.

10   9   8   7   6   5   4   3   2   1

FOR MY PARENTS

Contents

Tables

Preface

In 1974 Congress adopted the Federal Election Campaign Act. This landmark legislation was designed to resolve, once and for all, the inequities and abuses of the political finance system. The act completely restructured the system for financing presidential campaigns: it required full public disclosure of all campaign funds, placed limits on political contributions, established ceilings on campaign spending, and created a program of public funding for presidential elections. These reforms stand as one of the most significant efforts in American history to legislate political change. This book explains why the reforms failed.

The Federal Election Campaign Act dramatically altered the strategic environment of presidential elections, forcing candidates to conduct their campaigns within strict parameters. Presidential contenders, however, found it difficult to abide by the new rules of the game, because the law produced a conflicting set of strategic demands: some provisions of the law encouraged candidates to begin campaigning early; others encouraged them to restrict the length of their campaigns. Throughout the 1980s, as presidential campaigns became more complex and the financial demands of the modern nominating process grew, an increasing number of candidates decided that they could no longer resolve the conflicting strategic demands of the reforms and remain within the parameters of the law. As a result, the campaign finance reforms induced—and inspired—candidates to seek out creative methods of financing their campaigns outside the scope of the law. This book describes how they succeeded in their quest by using precandidacy PACs as shadow campaign organizations.

My central purpose is to describe how presidential candidates in the 1980s adapted their organizational and financial strategies in response to the changes in the presidential selection process that resulted from the campaign finance reforms and the party rules reforms of the past two decades. By doing so, I hope to explain the outcomes of the last three presidential nominating contests and illustrate why the campaigns of the 1980s were such long, drawn-out affairs. Such an analysis highlights the unique characteristics of the 1992 race and reveals the factors that are likely to cause the 1996 election to follow the patterns of the elections of the 1980s.

The idea for this book began during the 1984 presidential campaign while I was serving as deputy to the campaign manager and later assistant to the treasurer of the Mondale campaign, an experience that helped me understand the strategic problems generated by the campaign finance laws and gain an awareness of the substantial amount of time spent by political practitioners in attempting to fulfill the requirements of the law. For this experience I thank my friends Tom Donilon, who first encouraged me to become involved in presidential politics, and Tad Devine. Through three presidential campaigns they have supported my efforts and generously shared their extraordinary knowledge of the rules of the nominating process. Bob Beckel also played an important role in helping to frame the idea for this book, as did Michael Berman, who first introduced me to the complexities of the campaign finance regulations and taught me much in the process.

The research for this book would not have been possible without the assistance of Michael Dickerson of the Federal Election Commission's Public Records Office, who expertly guided me through the commission's files and indices and took care to ensure that the information in Washington was available to a scholar working in Maine. Other members of the commission staff, including Kent Cooper, Sharon Snyder, Bob Biersack, and Jennifer Fitzpatrick, also assisted with this study. Closer to home, Chuck Lakin of the Colby Library reference staff proved to be an invaluable friend and resource. Sunny Pomerleau of the interlibrary services staff helped locate materials. Ellyn Paine served as my research assistant for the past three years; her contribution is fondly acknowledged. I would also like to thank David Philbrick, Cynthia Hudson, Janet Boudreau, and Robert Lian for their assistance. Erik Belenky provided critical support in the final stages of the project.

Larry Dodd, the editor of the series in which this book appears, supported this project from its initial stages. His comments and insights substantially refined my argument. I am fortunate to have worked with such a talented editor as Jennifer Knerr. Her keen interest in this topic and thoughtful suggestions are deeply appreciated. I also appreciate the efforts of the others at Westview who assisted in the production of this book, especially Martha Leggett, who supervised this work through its various stages of production.

My thinking about American politics has benefited from the discussions and comments of my academic colleagues. My colleagues in the Department of Government at Colby College have provided the type of supportive and intellectually challenging community that every scholar seeks. I would especially like to express my gratitude to Sandy Maisel and Calvin Mackenzie, who have provided me with exemplary models of teaching and scholarship. Rob Weisbrot of the Department of History must also be counted among those who have influenced me. Marc Landy, Robert Scigliano, and Kay Lehman Schlozman of Boston College read the doctoral thesis from which this book evolved and significantly improved its content and expanded the scope of its inquiry.

I am grateful to Marlene Cameron, who very kindly allowed me the use of her summer home in Muskoka, Ontario, where much of the first draft of this manuscript was completed. Grace Von Tobel of Colby College was responsible for preparing the final version for publication.

I would like to acknowledge my parents, Jeannette and Anthony Corrado, for their steadfast support throughout the years. And finally, I would like to thank my wife, Lori Cameron, for the critical insight she has provided, along with her enduring love and support.

Anthony Corrado

1

Introduction

On April 25, 1985, less than six months after being reelected vice president, George Bush began his quest for the 1988 Republican presidential nomination. On that date, a statement of organization was filed with the Federal Election Commission for the Fund for America's Future, a political action committee (PAC) sponsored by Bush and chaired by Lee Atwater.[1] The avowed purpose of this group was to help elect Republican candidates and promote state and local party-building activities. The group's true purpose, however, was to advance Bush's personal ambitions: it was primarily created to provide Bush with an organization that could be used to raise funds for activities designed to benefit his future presidential campaign without being subject to the campaign finance limits imposed on presidential candidates.

From its formation through 1987, the Fund for America's Future raised over $11 million but donated less than $850,000 to federal candidates. Most of the remaining $10 million was used to pay office expenses, hire staff and political consultants, develop a fundraising program, sponsor political receptions, establish a nationwide network of state and local supporters, and finance state-level political operations. In short, the committee functioned as a shadow campaign organization concentrating its resources on activities designed to build a foundation for Bush's 1988 presidential candidacy. But because Bush had not publicly declared his intention to run, the monies raised and spent by his PAC were not considered to be campaign-related. These funds were therefore exempt from the contribution and spending limits established by the campaign finance reforms of the 1970s. The Fund for America's Future thus provided Bush with a significant head start on his 1988 nomination campaign and in the process allowed him to spend more than $10 million dollars outside of the limits mandated by federal law.

Bush was not the only 1988 candidate to recognize the value of a political action committee. By April 30, 1986, nine other presidential aspirants had organized similar committees in anticipation of the 1988 contest. These committees spent approximately $15 million, none of which was disclosed on campaign spending reports. Nor was Bush the first candidate to adopt this approach. He and other presidential hopefuls patterned their actions on the model established by Ronald Reagan, who began his successful 1980 campaign by forming Citizens for the Republic on January 28, 1977.[2]

Reagan initially established Citizens for the Republic as a means of disbursing $1.6 million in surplus funds from his unsuccessful 1976 presidential campaign. Rather than give the money away or keep it and pay taxes on it, he decided to convert his campaign committee into a political action committee and use the funds to support conservative Republican candidates and causes.[3] The committee sought to fulfill this objective by making contributions to Republican candidates who shared Reagan's political views, by providing assistance to state and local party organizations, and by funding Reagan's public appearances at events sponsored by candidates and various political groups.

Reagan and his advisers soon realized that this committee could also be used to conduct a wide range of campaign-related activities that would keep Reagan in the public spotlight and allow him to expand his political organization in preparation for a possible run in 1980. This insight became the operative principle that determined most of the PAC's subsequent actions. The surplus funds from the 1976 campaign were used as "seed money" to finance an extensive fundraising operation, which raised close to $5 million and developed a list of approximately 300,000 active donors, all of whom were likely prospects for future campaign contributions.[4] The PAC used some of these funds to hire a staff, cover administrative costs, and make contributions to Republican candidates and party organizations. Most of the funds, however, were used to retain professional consultants, finance political outreach programs, organize volunteer recruitment efforts, publish a committee newsletter, subsidize Reagan's travel and public appearances, and host receptions. These operations were aimed at increasing Reagan's presence in crucial primary states, improving his support among party activists, and maintaining his public visibility. The committee thus served as a scaled-down campaign committee, providing Reagan with the essential resources and services needed to launch his 1980 campaign.

More importantly, Citizens for the Republic offered Reagan a number of advantages that he could not have achieved as a declared candidate for the presidential nomination. Because the federal campaign finance laws set forth different regulations for PACs and candidate campaign committees, a PAC can be used to conduct financial activities that are prohibited in presidential election contests. Whereas a formal campaign committee must adhere to specified expenditure ceilings, there is no limit on the amount a PAC may spend. Citizens for the Republic could therefore spend as much money as it could raise. And it raised a substantial amount, largely as a result of the more permissive contribution limits established for PACs. Although an individual donor may contribute no more than $1,000 to a candidate's campaign, he or she may donate up to $5,000 per year to a PAC. Accordingly, over the four-year period of a presidential election cycle, an individual may give up to $20,000 to a candidate's PAC and still be eligible to donate the maximum of $1,000 to that candidate's campaign because the campaign organization is a legally distinct entity from the PAC. Citizens for the Republic thus provided Reagan with a means of accepting contributions that would be considered illegal if given to his presidential campaign. It also allowed him to avoid the strict public disclosure requirements established for federal candidates. Because the PAC was not legally affiliated with Reagan's campaign operation, he did not have to include any of the monies raised and spent by the committee in his campaign disclosure reports. Consequently, the PAC's greatest benefit was not that it allowed Reagan to conduct campaign activities before he declared his candidacy but that it allowed him to do so without having to be concerned with the restraints imposed on candidates by federal law.

Reagan was able to use his PAC as a vehicle for circumventing the presidential campaign finance regulations by deftly exploiting some of the technicalities embedded in the law. A prospective candidate, or any individual or group associated with a prospective candidate, may legally organize a PAC. The PAC is considered to be independent of any future campaign committee established by an individual associated with the PAC so long as the PAC or any of its members avoid certain activities specified by law as indicative of a formal candidacy. For example, a PAC may not identify a member or sponsor as a future candidate in its publications or public statements; it may not amass funds for a future campaign or use general public political advertising to promote that individual's future intention to seek office; nor may it attempt to qualify that person for a state ballot.[5] If a member of the PAC does engage in any of these activities, then the committee's actions may be judged to be campaign-related and its receipts and expenditures must be reported in the campaign disclosure reports of the individual concerned.

Reagan and his associates deliberately avoided any actions that would cast Reagan as a legally qualified candidate. While he served as chair of Citizens for the Republic, Reagan never publicly declared his intention to enter the 1980 nomination contest nor did he ever refer to himself as a candidate. The committee's public statements and written materials never explicitly mentioned a possible Reagan candidacy. Nor did the PAC amass funds for Reagan's future use in a campaign or attempt to qualify him for the ballot under state law. As far as the law was concerned, Citizens for the Republic's sole purpose was to assist Republican candidates and help build state and local party organizations. By maintaining this facade, Reagan was able to spend two years running for president in direct violation of the spirit of the presidential campaign finance regulations and the major provisions of the Federal Election Campaign Act (FECA). A new loophole in the campaign finance system was thus created.

Reagan's use of Citizens for the Republic revolutionized the way in which presidential candidates organize and finance their campaigns. By March 1, 1978, three of his prospective opponents, George Bush, Robert Dole, and John Connally, had created PACs of their own. The activities of these committees demonstrated that any candidate could benefit from a precandidacy PAC. As a result, the use of such committees rapidly increased, and they are now a central component of most presidential campaigns.

In each of the last two elections, a majority of the candidates for the presidential nomination have sponsored PACs as the first step in initiating their candidacies. These committees have spent tens of millions of dollars and facilitated an inordinate amount of unregulated campaigning. Candidate-sponsored PACs thus represent one of the largest loopholes in the federal campaign finance system. The use of these committees as surrogate campaign organizations is making a mockery of the financial restraints established by the Federal Election Campaign Act and raises serious questions as to the ability of the current regulatory approach to control campaign finances in the future. Why these committees have become so prevalent and why the present system has failed to control this abuse of the law is the primary topic to be explored in this book.

PURPOSE AND OVERVIEW

Since the 1976 election, the financing of presidential campaigns has been governed by the provisions of the Federal Election Campaign Act of 1971 and its subsequent amendments, which were adopted in 1974, 1976, and 1979.[6] These statutes were the result of a reform impulse that swept through the Congress in the 1970s, an attitude spurred by growing concern over the role of money in federal elections. Rapidly rising campaign costs, an alarming increase in the role of wealthy contributors in the financing of election contests, and the financial abuses revealed through investigations of the 1972 election combined to generate a wave of support for fundamental reform of the methods of funding elections. Congress responded by placing campaign finance reform at the top of its agenda and passing legislation that completely restructured the federal political finance system.

The most important of these statutes is the Federal Election Campaign Act Amendments of 1974. Although technically a set of amendments to the 1971 law, this landmark piece of legislation actually stands as the most comprehensive reform of the campaign finance system ever adopted. These amendments required full public disclosure of the financial activities of federal candidates, set strict limits on political contributions, established spending ceilings for presidential primary and general election campaigns, created a system of public financing for presidential elections, and formed the Federal Election Commission (FEC) to administer and enforce the law.[7] These provisions were designed to improve the efficacy of campaign disclosure laws, limit the influence of large donors on electoral outcomes, reduce the rapid growth in campaign spending, and minimize the emphasis on fundraising in presidential campaigns.

This book argues that these reforms have failed to achieve their goals and that a new approach is needed for the regulation of political finance. The Federal Election Campaign Act and its amendments have not fulfilled their purpose, which was to resolve, once and for all, the problems inherent in a private system of financing elections. Instead the reforms have simply encouraged candidates to seek out unregulated methods of funding their campaigns. Candidates have responded to the new regulations by developing innovative organizational and financial schemes based on legal technicalities that allow them to circumvent most of the law's major provisions. As a result, the ills that Congress sought to cure by changing the law, such as unlimited spending and the use of undisclosed campaign accounts, continue to plague the system.

This argument, to a certain extent, is not unique. In recent years, many scholars and observers of the political process have noted this unintended outcome of the reforms.[8] The common conclusion of these analyses is that the law is generally fulfilling some of its objectives but that its overall effectiveness is being undermined by a number of loopholes that provide candidates, individuals, and groups with a variety of means through which they can circumvent the law's proscriptions.[9] While a number of problems have been identified, most of the scholarly and public attention has focused almost exclusively on two types of unregulated activity, spending money independently[10] and using "soft money."[11]

As concerns presidential elections, both of these practices primarily affect the financing of general election campaigns. Independent expenditures are monies spent by an individual or group to advocate the election or defeat of a candidate that are disbursed without any prior consultation, suggestion, or coordination with a candidate or a member of a candidate's authorized campaign committee. Although an individual or group can spend funds independently in either a primary or general election, only a minor percentage of the monies spent in this manner have been disbursed during the primaries. Most of the groups or individuals who spend their own funds to advocate the election or defeat of a candidate focus their resources on attempting to influence the outcome of the general election. As Xandra Kayden of the Harvard Campaign Finance Study Group has noted, "typically, those organizations which made up the bulk of independent spenders spent somewhere between 80 to 90 percent of their funds during the general election."[12] In the 1980 presidential election, for example, approximately $10.9 million of the $13.7 million spent independently was devoted to influencing the outcome of the general election.[13] In 1984, approximately $17 million of the $17.4 million spent independently was designed to influence the general election outcome.[14]

"Soft money" is the colloquial term used to refer to funds that are not subject to the provisions of the Federal Election Campaign Act but are used to influence the outcome of a federal election. As with independent spending, soft money activities can take place in a primary or general election. In presidential elections, however, such funds are used almost exclusively to supplement the public funds available to general election candidates. This is commonly accomplished by using the national party committee as a "coordinator" for soft money activities. The national party asks individuals and groups to donate unregulated monies to state and local party organizations. These committees then spend the funds on activities designed to assist the party's nominee. National party committees thus use soft money to channel private funds indirectly into presidential general election campaigns.[15]

This emphasis on independent expenditures and soft money in scholarly and journalistic assessments of the shortcomings of the campaign finance reforms has played a critical role in focusing public attention on these loopholes and in clarifying their effects on the financing of presidential elections. But it has also served to minimize concern about the financing of presidential nomination contests. The general impression created by the current discussions of presidential campaign finance is that the major problems with the system lie in the area of financing general election campaigns. The tactics employed by presidential candidates to avoid the law during the nomination phase of the selection process have not been a focal point of public concern and have certainly not become a central issue in the legislative debates over the need for further campaign finance reform.

Indeed, since the passage of the Federal Election Campaign Act Amendments of 1979, Congress has devoted relatively little attention to the unresolved problems in the financing of presidential campaigns. Congressional debate throughout the 1980s has been dominated by the issues associated with the financing of House and Senate campaigns, especially the issues surrounding the increasing role of PACs as a source of congressional campaign income.

This obsession with PACs is evidenced by the campaign finance reform bills submitted in recent congresses. For example, in the 98th, 99th, and 100th congresses, approximately 173 bills and amendments were proposed that called for some change in the federal campaign finance regulations.[16] Most of these measures were primarily concerned with the financing of congressional campaigns. At least 61 of the bills contained provisions designed to limit the influence of PACs in congressional elections directly by requiring a ceiling on the amount of PAC money a candidate may receive (33 bills), a lower limit on PAC contributions (26 bills), or a prohibition against the bundling of individual contributions by a PAC (26 bills).[17] Approximately 29 of the proposals attempted to limit the influence of PACs indirectly by raising the contribution limit for individual donors (16 bills), providing tax-credits for non-PAC donations (10 bills), or recommending some other change that would serve this purpose (11 bills). Others sought to reduce the role of PACs and limit the cost of congressional campaigns by establishing some form of public financing (37 bills) or by allowing Congress to limit campaign spending without public funding (19 bills).

The problems that have developed in the presidential campaign finance system have received significantly less attention. If one were to base a judgment solely on the proposals submitted to these 3 congresses, it would appear that the legislature sees no urgent problems with the system or has been negligent in addressing its shortcomings. Although 43 bills included provisions concerning presidential elections, 32 of these were for the most part concerned with reducing the influence of independent expenditures, a practice that affects congressional as well as presidential candidates. About 20 bills advocated some other change in the current presidential system, with almost half of these aimed at repealing major aspects of the law, such as public financing (5 bills) or state spending limits (4 bills). Only 11 proposals offered a remedy for the problems posed by soft money, despite the fact that the use of these funds wholly violates the purposes of the Federal Election Campaign Act and has been a major issue in the press coverage of recent elections.

What is particularly noteworthy, however, is that the demand for further reform has not encompassed the unregulated campaigning that occurs in presidential nomination contests. Since the 1980 election, presidential aspirants have been evading the campaign finance regulations by using precandidacy PACs to finance campaign-related activities. Despite the extensive operations of such committees prior to the 1984 election and the proliferation of these organizations in 1985 and 1986, only 2 of the 173 bills included in this analysis, H.R. 2464 and H.R. 2717, which were submitted to the 100th Congress, included a major provision designed to end this practice. This clearly demonstrates Congress's failure to comprehend the extent to which candidates have relied on PAC operations to circumvent the law's proscriptions. Moreover, even if this problem had engendered greater interest, it is unlikely that a solution would have been adopted, because not one of these congresses was able to produce a majority in either house in support of any proposal advocating a significant change in the present system.[18]

This book represents an effort to expand our understanding of the effects of the campaign finance laws of the 1970s and refocus the current debate over campaign finance reform by demonstrating that the laws governing political finance have not only failed to control the flow of unregulated monies into general election campaigns but have also been ineffective in regulating the funding of presidential nomination contests. It does so by describing how presidential aspirants have subverted the regulations by using precandidacy PACs to finance their campaigns. Some scholars and a handful of journalists have taken note of this phenomenon and condemned the use of these committees by prospective candidates,[19] but their arguments have been based largely on limited data or anecdotal evidence. They have therefore failed to define the extent of the problem and provided few authoritative conclusions as to the overall effect of these committees on the system of financing campaigns.

This book provides the first detailed analysis of candidate-sponsored PACs and their role in the presidential selection process. The origins and proliferation of these committees in recent elections are traced, their financial and political activities are examined, and the strategic advantages that presidential aspirants hope to achieve by forming these groups are explained. This analysis thus reveals the reasons that most of the recent presidential contenders have established PACs and documents how these committees have been used to circumvent federal law and channel more than $40 million in unregulated monies into presidential campaigns.

An examination of the role of candidate PACs in presidential elections highlights the major changes that have taken place in the organization and financing of nomination campaigns. It also sheds light on recent electoral outcomes. One of the primary differences between the presidential contests of the 1980s as compared to those of the 1970s is that in the more recent period the preelection frontrunner won the nomination in almost every instance. This was not the case in the 1970s. During this period, lesser-known challengers enjoyed great success as evidenced by the victories of George McGovern in 1972 and Jimmy Carter in 1976, as well as by the serious challenge for the party standard waged by Ronald Reagan against then-President Ford in 1976. This ability of lesser-known challengers to mount competitive campaigns for our nation's highest office was widely viewed as a consequence of the reforms that were adopted in the late 1960s and early 1970s. These reforms created a more open and representative selection process and reduced the role of money in presidential campaigns by imposing limits on contributions and spending and by establishing a system of public subsidies to supplement private donations. These changes were designed to "level the playing field" and thus provide lesser-known challengers with a more equitable chance of competing against well-known challengers who often enjoyed strong support among party officials.

In the 1980s, however, lesser-known challengers enjoyed little success in the presidential sweepstakes, with the possible exceptions of Democrat Gary Hart's surprisingly strong challenge to Walter Mondale in 1984 and the victory of Democrat Michael Dukakis in 1988 (who won after the candidacy of the early frontrunner, Gary Hart, fell apart in the wake of intensive media scrutiny of his private life). The reason for this change is in large part due to the advent of candidate-sponsored PACs. Well-known candidates, especially Reagan in 1980, Mondale in 1984, and Bush in 1988, adapted to the reforms by forming PACs that could be used to capitalize on their public name recognition and broad bases of support. This tactic allowed them to avoid the level playing field dictated by the rules and thus gain a substantial head start in the race for the White House. That this was a logical outcome of the reforms is the central argument of my analysis.

My central thesis is that presidential aspirants establish PACs in order to resolve the strategic problems generated by the campaign finance reforms. These new rules of the game fundamentally altered the strategic environment of the selection process, thus forcing candidates to develop new organizational and financial approaches in seeking the nomination. Specifically, the reforms place conflicting strategic and operational demands on presidential contenders. On the one hand, some provisions of the law, such as the contribution limits and the public subsidies program, compel candidates to begin campaigning early and increase the length of their campaigns. On the other hand, the legal spending limits imposed on nomination contests encourage contenders to delay the start of their campaigns and restrict their activities. The campaign finance regulations thus present candidates with a fundamental problem in developing their campaign strategies: how to conduct the early campaigning required by the system yet avoid violating the expenditure limits.

This strategic problem has intensified throughout the 1980s as a result of changes in the delegate selection process. Party rules reforms have produced a "front-loaded" primary calendar in which most of the delegates to the national nominating conventions are chosen before the end of March. As a result, candidates must engage in an extensive amount of preelection-year campaigning in order to generate the funds and political support needed to advance a viable candidacy in this front-loaded system. In recent elections, candidates have found it increasingly difficult to fulfill their political objectives yet adhere to the financial parameters established by the Federal Election Campaign Act. To resolve this problem, presidential hopefuls began to search for ways to circumvent the restraints imposed on their campaigns. The best method discovered to date is to establish a precandidacy PAC.

By establishing a PAC prior to becoming a candidate, an individual can resolve the strategic problems created by the campaign finance reforms because a PAC's financial activities are not governed by the regulations established for presidential campaign committees. A PAC can accept large contributions that would be deemed illegal if given to a federal candidate. It can raise and spend an unlimited amount of money. And, most importantly, its expenditures do not have to be included on a candidate's financial disclosure reports or be allocated against a campaign's spending limits. This type of committee therefore provides a candidate with a means of raising and spending funds without having to worry about the campaign contribution and spending limits.

A PAC operation is particularly valuable to a prospective candidate because it can function as a surrogate campaign committee. Although the Federal Election Campaign Act specifically states that a PAC may not serve as a candidate's authorized campaign committee, this type of committee can undertake most of the activities that are normally conducted at the outset of a presidential campaign. It can be used to develop a campaign organization because it can hire staff and consultants, develop state and local subsidiaries, and recruit volunteers. It can initiate and develop a nationwide fundraising network through its own fundraising devices and direct mail programs. It can recruit support for its sponsor by financing his or her public appearances, party activities, and political outreach programs. A prospective candidate can thus use a PAC to accomplish all of the basic tasks needed to launch a presidential candidacy. And, by taking advantage of some of the technicalities in federal regulations, the PAC can fulfill these tasks without having to report the monies spent on these activities as campaign-related expenditures subject to federal limits.

Potential candidates who sponsor PACs claim that the sole purpose of these committees is to assist candidates and promote party-building. The primary reason these committees are formed, however, is to facilitate unregulated campaigning. Indeed, the amount of campaigning in recent elections conducted through PACs is so significant that no analysis of the strategies and tactics employed in presidential nomination contests is complete without a discussion of the roles and purposes of these groups. An understanding of the behavior of these committees thus illustrates not only how candidates have adapted to the increasingly burdensome requirements of federal law but also the extent to which these PACs have been used to undermine the efficacy of the campaign finance reforms.

CANDIDATE PACs AND
THE REGULATION OF POLITICAL FINANCE

In addition to highlighting the changing organizational and financial tactics employed in presidential campaigns, an analysis of candidate PAC operations provides a framework for assessing whether the government's current regulatory approach is capable of resolving the problems that persist in the financing of presidential campaigns. For more than a decade, presidential aspirants have exploited the PAC alternative so that they may raise and spend funds in defiance of the regulations. During this period, however, federal regulators have taken little action to prohibit this practice. Rather, the opposite has occurred. Instead of preventing further abuse of the law, the Federal Election Commission has essentially sanctioned the use of these committees by prospective candidates, even though they serve as a primary means of subverting the law.

One of the fundamental differences between the precandidacy PAC option and other major forms of unregulated campaign financing is that the growth of candidate PACs has been spurred by regulatory decisions issued by the Federal Election Commission. Independent spending is a result of the Supreme Court's ruling in *Buckley* v. *Valeo*.[20] The original provisions of the Federal Election Campaign Act Amendments of 1974 sought to reduce the influence of independent expenditures in federal elections by limiting the amount a person could spend independently to $1,000.[21] But in its 1976 decision in the *Buckley* case, the Court ruled that this limit violated the constitutional guarantee of freedom of speech and struck down the provision.[22] Individuals or groups seeking to influence the outcome of an election are therefore free to spend as much money as they desire to advocate the election or defeat of a particular candidate, provided that they do so without consulting or associating with a candidate or authorized campaign committee.

The soft money problem is, for the most part, a consequence of a decision made by Congress in 1979 when the Federal Election Campaign Act was once again revised. At the time, one of the primary criticisms advanced against the regulations was that they reduced the traditional role of state and local party organizations in federal elections and discouraged certain party-building activities. In order to redress this grievance and increase the role of parties in federal contests, the 1979 legislation exempted certain state and local party activities from the act's definition of "contribution" and "expenditure."[23] This allowed party organizations to raise and spend unlimited amounts of money for voter registration, campaign materials, get-out-the-vote drives, and other activities without having to disclose these funds to the Federal Election Commission. Presidential candidates quickly adapted to this change by learning how to rely on this exemption to channel unregulated funds into state and local party efforts designed to benefit their campaigns.

Congress and the courts, however, share little responsibility for the proliferation of candidate-sponsored PACs. These committees have become a common feature of presidential nomination campaigns largely due to decisions rendered by the Federal Election Commission in the 1980s that sought to clarify the status of these groups under federal law. These decisions approved the creation of PACs by potential candidates and expanded the scope of activities that these groups could conduct. Moreover, the commission ruled that the monies spent by a candidate's PAC need not be reported as campaign-related funds so long as the avowed purpose of the committee was to assist other candidates or promote party-building and provided that the committee avoided certain types of activities that would be viewed as indicative of a formal candidacy on the part of its sponsor. The commission thus honored this breech in the law by sanctioning the establishment of PACs by prospective candidates. Further, it provided these candidates with administrative guidelines that essentially told them how to structure their PAC activities in order to circumvent the law.

Most observers of the campaign finance system would argue that the experience with precandidacy PACs represents yet another example of the failure of the Federal Election Commission to uphold its regulatory responsibilities. Since its creation, the agency has been widely criticized for its unwillingness or inability to enforce the law. Critics, such as Brooks Jackson, argue that candidates continue to violate the law or exploit loopholes in the system because the commission "has neither the will nor the means to deter wanton violators" and has therefore "made the campaign finance laws a fraud on the public."[24] This lack of aggressive and rigorous policing of federal elections is usually explained by citing the commission's institutional characteristics. These include the agency's bipartisan structure (six commissioners, three from each party, which often results in tied votes that produce no decision); its lack of adequate resources (budget, staff, and enforcement authority); its unique relationship to the group it is supposed to regulate (the agency is charged with regulating congressional campaigns, but Congress determines its budget and legal authority); and the piecemeal approach to administrative rulemaking required by the agency's advisory opinion process and enforcement procedures.[25]

The commission's efforts to administer and enforce the law have been hampered by its unique institutional arrangements; my analysis, however, seeks to highlight a more fundamental obstacle to the effective regulation of political finance. The experience with precandidacy PACs reveals that the failure to prohibit this form of unregulated campaigning may not solely be a matter of a lack of will or means on the part of the commission. Rather, the cause may be an inherent problem in the law itself: the conflicting values and policy demands that the regulations force the commission to confront in carrying out its mandate to administer and enforce the law.

The primary goal of the campaign finance regulations is to protect the integrity and legitimacy of the electoral process. The law seeks to eliminate corruption in federal elections or the undue influence of money on electoral outcomes primarily by banning large "fat cat" donations and direct corporate and labor union contributions to candidates. This reduces the possibility of an individual or group using their ability to contribute funds as a means of unduly influencing the outcome of an election or gaining privileged access to a federal politician. More importantly, it reduces the likelihood of a legislative quid pro quo in exchange for a hefty campaign gift. The law therefore helps to ensure electoral outcomes that the public will perceive to be legitimate, which is a prerequisite for the maintenance of public faith in the electoral system.

The reforms further protect the integrity of the system by improving the accountability of political finances. The law eliminates the possibility of undisclosed campaign funds by mandating full public disclosure of all campaign finances. It requires that each candidate register one central campaign committee, identify any subsidiary or affiliated committees, and provide a complete accounting of all monies raised and spent by the committee(s). These provisions are designed to ensure that every federal candidate is held accountable for all monies raised and spent in conjunction with his or her campaign. They also seek to improve the public's knowledge of the financial aspects of federal campaigns so that voters can make more informed decisions when judging particular candidates. The law thus promotes the development of a more informed citizenry, which is essential to the proper functioning of a democratic society.

Another purpose of the law is to create a system of political finance grounded on the principle of political equality. The regulations seek to equalize the potential influence of individual citizens on electoral outcomes. This objective is based on the assumption that gross disparities in political giving (such as those that occurred in the 1972 election, where W. Clement Stone contributed $2 million to President Nixon's campaign while many others contributed $100 or less) violate the central principle upon which the electoral system is founded, the principle of "one person, one vote." This principle dictates that each individual have a relatively equal ability to influence electoral outcomes. The law is predicated on the belief that a campaign donation is comparable to a vote in that it can also influence electoral outcomes.[26] Individuals who donate funds to a candidate thus, in effect, engage in "a form of multiple voting; they seek to expand their influence beyond the single ballot to which all citizens are entitled."[27] By limiting the amount each individual may contribute, the law attempts to equalize the relative influence of individual citizens on electoral outcomes.

The regulations are also designed to enhance the equity and representative character of the electoral process by equalizing the resources available to federal candidates and reducing some of the financial barriers that might limit candidate participation. The Federal Election Campaign Act established aggregate and state-by-state spending ceilings on presidential campaigns and limited the amount a candidate may personally contribute to his or her campaign. These ceilings are designed to reduce the role of money in federal elections by restricting the amount a wealthy candidate may spend and ensuring that all candidates compete on a level playing field with respect to the maximum amount each may legally spend. These restrictions decrease the possibility of a wealthy candidate or campaign winning an election by simply capitalizing on an ability to outspend an opponent by a substantial sum, thereby essentially "buying" the election.

By improving the equity of the process, the regulations also encourage an increase in political participation. The limit on individual contributions forces candidates to finance their campaigns by soliciting gifts from thousands of small donors instead of a relatively elite group of wealthy contributors. This objective is reinforced by the public financing program established for presidential campaigns, which provides government subsidized matching payments on a dollar-for-dollar basis for contributions of $250 or less in presidential nomination contests.

Another way in which the reforms seek to broaden participation is by facilitating political candidacies. The public matching funds program is designed to ease the burden of fundraising, thereby reducing one of the barriers that might discourage individuals from running for office. These subsidies also assist candidates who do not have large campaign war chests by providing additional revenues that can be used to help such an individual promote his or her candidacy. This purpose is also served by the state spending limits, which were adopted in order to improve the level of competition in presidential primaries by preventing better-known and better-financed candidates from gaining an insurmountable advantage in a particular contest by dramatically outspending an opponent in that state.[28] The law thus improved the chances of lesser-known politicians entering the presidential race, which would in turn provide the electorate with a broader choice in nomination contests.

In addition to encouraging individual participation, federal regulators must also consider methods of increasing the role of political parties in elections; or at least they must avoid regulatory approaches that diminish traditional party roles. This policy goal arose out of the early experience with the reforms in the 1976 and 1978 elections. Analyses of these elections revealed that the regulations had served to discourage grass-roots campaigning and other party-building functions because candidates were unwilling to devote a significant portion of their limited resources to these types of activities.[29] The Congress responded to this problem by adopting a number of changes designed to promote party-building and volunteer activities. The most important revisions exempted funds spent on voter registration, volunteer programs, voter mobilization efforts, and certain other party activities from the legal limits on contributions and expenditures. These provisions, which led to the soft money problem in presidential contests, are designed to expand the role of party organizations and the level of grass-roots campaigning in federal elections.[30] By doing so, they may stimulate increased local participation and stronger political parties, two essential components of a democratic electoral system.

The Federal Election Commission therefore faces the unenviable and difficult task of trying to fulfill a diverse set of policy demands. It is responsible for controlling campaign costs, limiting the financial influence of individuals and groups in federal elections, and enforcing strict public disclosure requirements. It is also supposed to enhance the equity of the process, encourage political participation, promote the development of political parties, and pay homage to essential First Amendment rights such as freedom of speech and freedom of association. The problem is that these diverse goals are often in competition with each other. For example, stringent enforcement of the law may discourage participation because some candidates and donors may find the compliance procedures overly burdensome. Or it may encourage individuals to pursue unregulated and unaccountable methods of expending funds. Contribution limits reduce the influence of large donors but increase the costs of fundraising, which undermines efforts to limit campaign spending. Vigorous attempts to control political spending may inhibit the development of state and local parties by reducing the resources available to these organizations. Thus, in carrying out its duties, the commission is often forced to make relative judgments over competing values.

The problems inherent in this type of regulatory decision-making are clearly illustrated by the experience with presidential candidate PACs. These committees are established by individuals who are simply exercising their right of political expression. The avowed purpose of these groups is to promote party-building activities and assist candidates. As such, they enhance political participation, help to develop party organizations, and provide valuable resources to those seeking federal office. Yet, in recognizing the legitimacy of these committees, the commission has sanctioned an organizational alternative that allows prospective candidates to violate every major financial restraint imposed on presidential nomination campaigns.

An analysis of the operations of candidate-sponsored PACs sheds a bright and harsh light on the latest attempt to reform the campaign finance system. The role of these committees in recent elections highlights the failure of the current regulatory approach. Instead of enhancing the accountability, equity, and integrity of the process, the regulations have induced candidates to act in ways that undermine the goals of the reforms and threaten the legitimacy of the political finance system. The experience with precandidacy PACs demonstrates the pressing need to rethink the objectives of the current regulatory structure. The time has come for new approaches. And these efforts must be based on a more realistic understanding of the strategic and organizational pressures candidates face.

SUMMARY OF CHAPTERS

This book documents the need for further reform by analyzing the legal, financial, and political aspects of candidate-sponsored PACs. Chapter 2 provides a brief overview of the conflicting pressures that the campaign finance regulations place on candidates. It thus describes how the regulations have altered the strategic environment of the nominations process and why candidates have felt it necessary to pursue unregulated means outside of the intent of the law for conducting their campaigns. Chapter 3 presents a detailed analysis of the regulations applicable to different types of political committees and reviews recent Federal Election Commission advisory opinions relevant to the operations of candidate-sponsored PACs. This chapter traces the origins of the precandidacy PAC loophole and demonstrates how the commission's regulatory decisions have served to sanction the use of these committees.

Chapters 4 through 6 cover the operational aspects of PACs and the campaign-related benefits their sponsors' achieve as a result. Chapter 4 is an examination of the use of these committees in the 1980, 1984, and 1988 presidential elections and presents an analysis of their financial activities based on the disclosure reports filed with the Federal Election Commission. This chapter documents the growth of this phenomenon and defines the extent to which candidates have relied on PACs to raise and spend funds beyond the limits established by the Federal Election Campaign Act. Chapter 5 is an analysis of the financial benefits that candidates achieve through their PACs' activities; Chapter 6 is a discussion of the use of PACs as surrogate campaign committees. Finally, Chapter 7 covers the role of these committees in the organization and financing of presidential campaigns and presents an assessment of their effects on the campaign finance system. This chapter highlights the need for fundamental reform of the current regulations, and Chapter 8 attempts to answer that call with its suggestions for a program of reform designed to ensure a realistic and practicable system for regulating political finance in the future.

2

The Strategic Environment of the Modern Nominating Process

The changing political realities and turbulent events of the late 1960s and early 1970s produced a new era in American politics. During this period, the presidential selection system was essentially transformed from a loosely governed, closed process dominated by party leaders to a strictly regulated, open process based on popular participation and the representation of rank-and-file candidate preferences in the selection of convention delegates. This transformation was a result of the social and political turmoil generated by the Vietnam War, the 1968 election, and the Watergate scandal, which sparked a "virtual explosion of antigovernment sentiment"[1] and created a political climate singularly conducive to fundamental reform.

The American public reacted to the Vietnam War and events of the late 1960s by becoming increasingly disaffected and cynical toward the government. This attitudinal change was reflected in popular opinion polls, which recorded a steep decline in the level of public confidence in political institutions and elected officials. This erosion of confidence accelerated in the wake of the Watergate scandal because the investigations into the activities of President Richard Nixon's 1972 reelection campaign revealed illegalities and other financial abuses that highlighted the corruptive influence of money in elections. Consequently, public faith in the electoral process began to plummet while the demand for change continued to rise.[2]

Congress responded to this crisis of confidence with a wave of regulatory reform. Over a five-year period, four major statutes were adopted: the Revenue Act of 1971, the Federal Election Campaign Act of 1971, and the Federal Election Campaign Act Amendments of 1974 and 1976. This legislation completely restructured the federal campaign finance system in an effort to curb the spiraling increase in campaign costs that had occurred throughout the 1960s and prevent the abuses that had tainted the 1972 election. The Federal Election Campaign Act, as amended, strengthened the disclosure provisions of federal law, placed stringent ceilings on political contributions and campaign spending, established a program of public financing for presidential elections, and created a bipartisan agency, the Federal Election Commission, to administer and enforce the law. The Revenue Act established a checkoff provision on federal income tax forms for financing the public subsidies program and set up a system of tax credits for political contributions. The overall effect of these laws was to create a campaign finance system that held candidates accountable for their campaign monies, forced them to rely on small donations in financing their campaigns, and encouraged financial participation by offering incentives to individuals to make political contributions.

This period also witnessed major changes in the presidential selection process, an outcome of the Democrats' fractious 1968 nomination contest. This election created a deep rift in the Democratic party as the younger and more liberal wings split from the party leadership and coalesced behind the antiwar candidacies of Eugene McCarthy and Robert Kennedy. McCarthy's surprisingly strong showing in New Hampshire forced President Lyndon Johnson out of the race, leaving McCarthy and Kennedy as the main contestants in the fourteen remaining primaries. Kennedy won eleven primaries to McCarthy's four, but the convention delegates selected Vice President Hubert Humphrey, the party's heir apparent, who avoided the primaries and relied on his ties to party leaders to secure the nomination. Humphrey's victory demonstrated the unrepresentative character of the party's selection process and led the McCarthy supporters to demand reform. As a result, the party significantly altered its method of selecting a presidential nominee.

The changes adopted by the Democrats after the 1968 election established an open and representative nomination process governed by formal rules that shifted the ultimate responsibility for choosing the party's nominee from the party leadership to its rank-and-file membership. The new rules require that each state select its national nominating convention delegates through a primary or caucus open to all party members. The results of these contests determine the allocation of delegates among candidates: each state's delegates are apportioned on the basis of the percentage of the vote each candidate receives in that state's election. Presidential aspirants must therefore enter state primaries and caucuses in order to win delegate support. The rules also require that states hold their delegate selection contests within a certain time frame established by the Democratic National Committee. This provision, commonly called "the window," prevents states from selecting delegates before the voters have had a chance to assess the candidates. It is also intended to serve as a means of limiting the length of presidential campaigns since it concentrates the fifty state selection contests into a four-month period. Although these reforms were designed to affect only the Democratic selection process, the Republicans generally followed suit, especially with respect to the scheduling of primaries and caucuses. This occurred largely as a matter of convenience: it eliminated the expense and confusion that would result from separate party delegate selection contests held on different dates.

The reforms of the 1970s forced candidates to adopt new strategic approaches in their nomination campaigns. A presidential hopeful could no longer declare a candidacy late in the process, avoid the primaries, depend on large donors to finance a campaign, or rely on the support of party leaders to secure the nomination. Instead, candidates must pursue strategies that allow them to develop a broad base of financial and political support among the party's rank-and-file members. Such a base is the key to generating the large number of small contributions needed to finance a national campaign and to mobilizing the electoral support needed to win primary elections in various regions of the country.

The campaign finance laws and changes in the nominating process thus promote strategies that increase participation and improve the prospects for a representative outcome. But, as will be noted in this chapter, they also create strategic problems that are not easily resolved. The current selection process places conflicting demands on presidential candidates: the contribution limits and delegate selection system force candidates to increase the length of their campaigns; the expenditure ceilings require that they restrict their campaign activity. In recent elections, candidates have found it increasingly difficult to conduct the early campaigning that is required by the system and yet remain within the spending limits established by the Federal Election Campaign Act. They have therefore begun to pursue strategies that allow them to carry out their campaigns without being subject to the regulations. This chapter examines some of the strategic consequences of recent reforms in order to explain why the modern nominating process encourages candidates to seek out organizational alternatives that are designed to circumvent federal regulations. It thus highlights the strategic considerations that have inspired candidates to conduct their campaigns through precandidacy PACs.

THE CAMPAIGN FINANCE REFORMS

One of the primary reasons the Federal Election Campaign Act was adopted was to reduce the emphasis on fundraising in federal elections. Throughout the 1960s, campaign costs had skyrocketed, largely as a result of the increased role of media advertising in political campaigns. In the 1956 elections, the amount spent on political campaigns at all levels was estimated at $155 million. By 1972, total spending had risen to $425 million, or almost three times the amount spent less than twenty years earlier and significantly more than the estimated $300 million spent in 1968.[3] The costs of presidential campaigns rose at an even more rapid rate. Dwight Eisenhower and Adlai Stevenson spent a total of $11.6 million in the 1956 presidential election. In 1972, Nixon spent a staggering $61.4 million, more than twice the amount disbursed by his 1968 campaign committee, which had spent more than any previous presidential campaign in winning the election. McGovern spent approximately $30 million in 1972, or almost three times the amount spent by Humphrey four years earlier.[4] The 1972 presidential candidates thus expended more than eight times the amount disbursed by their 1956 counterparts, and there was every indication that this alarming trend would continue in the future.

The increase in the costs of campaigns led to a greater emphasis on fundraising since candidates had to devote significant amounts of their time to the burdensome task of soliciting funds. In an attempt to ease this burden and at the same time raise the enormous sums of money needed to finance their campaigns, candidates increasingly relied on large donors or "fat cats" as their primary source of campaign revenue. In 1952, 110 individuals contributed $10,000 or more to a political candidate. These individuals contributed a total of $1.9 million. In 1972, 1,254 individuals contributed $10,000 or more. These individuals gave more than $51.3 million to candidates. In addition, the number of individuals donating $500 or more increased from 9,500 in 1952 to 51,230 in 1972.[5]

This growing dependence on large contributors raised fundamental concerns about the health of the campaign finance system. Critics claimed that a system permitting such large donations encouraged intolerable inequities in the relative influence of individual citizens on electoral outcomes, led to enormous disparities in the resources available to candidates, and undermined the integrity of the political process. These issues became a focal point of public and congressional concern during the Watergate investigations because the inquiries revealed that President Nixon's fundraisers had accepted a number of extraordinarily large gifts, solicited illegal contributions from corporations, and attempted to secure donations by promising ambassadorial appointments, guaranteeing legislative favors, and offering other forms of undue influence.[6]

Congress took a major step toward addressing the problems of the campaign finance system in 1971 when it adopted the Federal Election Campaign Act, the first significant revision of federal campaign finance regulations since the passage of the Corrupt Practices Act of 1925. The 1971 law required full public disclosure of the receipts and disbursements of federal campaign committees, set a limit on the amount a candidate could personally contribute to his or her campaign, and established specific ceilings on media expenditures by candidates for federal office in both primaries and general elections.[7] But the experience of the 1972 election demonstrated that the revisions had not gone far enough. Congress therefore adopted a more comprehensive package of reforms, the Federal Election Campaign Act Amendments of 1974, in order to resolve the problems associated with increased campaign costs, the role of large contributors, and the emphasis placed on fundraising in presidential campaigns.

The 1974 legislation set forth a number of major provisions designed to restore the integrity of the system of financing presidential campaigns. It addressed the problems associated with large contributions by placing a limit of $1,000 per election on the amount an individual could contribute to a presidential candidate and limited an individual's total annual contributions to all federal candidates to $25,000. Donations from a candidate's campaign committee to other candidates were limited to $1,000 per election per candidate with no aggregate limit. The act also restricted the amount a candidate could personally contribute to his or her campaign by retaining the $50,000 limit enacted under the 1971 law.

The amendments imposed stringent ceilings on expenditures in an effort to restrain the spiraling costs of presidential campaigns and equalize the potential resources available to candidates. An aggregate spending limit of $10 million per candidate was established for nomination campaigns and a ceiling of $20 million per candidate for general elections.[8] In addition, candidates were allowed to spend an amount equal to 20 percent of the overall expenditure ceiling for fundraising costs.[9] The act also established individual state expenditure ceilings so that relatively unknown candidates would have an opportunity to compete effectively against better-known or better-financed candidates.[10] These limits were set at the higher amount of either sixteen cents times the voting age population of the state or $200,000. All of the ceilings are adjusted according to increases in the Consumer Price Index.

Another provision of the law sanctioned the creation of political action committees by labor unions, corporations, and other groups or individuals interested in raising and spending money in order to attempt to influence election outcomes. These committees originally developed in response to the long-standing legal prohibitions against the use of general treasury funds by labor unions or corporations for political contributions. Labor unions and other groups circumvented these prohibitions by establishing distinct committees with separate bank accounts to collect and distribute voluntary political donations from their members.[11] The 1974 amendments brought these committees under the purview of the law and established regulations governing their financial operations. These provisions included contribution limits that were less restrictive than those established for candidate campaign committees. A PAC may accept contributions of up to $5,000 from individuals and may contribute up to $5,000 per election to federal candidates. In addition, the law did not limit the aggregate amount a PAC could spend in a given year or election. In order to prevent candidates from capitalizing on these disparities, the act specifically prohibited any federal candidate from using a PAC as a campaign committee.

The most innovative aspect of the 1974 law was the creation of a system of public financing for presidential elections. This program was adopted in order to reduce the emphasis on private fundraising in presidential campaigns and allow candidates to spend more time informing the electorate of their policy views and proposals. A system of voluntary public financing was established for presidential general elections in which a major party candidate could receive the full amount authorized by the spending limit provided that he or she refused to accept private contributions and agreed to abide by the spending limit. Minor party candidates could receive a proportionate share of this amount with the size of their subsidy determined on the basis of the proportion of the vote they received in the prior election calculated in comparison to the average vote of the major parties.

For the primary election, the act established public matching subsidies for candidates who fulfill certain eligibility requirements and agree to adhere to the spending limits. In order to qualify, a candidate has to raise at least $5,000 in contributions of $250 or less in at least twenty states. Eligible candidates would then receive public monies on a dollar-for-dollar basis on the first $250 received from an individual, provided that the contribution was received after January 1 of the year before the election year. The maximum amount a candidate can receive in such payments is half of the overall spending limit, or $5 million under the original provisions of the act.[12]

Finally, in order to strengthen the disclosure and enforcement procedures of the 1971 act, the 1974 amendments created the Federal Election Commission, a six-member full-time bipartisan agency that was given the responsibility of administering and enforcing the regulations and implementing the public financing program. This agency was empowered to receive all campaign financial reports, interpret the statutes, promulgate rules and regulations, conduct audits and investigations, and take actions to ensure compliance with the law. To assist the commission with its tasks, the 1974 legislation tightened the reporting and disclosure requirements of the 1971 act and required that each candidate establish one central campaign committee through which all contributions and expenditures had to be reported.

The initial implementation of these amendments was disrupted by President Gerald Ford's delay in appointing members to the Federal Election Commission and by the Supreme Court's decision in *Buckley* v. *Valeo*, which deemed certain provisions of the law unconstitutional and forced Congress to adopt further amendments in the midst of the 1976 primaries.[13] The 1976 legislation modified a number of the provisions concerning the financing of presidential campaigns. It also changed the method of appointing commission members. The Court had ruled that the original process, which gave the president, Speaker of the House, and president pro tempore of the Senate the right to appoint two members apiece, violated the doctrine of separation of powers. The new law therefore called for the appointment of all six members by the president, subject to Senate confirmation and with the proviso that the appointments be bipartisan.

The law also amended some of the limits established by the act. The Court struck down the limits on contributions by candidates and members of their immediate families to their own campaigns unless a candidate had accepted public funding. Congress therefore reaffirmed the $50,000 ceiling on such contributions, but this limit only applied to presidential and vice-presidential candidates who had received public funds. Similarly, the ceilings on expenditures were retained but only applied to candidates who accepted public monies. The Court also ruled any limit on independent spending unconstitutional, so the amendments established a number of reporting procedures designed to ensure the public disclosure of independent expenditures. The act also increased the amount an individual could contribute to a PAC to $5,000 per year (as opposed to $5,000 per election) and stipulated that all political action committees created by a company or international union would be treated as a single committee for the purpose of determining compliance with the contribution limits in order to prevent circumvention of the law through the creation of multiple committees.

Finally, the 1976 legislation modified the provisions of the matching funds program for presidential nomination contests in order to ensure that these subsidies did not encourage a losing candidate to remain in the race.   Under the new requirements, a presidential candidate who receives less than 10 percent of the vote in two consecutive primaries in which he or she qualified for the ballot is ineligible for additional matching payments.   These subsidies are restored if that candidate receives 20 percent of the vote in a later primary.   The law also requires that candidates who withdraw from the nomination race after receiving matching funds must return any remaining public monies to the Treasury.

Once these issues were resolved, candidates and their advisers began to adjust to the law and abide by its proscriptions. All of the major party presidential candidates conducted their 1976 campaigns in accordance with the new regulations.[14] In the general election, both nominees accepted public financing and agreed to the expenditure limits that accompanied these subsidies. Since 1976, the law has gained widespread acceptance. All general election candidates have accepted public funding and acknowledged the spending ceilings applicable to their campaigns. Also, every candidate for the nomination, with the exception of Republican John Connally in 1980, has accepted matching funds and abided by the contribution and expenditure limits imposed by the act.

But despite this compliance with the law, many candidates have taken advantage of loopholes or organizational alternatives that allow them to avoid its proscriptions. This desire to circumvent the law is largely a consequence of the strategic problems generated by the reforms. The provisions of the Federal Election Campaign Act place operational demands on presidential campaigns that tend to conflict with each other. Some aspects of the law, such as the contribution limits, indexing of expenditure ceilings, and matching funds program, in effect require that candidates begin to campaign early. This need for an early start has been exacerbated by changes in the delegate selection process. But the expenditure ceilings discourage early campaigning because candidates who spend funds early risk having to restrict campaign activities later in the process in order to comply with the limits. The strategic implications of these competing operational demands are best understood by examining the effects of particular aspects of the law.

THE NEED TO CAMPAIGN EARLY

Given the current campaign finance regulations, presidential candidates must begin soliciting funds well in advance of the first primary contest. This is primarily due to the $1,000 limit on individual contributions, which forces candidates to finance their campaigns through small contributions. To raise the sums needed to mount a national campaign, a candidate must develop a broad base of potential donors and solicit tens of thousands of individual donations. This is a time-consuming and burdensome task, especially for those candidates who enter a campaign with a limited base of financial support. Candidates must therefore begin to develop a fundraising program and start to raise the "seed money" needed to initiate a campaign long before the commencement of the formal delegate selection contests.[15]

The most efficient means of performing this task is direct mail fundraising since this technique allows a candidate to make a direct, targeted appeal to hundreds of thousands of potential donors. Direct mail programs have therefore become an essential component of most presidential fundraising operations. But soliciting funds through direct mail appeals is expensive and usually requires lengthy lead times to produce the number of contributions needed to finance even the initial stages of a presidential campaign.[16] Consequently, even prospective frontrunners with well-established donor bases must begin raising funds early if they are to generate the revenues needed to meet the resource demands of the nomination process.

This need to start early has increased in recent elections as a result of the indexing of campaign spending limits. Under the provisions of the Federal Election Campaign Act, the expenditure ceilings applicable to candidates who accept public matching funds are adjusted to account for changes in the Consumer Price Index. Accordingly, the aggregate ceiling for presidential nomination campaigns, which was initially set at $12 million ($10 million plus 20 percent for fundraising expenses) under the 1974 amendments, had increased to $27.7 million (including fundraising costs) for the 1988 primary elections. The contribution limit, however, is not indexed: the maximum amount an individual can give to a candidate is still $1,000. Thus, in each succeeding election, candidates must raise a significantly larger number of contributions and devote more time to the task of fundraising if they are to raise the maximum amount that they may legally spend.

Early fundraising is also encouraged by the provisions of the public matching funds program. The eligibility requirements of the program necessitate the development of a fairly broad base of financial support since a candidate must raise at least $5,000 in small donations in at least twenty states. Whereas this is usually not a difficult task for well-known candidates, it can take time for a relatively unknown aspirant to meet this mark. Lesser-known candidates must therefore initiate their fundraising efforts early in the preelection year to give themselves time to build the broad donor base needed to qualify for the program and generate matchable contributions.

The matching funds program also promotes early fundraising because of the timetable it establishes for eligible donations. The law states that only those contributions made or received after January 1 of the year before the election are eligible for public subsidies. This encourages candidates to begin raising matchable contributions as early in the preelection year as possible. Candidates who solicit matchable contributions early, and do so successfully, normally receive a sizable sum when the Treasury Department issues the first matching payments in January of the election year. These initial subsidy payments can be a crucial source of campaign revenue and are particularly important in that they are received in the weeks just prior to the outset of the formal delegate selection process. A candidate, however, does not have to wait until January of the election year to gain access to these funds. If desired, an individual can, in effect, receive these funds earlier by using the Federal Election Commission's formal certification of matching funds (a document issued after each submission of eligible contributions by a candidate) to secure a bank loan for the amount accrued in public monies by posting the anticipated revenue or a portion of it as collateral for a loan.[17]

An early start on the solicitation of matchable contributions is especially important given the potential strategic consequences of such activity. Less well-known or well-financed candidates benefit from early fundraising activities because the matching funds they accumulate may help them to raise the sums needed to be perceived as credible candidates or to finance a competitive campaign in the crucial early primary elections. Or at least these funds can be used to secure bank loans that can provide additional "seed money" to develop more extensive fundraising operations.

A more important strategic advantage, however, may be realized by well-known candidates or others who successfully amass matching funds in the preelection year. These candidates will receive a large initial subsidy payment and may thereby achieve a substantial resource advantage over their opponents during the early primaries. The potential scope of this advantage is suggested by the initial matching payments issued in the 1988 election, which are summarized in Table 2.1. Among the Democrats, Dukakis had, by January 13 of the election year, amassed $3.49 million in matching funds, or approximately $1.5 million more than Gephardt and almost $2 million more than Paul Simon. Dukakis also realized a significant financial advantage, about $3.2 million, over his ultimate primary challenger,

TABLE 2.1
Initial Matching Funds Approved for Presidential Candidates, 1988

Party	Candidate	Amount Certified (million $)a
Democrat	Michael Dukakis	3.49
	Richard Gephardt	1.91
	Albert Gore	1.77
	Paul Simon	1.50
	Gary Hart	0.94
	Bruce Babbit	0.74
	Jesse Jackson	0.23
Republican	George Bush	6.16
	Marion "Pat" Robertson	5.53
	Robert Dole	5.27
	Jack Kemp	3.46
	Pierre "Pete" du Pont	2.04
	Alexander Haig	0.29

aAs of January 13, 1988.

Source: Federal Election Commission, *Record* 14:2 (February 1988), 1.

Jesse Jackson. The initial matching payments thus ensured that Dukakis would have the most money available to spend during the first weeks of the formal delegate selection process. The relative disparity among the leading Republicans was less substantial but still significant. Bush led all candidates with $6.16 million in certified matching funds, or approximately $600,000 more than Marion "Pat" Robertson and $900,000 more than Dole. Bush, however, gained a major resource advantage over his other challengers, amassing $2.7 million more than Jack Kemp, $4.1 million more than Pierre "Pete" du Pont, and close to $6 million more than Alexander Haig. The candidates who enjoyed the greatest success in soliciting matchable contributions in 1987 thus achieved an important financial advantage over their less well-financed opponents. The possibility of achieving such an important strategic benefit is the primary reason why candidates are eager to generate matchable contributions as early as possible.

This pressure to begin campaigning early is exacerbated by recent changes in the delegate selection system. These developments have dramatically increased the resource demands of the initial stage of the formal primary campaign, thereby making early fundraising a strategic imperative for every presidential aspirant. In this regard, two major changes in the presidential nominating process are of particular importance: the proliferation of primaries and the front-loading of the delegate selection calendar.

The reforms adopted by the Democratic party in the aftermath of the 1968 election required that all delegates to the national nominating convention be selected through open and representative processes. Many state party leaders believed that the easiest way to comply with the new guidelines was to select convention delegates through presidential preference primaries because primary elections permit broad and open participation by all party members.[18] Primaries have therefore become the predominant method of selecting delegates in both parties (because state law determines the selection system and most states are unwilling to support separate elections, the Republicans have generally accepted the Democratic rules changes in most states and followed suit). In 1968, there were 17 Democratic primaries and 16 Republican primaries in which approximately 37 percent of the Democratic delegates and 34 percent of the Republican delegates were selected. By 1980, there were 31 Democratic and 34 Republican primaries in which 71 percent of the Democratic and 76 percent of the Republican convention delegates were selected. In 1988, there were 34 Democratic and 35 Republican primaries, which determined at least two-thirds of the delegates in each party.[19]

This rise in the number of primaries has significantly increased the costs of presidential campaigns.[20] In order to appeal to the broad electorates eligible to participate in these contests, candidates have had to rely on television, radio, and other means of communication that can reach a mass audience. These forms of communication are expensive, certainly far more expensive than the approaches employed to solicit the support of the state and local party leaders who controlled the nomination process prior to the reforms. The increased costs of primary elections have therefore induced candidates to increase the emphasis on fundraising in their campaigns, which has intensified the need to start campaigning early.

The growing importance of delegate selection caucuses, especially Iowa's "first-in-the-nation" contest, has also driven the costs of presidential campaigns skyward. Iowa did not play a crucial role in the presidential selection process until 1976, when Jimmy Carter capitalized on the opportunity for media exposure afforded by this early event to catapult himself into the national spotlight and earn the status of a "serious" candidate in the race for the Democratic nomination. Since then, Iowa has joined New Hampshire as a focal point of media attention and a key stepping stone on the road to the White House. Accordingly, most presidential aspirants place great emphasis on "doing well" in Iowa and wage full-scale efforts in this state, using the same techniques for reaching the public as are used in primary campaigns. As a result, the costs of the Iowa campaign have risen dramatically. In 1976, Jimmy Carter spent less than $88,000 to "win" in Iowa (he actually finished second to "Undecided"). In the Republican contest, Ford and Reagan combined reported spending only $112,000. By 1988, a viable campaign in Iowa cost at least seven or eight times more. Congressman Richard Gephardt, the Democratic victor, reported spending at least $751,000 in Iowa; Senator Robert Dole, the Republican leader, reported more than $790,000. Moreover, nine of the candidates each reported spending more than $600,000 in their efforts to gain the support of Iowa's caucus participants.[21]

Changes in the nature of delegate selection contests have increased the pressure on candidates to raise large sums of money; changes in the scheduling of these events have made the financial demands of the process almost unbearable. In reforming its nomination process, the Democratic party sought to reduce the length of presidential campaigns by limiting the delegate selection period. The party ruled that all delegates were to be selected during a four-month period, known as the "window" for selection contests, which extends from the second Tuesday in March to the second Tuesday in June. A few states, particularly Iowa and New Hampshire, were exempted from this provision so that they could continue to hold their elections prior to the beginning of the "window."

Because early contests receive more media coverage and have a greater impact on the outcome of the nomination campaign than later contests, many states responded to this rule by moving the date of their primary or caucus to early March. Party leaders in these states felt that a move toward the front of the "window" would increase the influence of their state election on the nomination or at least ensure that their state received greater attention from the party's candidates.[22] In addition, in 1988, southern Democratic party leaders engineered efforts to schedule all of the southern states on the same day during the first week of the "window" period in order to increase the influence of the South in the nomination campaign, improve voter turnout, and promote the prospects of a southern candidate or ensure the selection of a nominee acceptable to southern voters. This led to the creation of "Super Tuesday," the Tuesday in the second week of March, which in 1988 witnessed twenty-one Democratic contests and twenty Republican contests.[23]

Consequently, the last three presidential elections have been characterized by a significant increase in the number of delegates selected in February and early March. By the third week in March in

1980, 29 percent of the Democratic delegates and 25 percent of the Republican delegates had been selected, based on the results of twenty-one state contests in the Democratic race and fifteen state contests on the Republican side.[24] At the same point in the 1988 election, 33 percent of the Democratic delegates and 42 percent of the Republican delegates had been determined as a result of twenty-seven contests in the Democratic race and twenty-five contests on the Republican side.[25]

This front-loading of the delegate selection process has not changed significantly in the 1992 election period. After the 1988 election, neither party made a serious effort to revise the primary calendar or to eliminate the unique position of Iowa and New Hampshire as the initial contests in the race. The Democrats, however, did adopt one rule change that altered the calendar. The party advanced the timetable for the beginning of the "window" from the second Tuesday in March to the first Tuesday in March and placed a limit on the length of the "prewindow" period. This revision was adopted in order to shorten the relatively long twenty-nine day "prewindow" period of 1988 that was produced by South Dakota's decision to hold a "prewindow" primary, which in turn led Iowa and New Hampshire to hold their contests a week earlier than expected. Under the revised 1992 rules, Iowa's caucus will be held twenty-two days before the start of the permissible scheduling period and the New Hampshire primary will take place one week later.

With respect to front-loading, the primary difference between 1988 and 1992 is that a few of the Super Tuesday states have changed the date of their elections and a number of states have moved to the first Tuesday in March. This will reduce the number of delegates selected in the first two weeks of March but will not have a significant impact on the front-loading of the process. A handful of states, including Colorado, Maryland, and Minnesota, scheduled their contests on the first Tuesday in March. At least five of the 1988 southern Super Tuesday states (Alabama, Arkansas, Kentucky, North Carolina, and Virginia) have moved to later dates. Super Tuesday will therefore not be as super as in 1988, but it will still be the day on which the largest number of delegates are selected. Overall, approximately 40 percent of the Republican delegates and more than 50 percent of the Democratic delegates will be selected by the end of the second week of March in 1992.[26]

Front-loading has drastically increased the resource demands of the initial stage of the formal campaign period. In order to compete for the crucial bloc of delegates at stake during the first few weeks of the process, a candidate must have the funds needed to mount an extensive national campaign operation months before the February Iowa caucus, which is the first state delegate selection contest. Separate state campaigns must be conducted in twenty to thirty states simultaneously, or at least in most of them, because candidates who fail to contest primaries will not receive a share of the delegates in those states. A candidate must therefore have the funds available to finance numerous state campaign organizations, purchase television and radio time in dozens of media markets, and cover the costs of traveling throughout the country while continuing to finance his or her national headquarters operation and fundraising programs. If a candidate hopes to accomplish all of these objectives, he or she must have several million dollars *in the bank* by the beginning of the election year.

Even candidates who hope to wage more "limited" campaigns by targeting particular states for intensive campaigning or relying on momentum from early victories to gain support in subsequent states must finance an extensive campaign operation well in advance of the first state contest because of the complex rules of the presidential selection process. Most discussions of front-loading emphasize the scheduling of elections and the need to run in many states simultaneously. But this emphasis fails to capture the true extent of the organizational burdens imposed on candidates by this phenomenon. Under the complicated procedures developed by Democratic reformers, candidates must complete a variety of organizational tasks long before the voting begins. They must therefore develop campaign organizations in states well in advance of the actual election.

The organizational demands of the delegate selection rules can be illustrated with a few examples. A candidate cannot compete in a primary or caucus without meeting the filing deadline and legal requirements to qualify for a state's ballot. In 1988, the deadline for qualifying for the ballot in at least twenty-nine states had passed before the final votes were cast in the New Hampshire primary. In five states (Virginia, New Hampshire, Illinois, South Dakota, and Maryland [Republican primary]) the filing deadline passed before January 1 of the election year.[27] In some of these states, candidates must file petitions or perform some other activity to qualify for the ballot. Candidates must also file affirmative action plans in some states or form and certify steering committees to demonstrate how they will ensure open participation and fair representation in recruiting delegate candidates. Other states require delegate candidates to file their candidacies very early in the process. Presidential campaigns therefore often have to begin the process of recruiting delegates in the year before the election. For example, in the 1988 Illinois primary, which was held on March 15, district-level delegate candidates had to file petitions with up to 1,000 signatures of Democratic voters with the

State Board of Elections by January 13. This forced presidential campaigns to begin recruiting possible delegate candidates as early as October and November of 1987.[28]

THE STRATEGIC CONSEQUENCES
OF SPENDING LIMITS

The pressures to begin campaigning early that are generated by the campaign finance and delegate selection reforms would not be of great concern to candidates if there were no limits on political spending. Without expenditure ceilings, candidates would simply adapt to the strategic and operational demands of the reforms by beginning their campaigns early enough to accommodate them. But this option is not readily available in a system that limits the amount a candidate can spend. The Federal Election Campaign Act's limits on aggregate and state expenditures are designed to encourage candidates to restrict the length of their campaigns and their level of early campaigning. Candidates who begin to campaign far in advance of the first primaries and spend substantial amounts in the preelection year may have to curtail campaign activities during the formal campaign period in order to comply with the limits. No candidate wants to face this possibility. Instead, candidates seek to limit early spending in order to maximize the amount they can spend in the primaries and caucuses. The current campaign finance regulations thus present candidates with a central strategic problem: how to accomplish the early fundraising and campaigning required by the process without violating the spending limits.

To a certain extent, the authors of the campaign finance reforms anticipated this problem and tried to address it by allowing each candidate to exempt fundraising costs (up to a total of 20 percent of the overall spending limit) when calculating the expenditures subject to the spending caps and by indexing the ceilings to account for inflation. These provisions were adopted in order to accommodate the additional fundraising costs that would accompany the shift to small donors as the primary source of campaign revenues and future increases in the costs of goods and services purchased by presidential candidates. But these provisions have done little to relieve the financial and strategic pressures these ceilings impose on presidential campaigns.

The problem is that the expenditure limits are not adjusted on a realistic basis that accurately reflects the factors that drive campaign spending. The advocates of reform did not fully anticipate the additional fundraising expenses that have accompanied small-donor financing. According to one Reagan campaign adviser, the general rule of thumb for estimating the costs of fundraising in the 1980 campaign was $1 for every $4 raised, or 25 percent; aides to other campaigns claimed the cost/return ratio may be even higher.[29] Nor did Congress account for the increased revenue demands generated by the proliferation of primaries and the front-loading of the primary calendar. The spending limits also fail to account for the rising costs of new campaign technologies such as polling, television advertising, and direct mail services, which have increased at a rate significantly greater than that of the Consumer Price Index.[30] For example, although the Consumer Price Index increased by approximately 40 percent between 1976 and 1980, the cost of such basic campaign items as mass mailings, television commercials, and air travel grew by 50, 100, and 300 percent, respectively.[31] The indexing of expenditure ceilings has therefore failed to relieve the pressures these limits place on candidates. Instead, in each succeeding election, candidates find it increasingly difficult to abide by these restraints as campaign costs continue to spiral upward at a substantial rate.

The limits are a central concern of every candidate because no candidate can accurately predict the overall resource demands of a campaign, the amount that should be spent in the preelection year to accomplish his or her strategic and organizational objectives, or the outcome of state delegate selection contests. It is therefore impossible to determine in advance whether a campaign will reach the limit in a particular state or approach the overall ceiling. Every campaign must therefore consider the potential effects of the limits when making strategic and organizational decisions. As Gary Orren has noted, "the stringent spending limit . . . has become a major strategic factor that preoccupies campaigns and colors most everything they do."[32]

The emphasis candidates place on the limits is supported by past experience. A few candidates have had to limit campaign activity because of the aggregate spending ceiling. In the four elections conducted under the act, five candidates have had to cut back significantly on staff or other anticipated expenditures or were reluctant to spend available funds because of the limit: Ford and Reagan in 1976, Reagan in 1980, Mondale in 1984, and Bush in 1988.[33] Reagan in 1980 and Mondale in 1984 actually exceeded the limit.[34] Six other candidates have effectively spent the allowable amount or come close enough to the ceiling that it may have affected their campaign spending decisions: Carter and Bush in 1980, Reagan in 1984 (who spent $20.1 million of the $20.2 million allowed by the law in an uncontested nomination campaign), and Dole, Robertson, and Dukakis in 1988.[35] That four candidates reached or approached the limit in 1988 reflects the competitiveness of the contest (this was the first election in which there was no incumbent in either party since the Federal Election Campaign Act was adopted) and may indicate that the aggregate ceiling will be of greater importance in future elections.

Although the state spending limits have generally had little effect on state campaign efforts, they have proven to be an increasingly important factor in the crucial early contests, especially in Iowa and New Hampshire. While it is difficult to assess the extent to which the state ceilings have influenced individual campaigns, an examination of spending patterns in recent elections provides one indicator of their potential effect. Table 2.2 lists the candidates who have reached the limit or spent at least 75 percent of the allowable amount in any state since 1976. It thus indicates the states wherein the ceiling may have impeded a candidate from spending additional funds as well as the states wherein candidate spending was close enough to the ceiling that excess spending may have been a concern.[36]

If the results of Table 2.2 are assessed in the context of a fifty-state campaign, the obvious conclusion is that the state spending ceilings have had a minimal effect on presidential campaigns. In 1976, candidates spent at least 75 percent of the allowable amount in only four states: New Hampshire, Florida, North Carolina, and Wisconsin. The only state in which the limit was achieved was in New Hampshire, where Carter and Morris Udall reached the ceiling and Reagan exceeded it. In 1980, candidates spent at least 75 percent of the limit in seven states: Iowa, New Hampshire, Maine, Massachusetts, Florida, South Carolina, and Connecticut. The limit was achieved in three of these states: Iowa, New Hampshire, and Maine. Howard Baker spent the limit in New Hampshire, and Edward Kennedy, Carter, and Reagan exceeded it. Carter and Kennedy also surpassed the ceiling in Iowa, and Carter violated it in Maine. In 1984, the Republican nomination was uncontested. Reagan therefore never approached any of the state limits. Democratic candidates met the 75 percent threshold in only three states: Iowa, New Hampshire, and Maine. But all of the candidates who met this criterion exceeded the state's ceiling, with the exception of Hart, who spent the limit in New Hampshire. Mondale violated the limit in Iowa, New Hampshire, and Maine; John Glenn in Iowa and New Hampshire; and Alan Cranston in Iowa.

Again in 1988, despite highly competitive contests in both parties, candidates achieved the 75 percent threshold in only three states: Iowa, New Hampshire, and South Dakota. All of these states held their elections in the initial stage of the process. South Dakota, which staged its primary on the first Tuesday in June in 1980 and 1984, took

TABLE 2.2
State Expenditures by Major Presidential Candidates, 1976-1988[a]

Election	State	Date of Primary	Candidates Spending Limit	Candidates Spending 75% or More of Limit
1976	NH	Feb. 24	Carter Udall Reagan[b]	Ford
	FL	Mar. 9		Ford Reagan
	NC	Mar. 23		Reagan
	WI	Apr. 6		Udall
1980	IA	Jan. 21	Carter[b] Kennedy[b] Baker	Bush Reagan
	NH	Feb. 26	Carter[b] Kennedy[b] Reagan[b]	Anderson Baker Bush
	ME	Feb. 10	Carter[b]	
	MA	Mar. 4		Bush
	FL	Mar. 11		Reagan Bush
	SC	Mar. 15		Reagan
	CT	Mar. 25		Bush
1984	IA	Feb. 20	Cranston[b] Glenn[b] Mondale[b]	
	NH	Feb. 28	Glenn[b] Hart Mondale[b]	
	ME	Mar. 4	Mondale[b]	

(Continued)

TABLE 2.2 (Continued)

Election	State	Date of Primary	Candidates Spending Limit	Candidates Spending 75% or More of Limit
1988	IA	Feb. 8	Bush[c] Dole[b] du Pont[b] Kemp[b] Robertson[b] Simon[b] Gephardt[b]	Babbitt Dukakis[c]
	NH	Feb. 16	Bush[b, c] Dole[b] Kemp[b] Simon[b]	du Pont Robertson Dukakis[c] Gephardt Gore
	SD	Feb. 23		Dole

[a]Analysis does not include Ellen McCormack, a candidate for the Democratic nomination in 1976; Lyndon Larouche, a candidate for the Democratic nomination in 1980, 1984, and 1988; or minor candidates. In 1988, Larouche reported $496,397 in expenditures in New Hampshire, $35,397 over the state limit (Federal Election Commission, "Presidential Primary Spending at $200 Million Mark," press release, August 18, 1988, 6).

[b]Exceeded state spending limit.

[c]Based solely on candidate's reported spending. Federal Election Commission audit of candidate's expenditures not completed as of November 1, 1991.

Source: Based on the Federal Election Commission's final reports on presidential campaign spending for each election and final audit reports released by the Commission's Audit Division through October 1991.

advantage of a gap in the delegate selection calendar and moved to February 23, a week after New Hampshire and two weeks before the commencement of the "window." Despite this prominent position, only Robert Dole spent at least 75 percent of the limit in South Dakota. Nine of the fourteen major party candidates, however, approached or achieved the cap in Iowa and New Hampshire. In Iowa, two candidates spent at least 75 percent of the limit, Bush reached the limit, and Dole, du Pont, Kemp, Robertson, Simon, and Gephardt exceeded the cap. In New Hampshire, five candidates passed the 75 percent mark; Bush, Dole, Kemp, and Simon each exceeded the limit.

Although the effect of state spending ceilings is not extensive and the number of states in which they may influence campaign spending decisions has declined in recent elections, Table 2.2 indicates that these ceilings are an important factor in the early contests that are essential to the viability of a candidacy and the momentum of a campaign. With the possible exception of the 1976 Wisconsin primary, which was a critical battleground in the 1976 race, and the 1980 Connecticut primary, which was important to Bush because he pursued a "New England strategy" and his father had represented the state in the U.S. Senate, all of the states in which candidates have spent or approached the limit held their nomination contests early in the primary calendar.[37] Of the states where candidates have spent or approached the limit, candidates must be most concerned about the ceilings in Iowa and New Hampshire. Since 1980, more than half of the presidential campaigns conducted in Iowa have approached the spending limit and 13 of the 31 major party candidates have achieved it. Since 1976, more than half of the presidential campaigns conducted in New Hampshire have approached the state limit and 13 of the 40 major party candidates have achieved it. Only two other states, Florida and Maine, have ever had their limit approached in more than one election. Reagan and Ford each spent at least 75 percent of the allowable amount in Florida in 1976, as did Reagan and Bush in 1980. Carter in 1980 and Mondale in 1984 exceeded the limit in Maine, making it the only state other than Iowa and New Hampshire in which the ceiling has been violated.

These data demonstrate that candidates cannot safely assume that spending ceilings will not affect their campaigns. This is especially true with respect to the early contests that play a crucial role in the nominating process. The data thus provide some evidence as to why candidates are so concerned about the spending limits. But they do not explain why candidates do not simply spend whatever amount they feel is necessary to achieve their objectives and, if this results in a violation of a spending limit, so be it. After all, the legal penalty for exceeding the limit is not unduly severe. The Federal Election Commission usually requires that a candidate simply repay to the Treasury the percentage of the amount overspent that it believes represents public funds. Because the final determination of a candidate's actual expenditures is based on the commission's audit of a campaign's disbursements, this fine is normally assessed a year or more after the election. For example, the commission's initial determination that the 1988 du Pont campaign had to repay $23,255 for excess spending in Iowa was not issued until March 1989.[38] By November of 1991, the audit reports on the Bush and Dukakis campaigns had not even been completed, so any violations were yet to be determined. Candidates, of course, want to avoid such fines, and this is one reason why they try to adhere to the limits. But these penalties alone are not severe enough or timely enough to explain the amount of attention candidates devote to the caps when developing their campaign strategies.

Candidates and their staffs constantly worry about their level of spending and the amounts being allocated against state spending limits because they fear the political consequences of excess spending. This aspect of the regulations, not the possible penalties, is the source of the almost obsessive fear of violating the spending ceilings that dominates the thinking of those who manage presidential campaigns. Most importantly, candidates fear the negative press coverage that would accompany excess spending in a state, especially if the limit was exceeded prior to that state's election or before the completion of the delegate selection process. Stories reporting that a candidate had "broken the law" or "failed to abide by federal regulations" might raise questions about a candidate's integrity or generate negative perceptions of a candidate among voters. Such reports might also encourage investigations into other aspects of a candidate's finances, which would divert staff time from other matters. Opponents may attempt to convert such stories into a campaign issue, thereby forcing a candidate to spend time and money countering these charges. This tactic may also distract the public's attention from other issues or policy concerns that are central to an individual's candidacy. Press coverage of a campaign's spending could thus result in a loss of electoral support and weaken a candidate's prospects for the nomination. No candidate wants to face this possibility.

Candidates also fear that they may place themselves in a vulnerable strategic position by spending too much early in a race. A candidate who spends large sums early may be forced to face a situation in which he or she can be outspent by less extravagant opponents in the final weeks of a particular state contest and thereby suffer a defeat. Or perhaps a candidate may have to restrict campaign activities in the later stages of the process in order to comply with the limits and thus offer an opportunity to an opponent to climb back into the race. Another concern is that the spending limit will become an issue in the press and lead to speculation that a particular candidate is at a strategic disadvantage because he or she will not be able to spend as freely as other competitors. Given these possibilities, all candidates must plan their campaigns on the assumption that the limits may affect their prospects.

CONCLUSION

The reforms of the 1970s fundamentally altered the strategic environment of presidential nomination campaigns. Changes in the campaign finance laws and delegate selection procedures resulted in an electoral system in which candidates must begin to campaign early if they are to fulfill the strategic and operational demands generated by the new rules governing the process. These changes, combined with the rising costs of campaign technologies, place great pressure on candidates to raise and spend substantial amounts of money in the preelection year. Candidates who do not accept this strategic imperative or fail to accomplish the early fundraising and organizational tasks required by the reforms will, in all likelihood, lack the resources and organizational development needed to wage a competitive campaign during the initial stage of the formal selection process. In other words, it is highly unlikely that they will win the nomination.

But candidates who attempt to accommodate the demands of the system and begin to campaign early may find themselves in a political catch-22 because of the conflicting demands of the campaign spending limits. Candidates who raise and spend substantial amounts of money in the preelection year may be forced to curtail their activities during the formal campaign period in order to comply with the limits and thus risk defeat at the hands of a less extravagant opponent. The experience with campaign spending in past elections is such that no candidate can be certain that his or her prospects will not be negatively affected by these ceilings. The reforms of the 1970s have thus created a central strategic problem for presidential contenders: how to conduct the early campaigning required by the system without significantly reducing the level of resources that can be devoted to state contests during the formal selection process.

The modern nominating process encourages candidates to pursue strategic and organizational options that allow them to raise and spend money well in advance of the first primaries yet maximize the amount they may spend during the formal campaign period. A rational analysis of this problem suggests that a candidate who can raise or spend funds outside of the spending limits may resolve this dilemma and perhaps achieve an important strategic advantage over his or her opponents. The strategic environment created by the reforms thus induces candidates to seek out methods that allow them to maximize their resources or ease the legal restrictions imposed on their campaigns. That is, the reforms encourage candidates to take advantage of alternatives that allow them to circumvent the Federal Election Campaign Act's proscriptions. Consequently, in recent elections presidential aspirants have increasingly relied on precandidacy PACs in order to resolve the strategic problems generated by modern reforms. Why they have chosen PACs over other options can be explained by examining the federal regulations governing different types of political committees.

3

Federal Law and the New Alternatives

A presidential hopeful can initiate a bid for the White House by establishing one of three organizational structures: an authorized campaign committee, an exploratory committee, or a precandidacy PAC. According to the provisions of the Federal Election Campaign Act, only the first two options are available to candidates; the law specifies that a PAC is not to be used as a candidate campaign organization. Yet because of the less restrictive regulations governing PACs, this type of committee offers the best solution to the strategic problems created by the modern nominating process. Consequently, presidential aspirants, with the assistance of a number of administrative rulings by the Federal Election Commission, have discovered ways to employ these committees as surrogate campaign organizations. The purpose of this chapter is to explain why the current campaign finance regulations encourage this approach.

A PAC is a legal structure that can be used to develop a financial and political base outside of the statutory prohibitions and limits applicable to candidate campaign committees. A PAC can be used to hire staff, rent office space, finance candidate or staff travel, print certain types of materials, conduct polls, sponsor receptions, form state steering committees, identify potential supporters, develop a direct mail program, build contributor lists, raise funds for other candidates, and engage in party-building activities. In effect, it can serve as a front organization for a prospective presidential campaign. More importantly, as long as the committee adheres to the technical guidelines that have been established to control PAC behavior, these actions can be conducted without triggering the legal obligations imposed on candidates by federal election laws.

A PAC thus provides a presidential aspirant with a means of addressing the conflicting demands of the nominating process. It allows a candidate to engage in early fundraising and organizational activities, thereby accommodating the pressures to begin campaigning early. Because the funds expended on these activities are allocable to the PAC rather than to the candidate's campaign committee, the PAC also helps alleviate the restrictive pressures generated by the campaign spending ceilings. The establishment of a PAC thus constitutes a rational response to the conflicting pressures imposed on presidential campaigns by the campaign finance reforms and changes in the nomination process.[1]

This chapter examines three components of the regulatory framework governing different types of political committees in order to highlight the factors that have led prospective candidates to pursue the PAC option. It begins with an analysis of the statutory provisions and regulations concerning contribution and expenditure limits in order to clarify the financial advantages afforded by a PAC in comparison to an authorized campaign committee or exploratory committee, which are the two organizational alternatives recognized for use by candidates under federal law. Federal Election Commission decisions regarding the use of exploratory committees, which established the guidelines governing activities by an undeclared candidate in the preformal campaign period, are then considered in order to identify the range of activities that a prospective candidate can undertake without being subject to the legal restrictions placed on candidates. Finally, more recent commission decisions, which apply these guidelines to actions initiated by a PAC associated with an undeclared candidate, are reviewed in order to establish the activities that a PAC may perform during the preformal campaign period. An examination of these rulings is important because it highlights the kinds of competing value choices the commission must often confront in issuing regulatory decisions. The examination thus helps to explain why the commission has not foreclosed the PAC option. Moreover, the analysis also reveals the extent to which the commission now sanctions what was once considered "loophole" activity.

STATUTORY PROVISIONS

Three types of organizations recognized by the Federal Election Campaign Act are employed by presidential candidates: principal campaign committees, exploratory committees, and multicandidate political committees. A principal campaign committee, also known as an authorized campaign committee or authorized candidate committee, is the legal structure presidential candidates must establish for their primary and general election campaigns. It is the committee designated and authorized by a candidate for federal office to receive contributions or make expenditures on his or her behalf. It is required by law to file periodic reports of its activities to the Federal Election Commission.

Any individual who becomes a candidate for federal office must designate a principal campaign committee within fifteen days of becoming a candidate and register it with the Federal Election Commission. A candidate may also designate other authorized committees, which also must be registered with the commission.[2] An individual becomes a candidate under federal law when either (1) the individual receives contributions or makes expenditures, either of which aggregate over $5,000; (2) the individual authorizes another person to accept contributions or make expenditures on his or her behalf; (3) the individual fails to disavow unauthorized campaign efforts on his or her behalf within thirty days following notification by the Federal Election Commission that another person has received contributions or made expenditures on the individual's behalf in excess of $5,000; or (4) the aggregate of contributions received or expenditures made in any combination of the first three circumstances exceeds $5,000.[3]

An exploratory committee is not explicitly defined in federal election regulations. "Exploratory committee" is the term used by the Federal Election Commission to refer to a committee that receives contributions or expends funds to explore the feasibility of a candidacy under the commission's "testing-the-waters" regulations.[4] These regulations exempt certain activities from the law's contribution and expenditure provisions so as not to discourage an individual from considering a run for office. An exploratory committee need not file with the Federal Election Commission until the individual for whom it acts becomes a candidate under established legal definitions.[5] If this individual does become a candidate, all contributions received and expenditures made by an exploratory committee must be disclosed on the first financial report filed by the candidate's principal campaign committee.[6]

Unlike a principal campaign or an exploratory committee, a multicandidate political committee is not intended to serve as an organizational vehicle for a candidate. Indeed, federal law specifically prohibits the designation of such a committee as an authorized committee for a candidate for federal office.[7] This type of committee is one of the legal forms of what are commonly referred to as "political action committees," or PACs.[8] A multicandidate political committee is distinguished from other political committees on the basis of three characteristics: (1) it has been registered with the Federal Election Commission for at least 6 months; (2) it has received contributions from more than fifty persons; and (3) it has made contributions to five or more federal candidates.[9] All of the political action committees associated with presidential candidates qualify as multicandidate committees under the law. But expenditures made by such a committee on behalf of a candidate or prospective candidate, if directly related to the campaign of a declared candidate or individual qualifying as a candidate under the law, would have to be allocated to the candidate's principal campaign committee or the committee would be limited to a contribution of $5,000, depending on the circumstances.

Consequently, when PACs are organized by prospective presidential candidates or individuals considering a future presidential bid, their formal purpose is not to assist their particular sponsors. They are not authorized by a particular candidate and do not receive contributions or make expenditures on behalf of a particular candidate. Rather, the committee is structured in a way that allows the prospective candidate to maintain a highly visible position in the organization. For example, the putative candidate serves as chair, honorary chair, principal spokesperson, or primary fundraiser of a committee organized to raise and expend funds on behalf of others.[10] This tactic accentuates the relationship between the aspirant and the PAC without crossing the legal boundaries that would cause a PAC to qualify as some sort of campaign organization or be subject to the limits established for presidential contests.   By paying strict attention to such legal technicalities, an individual can avoid the reporting and filing obligations imposed on candidates and circumvent the restraints placed on presidential campaigns.

PACs Versus Campaign Committees

A PAC is a more appealing organizational alternative than an authorized campaign committee because it is subject to less restrictive limits on contributions and expenditures. Presidential hopefuls establish PACs in order to exploit the financial opportunities that arise from these diverse regulatory provisions. Perhaps the most important relative advantage between a PAC and a campaign committee lies in the regulations governing contributions.   This advantage is summarized in the listing presented in Table 3.1.

A multicandidate PAC may receive contributions from individual contributors in amounts up to $5,000 per calendar year. A campaign committee may receive contributions from individual contributors in amounts up to $1,000 per election. Assuming that a presidential nominee will accept public funding for the general election campaign, a candidate for the presidency is limited to receiving no more than $1,000 from an individual contributor, regardless of the calendar year in

TABLE 3.1
Contribution Limits for Multicandidate PACs and
Authorized Candidate Campaign Committees Under the FECA

Type of Contribution[a]	Multicandidate PAC of Unannounced Candidate	Authorized Committee of Announced Candidate
From individual	$5,000 per calendar year	$1,000 per election
From PAC[b]	$5,000 per calendar year	$5,000 per election
To congressional committee	$5,000 per election	$1,000 per election
To presidential committee	$5,000 per election	$1,000 per election
To PAC[b]	$5,000 per calendar year	$5,000 per calendar year
To national party committee	$15,000 per calendar year	$20,000 per calendar year

[a]These limits apply to in-kind contributions (the value of goods and services provided to a campaign) and loans (until they are repaid) as well as direct monetary contributions. See 2 U.S.C. 431(8)(A) and Joseph E. Cantor, *Campaign Financing in Federal Elections: A Guide to the Law and Its Operation*, Congressional Research Service Report No. 87-469 (Washington, DC: Library of Congress, August 8, 1986; revised July 20, 1987), 26.

[b]These limits apply to multicandidate PACs. Under the FECA, a political committee that does not qualify as a multicandidate committee is subject to the same contribution limits as an individual contributor (2 U.S.C. 431[11]).

Source: Adapted from Thomas M. Durbin, *Legal Analysis of Specialized Multicandidate PACs and Private Tax-Exempt Foundations of Potential Federal Office Candidates*, Congressional Research Service Report No. 86-844A (Washington, DC: Library of Congress, August 12, 1986), 4-5. See also 2 U.S.C. 441a(a)(1) and (2), and Congressional Quarterly, *Dollar Politics*, 3rd ed. (Washington, DC: Congressional Quarterly, Inc., 1982), 26.

which the contribution is made, because the entire prenomination campaign constitutes a single election under the provisions of the act.[11] Through a multicandidate PAC, a presidential aspirant and his or her supporters can circumvent this limitation. An individual contributor may donate $5,000 per year to the PAC of a prospective candidate in addition to contributing to the candidate's authorized campaign committee once it is established. If a prospective candidate establishes a PAC in the first year of a presidential election cycle (e.g., in 1985 for the 1988 election), an individual contributor could conceivably donate $15,000-20,000 to the PAC and $1,000 to the campaign committee.[12]

A similar advantage exists with respect to PAC contributions. A presidential candidate may receive no more than $5,000 from a multicandidate PAC for his or her primary campaign, regardless of the calendar year. But the same PAC may contribute $5,000 per calendar year to a multicandidate PAC sponsored by the candidate. A PAC could donate up to $15,000-20,000 to a prospective candidate's PAC (assuming that a candidate establishes it in the first year of a presidential election cycle) and $5,000 to the candidate's authorized committee. In addition, the candidate's PAC itself could contribute $5,000 to the candidate's authorized committee.

A PAC also provides a prospective candidate with a legal structure through which contributions may be made to other political committees. Both PACs and candidate committees may contribute funds to other federal candidates, but a PAC may contribute five times the maximum amount permitted a candidate committee. In practice, this advantage is even greater. Whereas PACs are commonly utilized as a vehicle for making contributions to federal candidates (by law they must contribute to at least five candidates to qualify for the $5,000 contribution limit), authorized candidate committees are not. Every contribution made by a candidate's campaign committee to another committee depletes the resources available to a candidate for his or her own election. An active presidential candidate would thus rarely, if ever, make contributions to another candidate or committee, particularly given the resource demands of a presidential primary campaign.[13] If such contributions were to be made, they would in all likelihood be made after the candidate was no longer a viable contender for the nomination or after the nomination was firmly secured. But even this latter possibility is unlikely because general election concerns would discourage the reduction in campaign resources that the donation of funds to other candidates would entail. The establishment of a PAC is thus the optimal vehicle available to a prospective candidate for generating contributions to other candidates or political committees.

The one important statutory advantage with respect to contribution limits that a presidential candidate's authorized committee has over a multicandidate PAC is that an authorized committee may receive contributions in an amount up to $5,000 per election from a multicandidate PAC whereas these committees are limited to contributions from another PAC of no more than $5,000 per calendar year.[14] Accordingly, in an election year, an authorized committee could receive contributions in an amount up to $10,000 ($5,000 in the primary campaign and $5,000 in the general election), but a PAC could accept a gift of no more than $5,000 in the same calendar year. But as Thomas Durbin of the Congressional Research Service has observed, in a presidential election this potential advantage is unlikely to be realized.[15] Because a presidential candidate would generally accept public financing in the general election (as has been the case with every major party nominee since the system was established), a PAC would not be allowed to contribute funds to the nominee's general election campaign. As a result, the maximum aggregate amount an authorized committee would receive from a PAC in an election year is $5,000 (since the individual state primaries in a presidential nomination campaign are considered one election for the purposes of the law), an amount equal to the maximum aggregate contribution a multicandidate committee may make in an election year. But over the course of an election cycle, an authorized committee would still be limited in practice to an aggregate contribution of $5,000 from a PAC, whereas a PAC sponsored by a prospective candidate could receive an aggregate of $20,000 ($5,000 for each year of the cycle) from that donor.

A PAC also affords a prospective candidate a distinct advantage with regard to spending limits. With the exception of John Connally in 1980, every presidential candidate eligible for public matching funds has chosen to accept these subsidies for the prenomination campaign.[16] Consequently, each of these candidates has been subject to the aggregate ceiling on campaign expenditures and the state-by-state limits that accompany the acceptance of matching funds. A PAC constitutes a legal structure through which an unannounced candidate can expend funds outside of the expenditure limits applicable to declared candidates seeking public monies. So long as the PAC adheres to applicable federal guidelines regarding the allocation of expenditures, it can spend an unlimited amount without having to allocate any of its expenditures to the candidate's campaign committee.

One of the primary reasons candidates establish PACs is therefore to ease the campaign spending restraints placed on their authorized committees. Although most candidates spend significantly less than the law allows, an ability to spend money outside of the limits may prove to be an important asset for particular candidates in a competitive race or in the crucial early contests. A precandidacy PAC helps a candidate to realize this potential advantage.[17]

The experience with aggregate and state expenditure limits is such that candidates cannot safely assume that these ceilings will not be a factor in their campaigns. This is especially the case with respect to early contests such as Iowa and New Hampshire, which play a crucial role in the nomination process. Funds expended by a PAC in the preformal campaign period, which are not allocable to a candidate's campaign committee, in effect supplement the resources expended during the nomination contest and mitigate the effect of expenditure limits in a number of ways. PAC spending facilitates a circumvention of the expenditure ceilings, which may allow a candidate to outspend opponents in a given state or in the election. It also helps minimize the amount of allocable funds reported by a candidate prior to a particular state contest, thereby reducing the possibility that the spending limit will become a focal point of press attention during the primary campaign. Finally, effective use of a PAC can help a candidate avoid violations of the law or at least reduce the amount of excess spending, which reduces the amount of any repayment penalties assessed by the Federal Election Commission for violating the limits. Given past experience, candidate perceptions, the importance of a successful campaign in the early primary contests, and the potential spending advantage that can be achieved, the establishment of a PAC is a rational response to the strategic problem generated by the expenditure ceilings.

One final advantage a multicandidate committee offers a prospective candidate is the ability to establish and utilize nonfederal financial accounts. Any PAC or campaign committee organized at the federal level must designate a depository(ies) for all funds and disclose its location to the Federal Election Commission.[18] A depository so designated constitutes the receptacle for contributions received by the committee for activities associated with federal elections. Contributions deposited in this account must meet the requirements of federal law and be reported on committee public disclosure statements. All funds disbursed from such a depository must adhere to the expenditure provisions of the law and must also be reported. Since presidential campaign committees are by definition only involved in federal elections, they are restricted to federal financial accounts. This restriction does not apply, however, to multicandidate committees under the Federal Election Commission's interpretation of campaign finance rules.[19]

A PAC may establish nonfederal accounts to raise funds and make contributions to state and local candidates or state and local party committees. These accounts need not be registered with the Federal Election Commission if they are kept entirely separate from any federal accounts the committee may have and if they are created solely for the purpose of financing political activity in connection with state or local elections. Such accounts are subject to the provisions of election laws in the respective states in which activities are being conducted. Such accounts thus provide a PAC with a means of shifting campaign finance activities from the sphere of federal regulation to the orbit of state laws.

State campaign finance laws, in general, are less rigorous than federal regulations. In most states, the restrictions applied to political contributions are more lenient than federal guidelines, and in many states, there are no limits whatsoever.[20] Twenty-nine states allow unlimited contributions by political action committees in state and local elections. Three others, Ohio, New Jersey, and Mississippi, allow unlimited contributions with exceptions. In Ohio, contributions by corporate political action committees are prohibited, but contributions by other types of committees are unlimited. In New Jersey, primary and general election campaigns for governor are partially financed by public funds, so political action committees are limited to contributions of no more than $800 per election to gubernatorial candidates. In Mississippi, contributions are unlimited except for contributions to judicial office primary candidates, which are limited to $250. In those states that do limit PAC contributions, only eleven set a limit lower than that established by federal law.[21]

Most states have also failed to adopt the federal restriction against corporate and union contributions.[22] Only twenty states prohibit corporate contributions (two of the twenty limit the prohibition to contributions to candidates) and only ten states prohibit contributions by labor unions. Twenty-seven states forbid contributions by any utility or business regulated by the state.[23] Overall, eleven states have no contribution limits and no proscription against contributions by corporations, labor unions, or regulated industries: California, Idaho, Illinois, Louisiana, Missouri, Nebraska, Nevada, New Mexico, Rhode Island, Utah, and Virginia. Another five states without contribution limits prohibit or otherwise restrict only contributions by regulated industries: Alabama, Colorado, Georgia, Oregon, and South Carolina. Six states allow unlimited contributions by political action committees but forbid corporate and union contributions: Arizona, North Dakota, Pennsylvania, South Dakota, Texas, and Wyoming.[24]

Because nonfederal accounts are governed by applicable state laws (so long as the funds are segregated from a committee's federal accounts and disbursed solely for state and local political activities), they provide a multicandidate committee with a number of avenues for avoiding the proscriptions of federal regulations. First, in a majority of states, a committee can contribute an unlimited amount from its nonfederal accounts to a state or local candidate, political committee, or party organization. Federal accounts are governed by federal law, which limits contributions to these recipients to amounts no greater than $5,000.

Second, in states that allow them, PACs can solicit and receive contributions that are considered illegal in federal elections. In states without contribution limits, a committee with a nonfederal account can receive contributions into this account that exceed the amounts permitted at the federal level. More importantly, this committee can receive contributions from sources that are banned under federal law. A majority of states allow contributions from corporations, labor unions, and regulated industries in limited or unlimited amounts. None of these sources are allowed to make contributions at the federal level. By establishing nonfederal accounts, a PAC can solicit these gifts and employ them in state and local political campaigns.

Third, a multicandidate PAC can undertake these activities without having to abide by the strict disclosure and reporting requirements of the Federal Election Campaign Act. If nonfederal financial activity is being conducted through a federal account or joint federal/nonfederal account, it must be reported to the Federal Election Commission. But if these transactions are independent of federal accounts and only used in connection with state and local activities, they are subject only to state disclosure and reporting requirements. Every state requires some form of campaign finance reporting from at least some candidates and political committees.[25] But these regulations are often not as stringent as those mandated by federal law, nor is the information they contain as accessible.

State reporting requirements vary greatly, especially regarding frequency of reporting and deadlines; but in the long run the major test of any reporting law is the availability of the data the candidates and committees report. Despite the universality of reporting, a survey of state statutes conducted by political scientist Frank Sorauf revealed that only twenty-two states publish aggregate data on receipts and expenditures.[26] The obstacle reporting requirements pose to those seeking information on the nonfederal activities of multicandidate committees is highlighted by Teresa Riordan, who notes that "often, the only way to discover whether these secretive accounts exist is either by sheer accident or by methodically searching for discrepancies between disclosure forms filed with the Federal Election Commission and those filed with state election offices."[27]

A nonfederal account provides a multicandidate committee with a means of expanding its contributor base, increasing its revenue potential, and enhancing its role in state and local elections. It is a legal mechanism that expands a committee's capacities beyond the parameters set by federal statute and that facilitates the receipt and disbursement of funds that would be deemed illegal in federal elections. Moreover, much of this activity can be conducted relatively free of public scrutiny. The establishment of such an account(s) thus augments the substantial statutory advantages a multicandidate committee is granted in comparison to an authorized candidate committee.

PACs Versus Exploratory Committees

Individuals who have not announced their candidacy for the presidential nomination may also choose to form an exploratory committee prior to authorizing a principal campaign committee. This type of committee is governed by the "testing-the-waters" regulations established by the Federal Election Commission.[28] These regulations were adopted to ensure "that an individual is not discouraged from 'testing-the-waters' to determine whether his [or her] candidacy is feasible."[29] They are designed to distinguish activities directed to an evaluation of the desirability and feasibility of a candidacy from conduct signifying that a private decision to become a candidate has been made.[30]

The key feature of the "testing-the-waters" regulations is that they establish exceptions to the provisions of the Federal Election Campaign Act for the purpose of allowing an individual to determine whether to become a federal candidate. The rules essentially exclude certain contributions and expenditures made to consider a possible candidacy from the legal definitions of "contribution" and "expenditure," permit certain activities to test the feasibility of a candidacy, and exempt candidates or committees engaged in such activities from the law's filing and reporting requirements during the testing period.

The regulation that exempts exploratory committee receipts from the definition of contribution provides that

Funds received solely for the purpose of determining whether an individual should become a candidate are not contributions. Examples of activities permissible under this exemption if they are conducted to determine whether an individual should become a candidate include, but are not limited to, conducting a poll, telephone calls, and travel. Only funds permissible under the Act may be used for such activities. The individual shall keep records of all such funds received. . . . If the individual subsequently becomes a candidate, the funds received are contributions subject to the reporting requirements of the Act. Such contributions must be reported with the first report filed by the principal campaign committee of the candidate, regardless of the date the funds were received.[31]

A parallel exemption from the definition of expenditure is included in the subsequent section of the regulations.[32] The commission originally set forth regulations to allow an individual or committee examining the feasibility of a candidacy to receive and expend funds that would otherwise be prohibited by federal law. In a number of administrative rulings in the early 1980s, the commission declared that the prohibitions, limitations, and requirements of the Federal Election

Campaign Act are applicable to funds received by an exploratory committee only after an individual becomes a candidate within the meaning of the statute.[33] An exploratory committee could therefore receive contributions from prohibited sources or in amounts beyond prescribed limits for testing-the-waters activities. Corporations and labor unions presumably could provide the seed money needed to initiate an exploratory effort. Wealthy individuals or the prospective candidate could contribute unlimited amounts.[34] When an individual became a candidate, his or her principal campaign committee was required to refund or repay any excessive or prohibited contributions previously received. These refunds or repayments had to be made within ten days after the individual became a candidate. All contributions received in connection with testing-the-waters activities and any repayments had to be disclosed on the first report filed by the candidate's principal campaign committee.[35]

In 1985 the commission revised the rules governing testing-the-waters activities in order to resolve the discrepancy between an exploratory committee and an authorized candidate committee with respect to allowable contributions and expenditures. The new regulations apply the contribution limits and prohibitions of the law to funds used to determine whether to run for office, regardless of whether the individual eventually becomes a candidate.[36] As of July 1, 1985 (the date the regulations took effect), an individual or exploratory committee may not accept unlawful contributions (either prohibited or excessive). A candidate or committee receiving such contributions prior to July 1 had to refund and report the contributions in accordance with the original regulation.[37]

An exploratory committee thus provides little relief to aspirants concerned with the strategic problems generated by the campaign finance laws. Under the revised regulations, an exploratory committee is essentially subject to the same restrictions as a campaign committee. It thus shares all of the relative disadvantages that exist between a campaign committee and a PAC. The only major advantage it holds over a campaign committee is that it does not have to file public disclosure reports unless the individual with which it is associated decides to become a candidate. This proviso was adopted to ensure that the reporting requirements do not serve to discourage an individual from considering a candidacy. But the regulations promulgated in 1985 require that an individual or his or her exploratory committee "keep records of the name of each contributor, the date of receipt and amount of all contributions received, and all expenditures made in connection with activities conducted [to test the waters] or the individual's campaign prior to becoming a candidate."[38] These contributions and expenditures must be disclosed on the first report filed by an individual's campaign committee. As a result, the advantage with respect to the law's reporting and disclosure requirements that a prospective candidate may obtain by establishing an exploratory committee is minimal.

Prior to the promulgation of the 1985 regulations, an exploratory committee offered a prospective candidate an advantage in raising seed money. An individual engaged in testing-the-waters activities could solicit contributions that are considered illegal under the statutory regulations governing federal candidates. Contributions of this sort, however, had to be refunded once an individual became a candidate. Since the adoption of the new regulations, an exploratory committee is subject to the same contribution limits as an authorized committee and any contributions it receives are allocable to an individual's campaign committee unless they qualify as exempt contributions (e.g., in-kind contributions related to party-building activities received prior to an individual's qualifying as a candidate). Likewise, any expenditures made by an exploratory committee are allocable to an individual's campaign committee unless they qualify as nonallocable expenses (e.g., expenses related to party-building activities made prior to an individual's qualifying as a candidate). Any allocable expenditures are applied to the overall and state spending ceilings imposed on authorized campaign committees accepting public funds. The exploratory committee alternative is therefore of limited benefit to a prospective candidate with respect to the act's contribution and expenditure limits.

While the Federal Election Commission has adopted a firm stance with respect to contributions, it has been less restrictive in defining the activities allowed under the testing-the-waters exemption. Permissable activities set forth in the regulations include, but are not limited to, expenses incurred to conduct a poll, make telephone calls, and travel.[39] The open-ended nature of this provision has led a number of candidates to seek clarification of its meaning. As a result, the scope of this provision has been significantly expanded by a string of advisory opinion rulings issued by the commission.

FEC RULINGS ON
EXPLORATORY ACTIVITIES

The advisory opinion procedure is the primary means employed by the Federal Election Commission to apply federal regulations to particular situations and encourage compliance with the law. This procedure allows any person affected by the Federal Election Campaign

Act or commission regulations, or an agent authorized by that person, to request the commission's advice on a specific activity pertaining to the law. Such a request must concern the application of the regulations to a specific transaction or activity involving the requester; it may not pertain to a general question of interpretation, a hypothetical situation, or a matter raised in regard to the activities of a third party who is not represented in the request. The law directs the commission to respond to a qualified request within sixty days of its receipt or within twenty days if the request is submitted by a candidate or campaign committee within sixty days of an election. The commission responds in an advisory opinion, which is a binding legal opinion drafted by the commission's legal staff and presented to the six commissioners for their consideration. An advisory opinion is issued only when it has been approved by at least four commissioners.[40]

Advisory opinions fulfill an important regulatory function in that they set forth the commission's interpretation of federal laws as applied to particular actions that are usually not specified in federal statutes or regulations. An advisory opinion thus serves two important purposes: it provides legal protection for the individual(s) who has made the request and it clarifies the law for persons who are in the same situation as the requester. Since 1981, prospective candidates have relied on this procedure to determine the activities that can be legitimately conducted under the testing-the-waters regulations and to define the role of PACs associated with potential candidates in the preformal campaign period. The commission's opinions in response to these requests have significantly expanded the range of activities that an undeclared candidate can pursue without being subject to the restrictions applicable to legally qualified candidates.

A significant expansion of the scope of allowable testing activities began in 1981 when the commission was asked for an advisory opinion on behalf of Reubin Askew, a former governor of Florida, concerning the permissibility of a variety of activities he sought to undertake to determine the feasibility and desirability of a candidacy for the Democratic presidential nomination.[41] Fourteen activities were proposed.[42] They were:

1. Travel throughout the country for the purpose of speaking to political and non-political groups on a variety of public issues and meeting with opinion makers and others interested in public affairs for the purpose of determining whether potential political support exists for a national campaign.
2. Employment of political consultants for the purpose of assisting with advice on the potential and mechanics of constructing a national campaign organization.

3. Employment of a public relations consultant for the purpose of arranging and coordinating speaking engagements, disseminating copies of the Governor's speeches, and arranging for the publication of articles by the Governor in newspapers and periodicals.
4. Rental of office space.
5. Rental or purchase of office equipment for the purpose of compiling the names and addresses of individuals who indicate an interest in organizing a national campaign.
6. Preparation and use of letterhead stationery and correspondence with persons who have indicated an interest in a possible campaign by the Governor.
7. Supplementing the salary of a personal secretary who is employed by the Governor's law firm but will have the additional responsibility during the testing period of making travel arrangements, taking and placing telephone calls related to the testing activities, assisting in receiving and depositing the funds used to finance the testing, and assisting with general correspondence.
8. Reimbursement of the Governor's law firm for the activities of an associate attorney who is employed by the firm but will have the responsibility during the testing period of researching and preparing speeches, and coordinating the arrangement of interviews of the Governor by the news media, answering inquiries of the news media, arranging background briefings on various public issues, and traveling as an aide on some of the testing trips.
9. Reimbursement of the Governor's law firm for telephone costs, copying costs, and other incidental expenses which may be incurred.
10. Travel to other parts of the country in order to attend briefings on various public issues, and reimbursement of those who travel to Miami for the purpose of providing briefings on public issues.
11. Employment of a specialist in opinion research to conduct polls for the purpose of determining the feasibility of a national campaign.
12. Employment of an assistant to help coordinate travel arrangements and also travel as an aide on some of the testing trips.
13. Preparation and printing of a biographical brochure and possibly photographs to be used in connection with speaking appearances by Governor Askew.
14. Solicitation of contributions for the limited purpose of engaging in such "Testing the Water" [sic] activities as the foregoing.

In considering this request, the commission had to weigh two aspects of the law. On the one hand, it had to maintain the integrity of the regulations by limiting the scope of action allowed under the "testing" exemption and maintaining the legal line between an individual testing a candidacy and one who was effectively a declared candidate. On the other hand, it had to ensure that the regulations did not impose limits that would prove to be overly burdensome and thus discourage individuals from considering candidacies or choosing to seek office.

The commission, given the rather basic actions listed in the regulations as examples of testing activities, expressed concern about some of Askew's proposals but ruled that all fourteen were permissible. The ruling thus expanded the range of allowable activities and ensured that individuals could broadly explore a possible candidacy before making a decision. At the same time, the commission tried to maintain some restrictions on this sort of activity by stating that the exemption does not include activities designed to "promote" a candidacy, such as those that entail public political advertising, represent the establishment of a campaign organization, amass funds for a future candidacy, or promote the possible candidate as a qualified candidate. If former Governor Askew or a committee established on his behalf conducted any of these activities, it would indicate that he had "moved beyond the process of deciding whether or not to become a candidate and into the process of planning activities to heighten his political appeal" to the electorate.[43] Engaging in testing-the-waters activities for a protracted period of time would also suggest that the effect of the activities is to build campaign support rather than ascertain the feasibility of a candidacy. In these circumstances, an individual could qualify as a candidate within the meaning of the law.[44] If so, all contributions and expenditures incurred by the individual or his or her committee would have to be reported as such and would be subject to the provisions established for legally qualified candidates.

The commission further extended the scope of the exemption in a 1982 advisory opinion requested by the Cranston Advisory Committee.[45] Senator Alan Cranston authorized the formation of this committee to advise him on the desirability of his becoming a candidate for the 1984 Democratic presidential nomination. In informing the commission of its role, the committee sought a ruling to determine whether the testing-the-waters exemption was applicable to certain planned activities. The committee's request noted that Senator Cranston "has not made a decision to become a candidate and will make no such decision until after the Committee has completed its exploratory work."[46] Furthermore, the committee did not intend "to engage in any activities to promote a campaign, to make expenditures or engage in activities for general public political advertising, or to raise any funds for any subsequent campaign that may develop should the Senator decide to become a candidate."[47] The committee therefore met the criterion established by the commission in its earlier ruling.

The Cranston committee proposed a number of activities similar to those submitted in the Askew decision. Many of the proposals, however, were broader and more akin to the types of organizational activities that would take place in a full-fledged presidential campaign. For example, the committee's proposed actions included travel by Cranston and committee members to speak to groups on a "variety of public issues," compiling and maintaining information on persons who indicated interest in a possible Cranston candidacy, and organizing "advisory groups on critical and substantive issues."[48]

The commission concluded that all of these activities were permissible under the exemption as long as they continued to take place in a "factual context" indicating that the senator had not "moved beyond the deliberative process of deciding to become a candidate."[49] The ruling thus maintained an expansive interpretation of the law that served to ensure that the regulations did not discourage a candidacy. At the same time, the commission sought to maintain the integrity of the regulations and improve enforcement of the law by clarifying the distinction between exploratory activity and campaign activity. As part of the revised testing-the-waters regulations, the commission defined the types of activities that would indicate that an individual had become a legally qualified candidate.[50]

This exemption does not apply to funds received for activities indicating that an individual has decided to become a candidate for a particular office or for activities relevant to conducting a campaign. Examples of activities that indicate that an individual has decided to become a candidate include, but are not limited to:

(A) The individual uses general public political advertising to publicize his or her intention to campaign for federal office.

(B) The individual raises funds in excess of what could reasonably be expected to be used for exploratory activities or undertakes activities designed to amass campaign funds that would be spent after he or she becomes a candidate.

(C) The individual makes or authorizes written or oral statements that refer to him or her as a candidate for a particular office.

(D) The individual conducts activities in close proximity to the election or over a protracted period of time.

(E) The individual has taken action to qualify for the ballot under state law.

A parallel provision for expenditures is also included in the regulations.[51] The commission has thus imposed certain limits on testing-the-waters activities. But these limits are so narrowly conceived and specific that they fail to close the door to a wide range of precampaign activity.

Commissioner Thomas Harris recognized this problem as early as 1982 and argued that the commission's decisions, instead of clarifying the difference between testing-the-waters activities and formal campaigning, would actually obscure the line between the two and make enforcement of the law more difficult. He disagreed with the commission's ruling in the Cranston decision and filed a sharply worded dissenting opinion. He argued that the decision "sanctions activities which go beyond those which the commission envisioned when promulgating its regulations and permits activity which borders on campaigning." The regulations, in his view, were "intended to be a narrow exemption" but the opinion serves to make the line between testing-the-waters and campaign activity "non-existent."[52] He concluded by expressing his concern that "one narrow . . . exemption will become broader and broader."[53] His fears were realized when the commission was asked to determine what sorts of activities PACs could undertake on behalf of undeclared candidates.

FEC RULINGS ON PAC ACTIVITIES

In 1985 the commission was asked for an advisory opinion on behalf of the Republican Majority Fund (RMF), a multicandidate PAC, and the testing-the-waters fund of Senator Howard Baker, an authorized presidential exploratory committee.[54] The Republican Majority Fund had been "closely identified" with Senator Baker since its inception in 1980; he had hosted committee fundraising events, signed direct mail newsletters to contributors, and been mentioned in the committee's newsletter.[55] RMF asked the commission for its opinion as to whether certain planned activities and expenditures would constitute contributions to the exploratory fund.[56] Specifically, the request sought to determine whether RMF could conduct or finance the following activities under the testing-the-waters exemption: (1) direct mail fundraising solicitations; (2) travel costs for public appearances and attendance at state and local party functions; (3) travel costs for private political meetings with state and local party leaders in states holding early primaries or caucuses; (4) travel costs of individuals who attend meetings, conferences, and receptions as Senator Baker's authorized representatives; (5) hospitality suites or receptions in conjunction with such travel; (6) establishment of steering committees in certain states to advise and consult with RMF on contributions to federal, state, and local candidates and to encourage Senator Baker to seek the 1988 Republican presidential nomination; (7) certain administrative expenses for salaries, consulting fees, and overhead costs incurred by RMF for meetings, travel, and other testing-the-waters activities; and (8) newsletter solicitations to its contributors and party officials.[57]

As opposed to the Cranston and Askew decisions, which concerned the types of activities that could be conducted by an exploratory committee, this decision raised the issue of whether a PAC organized independently of an exploratory effort could assist in testing activities. In Advisory Opinion 1985-40, the commission ruled that RMF could assist Senator Baker in his precandidacy activities. But it noted that expenditures made by RMF on Senator Baker's behalf would constitute "in-kind gifts of things of value" to his exploratory fund. As such, they would qualify as contributions to Baker's exploratory fund and, because an exploratory committee may receive only legal contributions as a result of the 1985 regulations, they would be subject to the law's $5,000 aggregate limit on PAC contributions to an authorized committee.[58] Moreover, for the purposes of the presidential campaign contribution limits, funds received by the exploratory fund from RMF, whether direct or in-kind, would be aggregated with any contributions to Senator Baker as a candidate or to his authorized campaign committee.[59]

The commission's ruling therefore limited the extent to which a multicandidate PAC could assist an individual involved in testing-the-waters. In general, a PAC can provide direct assistance up to the level allowed by federal contribution limits. Once again, the commission's decision sought to balance diverse values. The agency reaffirmed the goals of encouraging participation in elections and promoting party-building by allowing the committee to participate in exploratory efforts. Yet it did so in a way that upheld the integrity of the law's contribution and spending limits by limiting a PAC's assistance.

The commission also maintained its view that the regulations should not discourage candidacies by continuing to enlarge the sphere of activities permitted within the exemption. The decision broadened the scope of allowable travel expenditures that may be incurred in an exploratory effort. In prior opinions, the commission determined that the exemption encompassed travel and public appearances by individuals other than the prospective candidate, including advisory committee members. Here the commission decided that the exemption also included travel or public appearances by individuals associated with a multicandidate PAC assisting in testing activities and, presumably, by members of state steering committees established by that PAC or an exploratory committee.[60] The ruling further stated that any travel expenses defrayed by a PAC for trips to qualified party-building events, assuming that the prospective candidate has not yet decided to run for office and does not engage in testing-the-waters activities at the events, do not constitute in-kind contributions to the exploratory fund or in-kind contributions to the individual's candidacy.[61] A PAC can therefore make expenditures for such travel in amounts exceeding the law's limits. These expenses are not allocable to an individual's exploratory committee and need not be reported by the individual's campaign committee if he or she becomes a candidate. Once an individual becomes a candidate, however, any PAC expenditures on his or her behalf for travel to party-building activities constitute in-kind contributions to the individual's campaign and are subject to the limits and reporting requirements of the act.[62]

The commission also sanctioned the formation of state steering committees as a legitimate precandidacy activity. RMF's advisory opinion request asked whether it could expend funds to establish steering committees of twenty-five to one hundred persons in states such as Iowa and New Hampshire.[63] The commission accepted this proposal, although it cautioned that these committees could not engage in activities relevant to a Baker candidacy or the establishment of a Baker campaign organization if they were to avoid triggering Senator Baker's status as a candidate under the act.[64] An exploratory committee may therefore accept assistance from a PAC to identify and recruit a large group of individuals in each state to serve as a steering committee. Although this action may not constitute a state campaign organization, it certainly may provide the foundation for one. A steering committee may encourage an individual to become a candidate and, given the commission's ruling in the Cranston opinion, probably may compile and maintain information on individuals who indicate an interest in a possible candidacy. More importantly, a steering committee may serve as the upper tier in a state campaign organization when an individual becomes a candidate. Indeed, in its advisory opinion request, RMF noted the likelihood of this possibility. The committee informed the commission that "in certain circumstances, . . . steering committee members will be requested to accept such position with the understanding that such committees will become the official campaign organization supporting Senator Baker in such states if he decides to seek the 1988 Republican presidential nomination."[65] The formation of steering committees was deemed a legitimate testing-the-waters activity, but it is a function that clearly borders on campaign activity.

The commission also decided that direct mail solicitations by the exploratory committee to former contributors to RMF or to Senator Baker's previous campaigns qualify as testing-the-waters activity.

The commission reached this conclusion because (1) the solicitations would clearly state that Senator Baker had not determined that he would seek the 1988 nomination; (2) the funds raised would be used for testing-the-waters activities; and (3) the purpose of the solicitations were not to amass campaign funds.[66] The decision thus allows an exploratory committee to utilize a fundraising vehicle that can increase awareness of an individual's possible candidacy, develop a broad base of contributors, and generate a substantial amount of revenue. If used successfully, it could enhance a committee's ability to engage in a broad range of activities in determining the feasibility of a candidacy. It would also provide an individual's campaign committee with an important resource, a list of proven donors whom the committee could solicit for campaign contributions, assuming these individuals had not contributed the maximum allowable amount to the candidate's exploratory fund.

This aspect of the ruling is particularly interesting because it appears to contradict previous commission interpretations regarding direct mail solicitations. Commissioner Harris, in a dissenting opinion, noted that direct mail solicitations have customarily been considered "campaign activity."[67] Direct mail is defined in the regulations as "any mailing(s) by commercial vendors or mailing(s) made from lists which are not developed by the candidate [conducting the mailing]."[68] It is considered "a form of general public political advertising" under the provisions of the act, a determination that the commission has upheld in interpreting other sections of the law.[69] As such, it would appear to be prohibited by the guidelines affirmed in the Cranston opinion or at least should serve as an indication that a candidate may have moved beyond the process of determining whether to become a candidate.

The Baker decision thus further blurred the distinction between exploratory or "precampaign" activity and campaign activity. But it did not have a significant effect on the ability of the Federal Election Commission to enforce the federal contribution and spending limits because the decision was made in the context of the regulatory framework governing an acknowledged exploratory effort. And the financial limits on exploratory committees were fairly well defined. This decision did not address the related issue of the limits on the use of a multicandidate PAC by a presidential aspirant who has not engaged in testing activities or the legal treatment of a PAC that is not involved in activities with a prospective candidate's exploratory committee. These circumstances were not considered until 1986, when the commission was asked to answer a query made on behalf of the Fund for America's Future, a PAC closely identified with then-Vice President George Bush.[70]

The Fund for America's Future (FAF), whose founder and honorary chairman was George Bush, was a multicandidate political committee registered with the Federal Election Commission. Its declared purpose was "to build a stronger Republican Party at all levels of government" by supporting "the Republican Party and Republican candidates, including candidates for party office, state and local office, and for both Houses of the United States Congress."[71] The FAF asked the commission for its opinion concerning the application of the Federal Election Campaign Act and commission regulations to FAF expenditures for activities conducted during the 1986 election cycle in support of the Republican party and its candidates, and the treatment of such expenditures with respect to any potential future presidential candidacy by then-Vice President George Bush. The committee proposed expenditures for a number of activities, including: (1) appearances by the vice president on behalf of Republican candidates and the Republican party; (2) references to the vice president in FAF publications and solicitations; (3) the establishment and operation of steering committees; (4) a program to organize volunteers for the Republican party; and (5) recruitment and financial assistance to persons seeking election to party offices, particularly with regard to the August 1986 Michigan precinct delegate election.[72] The FAF sought to ensure that these activities would be in accord with commission rulings and that no expenditures made in connection with them would be allocable to any future campaign committee established by the vice president. With regard to this latter concern, the committee emphasized that Vice President Bush had not announced his candidacy for the office of the president, authorized FAF to make expenditures on his behalf, or engaged in activities as a potential presidential candidate.[73]

In a 4-2 decision, the commission ruled that the FAF may engage in certain activities and that the monies spent by the committee would not be allocable as contributions or expenditures to Bush's campaign committee should he become a candidate. It thus allowed a multicandidate PAC sponsored by a potential candidate to undertake certain activities without jeopardizing the sponsor's status as a noncandidate under the law. But the commission noted that its conclusions apply solely to expenditures and activities that "are indistinguishable in all material aspects" from those described in its opinion.[74] Furthermore, the ruling pertains only to expenditures and activities conducted by a PAC in the period before the individual with whom it is associated becomes a qualified candidate. Any expenditures or activities engaged in thereafter would constitute in-kind contributions to the candidate and would be subject to the act's $5,000 aggregate contribution limit.[75]

The commission approved all of the activities described by the FAF provided that the committee adhere to the requirements and guidelines set forth in its opinion.[76] Specifically, it ruled that

1. A PAC may make expenditures for a prospective candidate's travel and public appearances to party functions, candidate rallies, fundraisers, and hospitality suite gatherings. These expenditures are not allocable to a candidate's campaign if the appearances do not include (a) any public references to the individual's possible candidacy or to the candidacies of his or her opponents; (b) any solicitations on behalf of the individual's candidacy; (c) any meetings with individuals or with members of the press regarding the individual's candidacy or the formation of a campaign organization; and (d) the distribution of any campaign paraphernalia in support of the individual's candidacy.

2. A PAC may make expenditures for publications that describe its purposes and solicit contributions. Such publications may mention a prospective candidate's association with the PAC and his or her desire that individuals contribute to the PAC as a means of supporting other candidates or a political party. Expenses for such materials are not allocable to an individual's campaign if they do not contain references to an individual's potential candidacy or suggest that contributors will be early supporters of the individual's campaign.

3. A PAC may establish steering committees to involve party officials, leaders, and officeholders in its activities and to solicit their advice on candidate support. Expenditures for these committees are not allocable provided that (a) the committees do not promote an individual's potential candidacy by forming a campaign organization on his or her behalf or by influencing his or her nomination; (b) the committees do not make support of an individual's potential candidacy a condition for receiving aid from the committees.

4. A PAC may recruit volunteers and conduct volunteer programs to aid the Republican party and Republican candidates for party, local, state, and federal offices. In developing these programs, a PAC may hire personnel and establish local offices in order to identify, encourage, and organize volunteers. Expenditures related to these programs are not allocable to a potential candidate if the activities conducted through the programs do not establish a campaign organization or participate in the presidential nomination process (e.g., the delegate selection process) on the individual's behalf.

5. A PAC may recruit, assist, and make contributions to individuals seeking party office in various states, including the office of precinct delegate. Any expenditures made by a PAC in aiding precinct delegates are not allocable to a potential candidate if the granting of aid does not involve the soliciting of support for a potential candidacy

or any other campaign activity on behalf of a clearly identified candidate.

The commission thus decided that a PAC sponsored by a potential candidate who is not involved in testing activities can engage in many of the same precandidacy activities as an exploratory committee or, for that matter, a presidential campaign committee. All of these committees can support travel and public appearances by a potential candidate and other individuals, form steering committees, conduct direct mail solicitations, establish offices, sponsor polls, recruit volunteers, and hire personnel and political consultants. An exploratory committee can conduct these activities in order to determine whether an individual should become a candidate or to encourage an individual to do so. Here the commission ruled that a multicandidate PAC can conduct these activities in order to build support for a political party and its candidates.

The commission's decision essentially sanctioned an unintended form of political campaigning that presidential candidates had practiced since 1977. Instead of restricting the role of candidate-sponsored PACs in the presidential nominating process, the ruling approved of their activities. Moreover, the agency clearly stated that the funds raised and spent by these committees were not subject to the limits imposed on presidential campaigns so long as the groups did not engage in one of the handful of activities that would indicate a formal candidacy on the part of a PAC's sponsor. It thus opened the door to widespread abuse of the law by providing aspirants with guidelines that could be used to circumvent the law in the future. In essence, the commission authorized a means by which presidential hopefuls could conduct most of the activities needed to initiate a presidential campaign at no cost to their authorized campaign committees.

That this was the penultimate effect of the commission's ruling was clearly understood by Commissioner Harris, who issued a lengthy dissenting opinion highly critical of the majority view. Refusing to stand on legal technicalities or narrow decisionmaking rules, Harris declared that the commission's decision would seriously undermine the efficacy of the law.[77]

In its rulings on unannounced presidential aspirants the Commission has, step by step, gotten itself into the absurd position that it refuses to acknowledge what everyone knows: that Vice President Bush is running for President and is financing his campaign through the Fund for America's Future, Inc., which he organizes and controls. . . . Only persons just alighting from a UFO can doubt that activities of these sorts, which are engaged in over a period of many months, will promote the candidacy of the founding father. That, of course, is why so many would-be Presidents, of both parties, have created and utilized PACs of this sort in recent years. The Commission, however, is willing to turn a blind eye to the realities so long as the presidential hopeful announces periodically that he will not decide whether to run until some future date. . . .

This is just plain ridiculous. Disbursements for these activities are made for the purpose of influencing a federal election. They are contributions and expenditures under the Act, should trigger the requirement to register as a candidate with consequent reporting obligations, and should count against the national and state expenditure ceilings if the candidate opts for public financing. . . .

[I]f activities of the sorts envisioned by Mr. Bush's PAC were held to constitute "testing the waters," [sic] no substantial loophole would result. But, the Commission has held that these activities are not even testing. Worse, the present ruling, or non-ruling, is the first to leave it open to presidential aspirant PACs to spend money, without limitations, to influence the selection of delegates to a national party convention held to select a presidential nominee. This plainly undermines the contribution limits and expenditure ceilings of the statute.

Harris's final point in this passage was directed toward an especially controversial aspect of this ruling: the decision to allow Bush's PAC to help individuals seeking positions as precinct delegates in the 1986 Michigan elections.

The delegate selection process established by the Michigan Republican party for the 1988 national nominating system was a multitiered system that actually began with the election of precinct delegates in August 1986. Those selected as delegates were supposed to attend two conventions: one to select delegates to the state party convention and another, in November 1986, to select the party's county executive committees. Then the precinct delegates were scheduled to meet again in early 1987 in county or district conventions to select delegates to a state convention that would select party leaders. They were to meet yet again in January 1988 in county or district conventions to select delegates for the state convention that would select delegates to the 1988 Republican National Convention. This final meeting was the key to the controversy.

Harris opposed the commission's decision because the precinct delegates that Bush's PAC helped to select would play a role in influencing the outcome of the Michigan delegate selection process. These individuals, he wrote, "form the closed universe of persons who will participate in the process of selecting delegates to the Republican national nominating convention in 1988."[78] Accordingly, any assistance given to precinct delegate candidates should be considered campaign-related spending subject to the limits imposed on presidential candidates. This was the view of the commission's legal staff, whose draft opinion in this decision unequivocally stated that "it is . . . incontrovertible that the election of these precinct delegates is also the first level in the Michigan process of selecting delegates to the 1988 Republican national convention. . . . [T]he intra-party role of these precinct delegates does not alter, diminish, or dilute their key, influential role in the selection of national nominating convention delegates."[79] The draft argument thus concluded that funds spent in conjunction with these elections "constitute contributions under the Act as in-kind gifts" and will be subject to the campaign contribution and spending limits.[80] This argument was also accepted by Commission Vice Chair John Warren McGarry, who was the other member to vote against the majority in this case. In his dissenting opinion, McGarry argued that any funds spent to assist precinct delegate candidates should be subject to the limitations on contributions and spending if Bush became a candidate because these elections have an influence on the selection of national nominating convention delegates.[81]

The majority of the commission members, however, rejected the legal staff's position and instead allowed Bush's PAC to assist in the precinct elections. It thus essentially eliminated the line between precampaign and campaign activity. After all, if working to influence the process through which national convention delegates are selected is not presidential campaigning, what is? The commission's answer was that the five specific types of activities outlined in the regulations as indicative of a formal candidacy were the criterion for judging whether an individual had qualified as a candidate. Under these guidelines, participating in precinct elections was the sort of party-building activity that the regulations should encourage. Indeed, in the text of its decision, the agency highlighted the intraparty aspects of the precinct elections and noted that choosing convention delegates was not the sole purpose for which these individuals were selected.[82]

Why the commission rejected the argument of the legal staff with respect to the FAF's proposed activities is not clear from the text of the decision, the dissenting opinions, the memoranda proposing alternative language, or the published minutes of the commission meetings. Perhaps members were influenced by political considerations, a motive commonly advanced by critics in explaining commission decision-making.[83] What is clear is that the agency did not wholly abandon the objectives of the law in rendering its decisions. It tacitly acknowledged the rights of freedom of speech and freedom of association by affirming the right of any individual or group of individuals, even prospective presidential candidates, to organize and maintain a PAC. It recognized party-building and political participa-tion as important aspects of PAC operations. It ensured that the regulations would not be overly burdensome. But it did so at the expense of the efficacy of the contribution and spending limits. It advanced a very technical reading of the Michigan delegate selection process, further complicating its ability to determine a formal candidacy on the part of an individual. It also adopted a very narrow interpretation of the regulations that could be used to restrain precandidacy PAC activity. As a result, it sanctioned what was once considered "loophole" activity and seriously undermined the integrity of the campaign finance system.

CONCLUSION

The Federal Election Campaign Act, its amendments, and subsequent regulations establish a legal framework that imposes different requirements on the various types of political committees defined in federal campaign finance statutes. Under these regulations, an individual considering a presidential candidacy can choose to initiate a bid for office by establishing a principal campaign committee, approving the formation of an exploratory committee, or sponsoring a multicandidate political committee. Because of the legal provisions governing these organizational structures, a multicandidate PAC is the best alternative available to a prospective candidate for addressing the legal restraints and expansionary pressures generated by recent campaign finance reforms. A candidate-sponsored PAC can receive contributions and incur expenditures without triggering an individual's status as a candidate under the law and without affecting the contribution and expenditure limits that apply to a prospective candidate's future campaign. It can undertake activities that may improve the prospects of a potential candidacy and develop the resources needed to launch a successful presidential campaign. And it provides a vehicle through which a potential candidate can legally receive and expend funds that would be considered illegal in other circumstances.

The desirability of the PAC alternative has been enhanced in recent years as a result of a number of advisory opinion rulings issued by the Federal Election Commission. These opinions have limited the regulatory advantages that can be achieved by establishing an exploratory committee and have sanctioned the use of a multicandidate PAC by a prospective candidate for particular purposes. More importantly, a loophole once exploited by candidates without specific sanction from the commission has been legitimized. A legal structure employed by a few candidates prior to the 1980 presidential campaign is therefore now used by most candidates seeking their party's nomination.

4

The Rise of Presidential Candidate PACs

The Federal Election Campaign Act specifically prohibits the establishment of a PAC as a candidate campaign committee. The law does not, however, prohibit the formation of a PAC by a potential candidate or by an individual planning to become a candidate. Rather, the regulations seek to ensure that an aspirant does not take advantage of this option by discouraging the use of such a committee for "campaign-related" purposes. The statutory ambiguity concerning the definition of "campaign-related" activities has led some committees to seek prior approval of their proposed actions from the Federal Election Commission. In rendering its opinion in these instances, the commission has failed to discourage candidates from employing the PAC alternative. The commission's rulings have instead served to reinforce the use of PACs by sanctioning their sponsorship by potential candidates and by permitting activities that effectively allow an individual to initiate a political campaign prior to becoming a candidate. Rather than inhibit unintended activities, the commission's decisions have contributed to the trend toward candidate PACs and have thus fostered further abuse of the law.

Prospective presidential candidates, eager to advance their candidacies and initiate their campaigns, have responded to this permissive regulatory environment by expanding their reliance on PACs, especially during the early years of a presidential election cycle. This chapter traces the rise of these candidate-sponsored committees and highlights the extent to which prospective candidates have taken advantage of these structures in recent elections. It begins with a review of the growth in the use of these committees during the 1980s. Whereas none of the 1976 candidates established a PAC before organizing a campaign committee, most of the candidates in the 1988 contest launched a campaign in this manner. Those who did not exploit the PAC option often employed some other alternative to facilitate precandidacy campaigning.

The second part of this chapter presents an analysis of available Federal Election Commission data to determine the financial activity of candidate-sponsored PACs since 1977. These committees have raised and spent increasingly large sums of money in each of the last three presidential election cycles, with a dramatic rise in both receipts and expenditures in 1988. Most of this financial activity occurs in the first two years of the election cycle. This indicates that aspirants are primarily using these committees to conduct political activities in the earliest stages of the nomination process, well before they declare a candidacy. More importantly, it reveals the extent to which these committees have been used to avoid the legal restrictions imposed on presidential campaigns. Presidential hopefuls have relied on these committees to an alarming degree, raising and spending millions of dollars outside of the limits established by federal statutes. This financial activity violates the intent of federal campaign finance laws. It has undermined efforts to reduce campaign spending, provide greater equity in the resources available to presidential candidates, and shorten the length of campaigns. Yet it continues to grow, encouraged by a favorable regulatory environment and fueled by the competitive pressures of the nomination process.

PRESIDENTIAL CANDIDATE PACs

None of the 1976 presidential candidates established a PAC before forming a campaign committee or declaring a candidacy. This is not surprising given that the 1976 nomination campaign was the first conducted under the Federal Election Campaign Act. Candidates were uncertain of the provisions of the new law and the act's implementation was delayed by a court challenge and the legislative reconsideration necessitated by the Supreme Court's decision in *Buckley* v. *Valeo*.[1] Consequently, the 1976 candidates and their advisers devoted their time to determining the actions needed to comply with the new law rather than ways to take advantage of it.

After the 1976 election, Citizens for Reagan, Ronald Reagan's principal campaign committee, held surplus funds in excess of $1 million in its campaign accounts.[2] Rather than give the money away or keep it and pay taxes on it, Reagan and his advisers decided to convert the campaign committee into a multicandidate political committee that would support conservative Republican causes and candidates. The new committee, Citizens for the Republic, was filed with the

Federal Election Commission on January 28, 1977, with Reagan designated as the committee's chairman.[3] Other Republican presidential hopefuls soon recognized the benefits of Reagan's approach and formed PACs of their own. A new method of financing prenomination campaigns was thus born.

Table 4.1 lists the PACs registered with the FEC that were established by individuals who subsequently became presidential candidates. It documents the proliferation of such committees that has occurred in recent elections. It also indicates the temporal relationship that exists between the creation of these organizations and presidential elections. The timing of these operations is particularly important because, in most instances, the committees listed were active during a single presidential election cycle. This clearly suggests that the primary purpose of these groups was not to assist the party or other candidates but was to advance their respective sponsors' presidential ambitions.

The 1980 Election

During the period before the 1980 election, four of the ten major presidential candidates sponsored a PAC.[4] All four were contenders for the Republican nomination. George Bush, John Connally, and Robert Dole followed Reagan's lead and established PACs of their own by March 31, 1978. None of the three Democratic candidates (Jimmy Carter, Edward Kennedy, and Jerry Brown) chose to pursue this option. Carter and Kennedy, however, were assisted in their efforts by other sorts of precampaign activity.

President Carter effectively took advantage of the political opportunities that accompany the incumbency. Before announcing his candidacy for reelection, he visited twenty-four states in an official capacity or in order to appear at party-related functions. Eighteen of these states held presidential primaries in 1980.[5] But under the provisions of a 1975 FEC advisory opinion, none of the costs associated with these trips were allocable to Carter's campaign committee.[6] The president's candidacy also benefited from travel for official and political purposes by his cabinet members and other administration appointees. In these instances, Carter's campaign committee was responsible only for the costs associated with political travel. Such events as Secretary of Agriculture Robert Bergland's hearings on preserving the family farm, which were conducted in nine states in December 1979, were not allocable to the campaign, even though six of the nine states held early primary contests in 1980. The administration also sought to build support for the president's candidacy by adroitly

TABLE 4.1
Federal Multicandidate PACs Sponsored by Presidential Candidates, 1980-1988

Election Cycle	Name of PAC	Candidate (Party)	Date Filed with FEC
1980	Campaign America	Dole (R)	Mar. 1, 1978
	Citizens for the Republic	Reagan (R)	Jan. 28, 1977
	Fund for a Limited Government[a]	Bush (R)	Sept. 26, 1977
	John Connally Citizens Forum	Connally (R)	Oct. 7, 1977
1984	Citizens for a Competitive America	Hollings (D)	Feb. 25, 1982
	Citizens for the Republic[b]	Reagan (R)	Jan. 28, 1977
	Committee for a Democratic Consensus	Cranston (D)	May 19, 1981
	Committee for the Future of America	Mondale (D)	Feb. 4, 1981
	National Council on Public Policy	Glenn (D)	Sept. 15, 1982
1988	Americans for the National Interest	Babbitt (D)	Sept. 9, 1985
	Campaign America[c]	Dole (R)	Mar. 1, 1978
	Campaign for Prosperity[d]	Kemp (R)	Sept. 22, 1976
	Committee for America	Haig (R)	April 2, 1986
	Committee for Freedom/ Freedom PAC	Robertson (R)	June 25, 1985
	Effective Government Committee	Gephardt (D)	Oct. 3, 1984
	Fund for America's Future	Bush (R)	Apr. 25, 1985
	Fund for '86	Biden (D)	Apr. 25, 1986
	The Democracy Fund	Simon (D)	Dec. 3, 1984

[a]George Bush was also associated with a PAC called the Congressional Leadership Committee, but the Fund for a Limited Government was the principal vehicle used to conduct precampaign activities. The Congressional Leadership Committee raised only $5,216 in 1979 and 1980 (Federal Election Commission, Committee Index of Disclosure Documents [C Index], 1979-1980, computer printout, n.d.).

[b]Citizens for the Republic, the PAC established by Reagan prior to the 1980 nomination campaign, remained in operation throughout his first term.

[c]Campaign America remained in operation from the date of its formation prior to the 1980 campaign.

(Continued)

TABLE 4.1 (Continued)

dJack Kemp has been associated with a PAC since the Committee for Economic Strength was established on September 22, 1976. This committee never raised any money and changed its name to the Committee to Rebuild American Incentive in 1977. The committee again changed its name in October 1982, this time calling itself the Campaign for Prosperity.

Source: Federal Election Commission, "PACs Associated with Recognized Individuals," Memorandum prepared by the FEC Press Office, n.d.; and Federal Election Commission, Committee Index of Disclosure Documents (C Index), 1977-1987, computer printouts, n.d.

allocating discretionary government funds and by staging White House briefings for party and elected officials and political supporters.[7]

Senator Kennedy did not decide to challenge Carter for the Democratic nomination until October 1979.[8] He therefore did not engage in extensive campaigning before designating a principal campaign committee. His campaign, however, was assisted by the precampaign activities of a number of independent "draft" committees formed to advance his candidacy and convince him to enter the race. These committees began organizing on May 21, 1979, when five Democratic members of congress announced an effort to draft Kennedy as the party's nominee.[9] Kennedy disavowed the activities of these groups and the FEC ruled that as unauthorized political committees, they could receive individual contributions of up to $5,000 per calendar year and spend unlimited amounts in their draft effort.[10] By the time Kennedy declared his candidacy, more than seventy draft committees had been organized in thirty-eight states. Overall, these committees reported total receipts of $555,000 and expenditures totaling $543,000. Most important were the draft groups that targeted their efforts toward crucial early events in the Democratic nomination contest, particularly the Florida State Democratic party's presidential straw vote, the Iowa caucus, and the New Hampshire primary. The Florida for Kennedy Committee alone raised $266,000 and spent $264,000. The Iowa-based Committee for Alternatives to Democratic Candidates raised $38,600 and spent $37,000, and New Hampshire Democrats for Change raised $81,500 and spent $80,000.[11] These committees helped prepare the way for Kennedy's campaign, but none of their contributions or expenditures were allocable to his campaign committee because they acted independently without the senator's authorization.

The 1984 Election

During the period before the 1984 election, five of the nine major presidential candidates sponsored PACs.[12] Ronald Reagan's Citizens for the Republic continued to operate throughout his first term, even though his bid for reelection was uncontested. This committee no longer needed to conduct preannouncement activities, but it worked to further Reagan's political objectives. The group helped build support for the president and his agenda by assisting candidates supportive of his program and by engaging in party-building efforts. It also helped maintain the president's political network by defraying travel costs for former administration officials and by hosting meetings with former campaign workers.[13]

In October 1984, Citizens for the Republic merged with another PAC, Citizens for the Republic II, in order to facilitate a transfer of funds from Citizens for Reagan, the president's 1980 prenomination campaign committee. The 1980 committee ended the campaign with a surplus of $1.4 million. In September 1984, it changed its name to Citizens for the Republic II and then qualified as a multicandidate committee by making contributions to five federal candidates. This new PAC declared its affiliation with Citizens for the Republic in October and transferred its remaining funds to the original committee in accordance with federal law, which permits legally unlimited transfers between affiliated committees.[14]

The four other candidates who established PACs prior to the 1984 campaign were Democrats, marking the first use of these committees by contenders for the Democratic nomination. Former vice president Walter Mondale was the first Democrat to create a PAC, forming his Committee for the Future of America only two weeks after leaving office. Senators Alan Cranston, Ernest Hollings, and John Glenn followed Mondale's lead. In addition, Senator Kennedy founded the Fund for a Democratic Majority on February 20, 1981.[15] The declared purpose of the committee, according to the senator's press secretary, was "to help the Democratic Party in the 1982 midterm elections."[16] A more forthcoming explanation of the committee's purpose was noted by political reporter Adam Clymer, who stated that Kennedy and Mondale were forming PACs "to provide money for other Democrats and visibility for themselves."[17] The fund raised approximately $2.3 million and spent $2.1 million before Kennedy decided not to run for the 1984 nomination on December 1, 1982.[18]

Four Democrats did not capitalize on the political opportunities afforded by PAC sponsorship. One of these candidates, Reubin Askew, chose to conduct preannouncement activities and to test the waters for his prospective candidacy through an exploratory committee rather than a PAC.[19] This exploratory committee, in accordance with the commission's ruling in Advisory Opinion 1981-32, engaged in a wide range of activities on Askew's behalf. Askew converted this committee into his principal campaign committee on January 3, 1983.[20] Jesse Jackson also explored the possibility of becoming a candidate prior to his late entry into the race. Jackson first considered the idea of running early in 1983 and spent several months testing the desirability of a candidacy while he traveled around the country appearing at voter registration rallies, church assemblies, and campaign events for local candidates.[21] But his effort was less formal than Askew's and he never exercised the option of registering an exploratory committee with the FEC. Gary Hart and George McGovern (another late entrant in the race) were therefore the only 1984 Democratic hopefuls who neither employed an alternative organizational structure nor engaged in significant testing activities before authorizing a principal campaign committee.

The 1988 Election

A virtual explosion in the number of candidate-sponsored PACs occurred in advance of the 1988 prenomination contest. Nine of the fourteen major presidential candidates established PACs at the federal level.[22] Three others relied on some other type of organization to avoid federal limits. Republican Pierre "Pete" du Pont IV relied on a state-level PAC registered in Delaware rather than a federal committee. Democrat Gary Hart eschewed the PAC option but engaged in extensive precampaign activity through a tax-exempt, nonprofit foundation named the Center for a New Democracy. Reverend Jesse Jackson established a nonprofit, independent political organization called the National Rainbow Coalition. Democrats Michael Dukakis and Albert Gore did not establish some type of organization designed to circumvent federal restrictions, although Dukakis, the eventual Democratic nominee, took advantage of another regulatory provision to jump-start his campaign.

All of the 1988 Republican candidates sponsored political action committees. Three of these committees were formed during the 1988 presidential election cycle: George Bush's Fund for America's Future, Marion "Pat" Robertson's Committee for Freedom, and Alexander Haig's Committee for America. Robert Dole and Jack Kemp were assisted by committees established before the 1988 presidential election cycle. Dole's Campaign America was set up in advance of the 1980 presidential election and thereafter continued to operate. Kemp's

Campaign for Prosperity is the latest form of a multicandidate committee he organized in 1976 as the Committee for Economic Strength and then renamed the Committee to Rebuild American Incentive in 1977.[23] The committee was relatively inactive from 1976 to 1980, raising only $145,000 and spending $126,000 during this five year period. Prior to the 1982 midterm elections, the committee's name was changed to the Campaign for Prosperity and increased its activity, raising $244,000 during the 1981-1982 election cycle and $2.2 million during the 1983-1984 cycle.[24] This increased activity in 1983-1984 constituted an initial step toward a 1988 candidacy.[25] The PAC sustained this heightened level of activity until Kemp became a candidate.

Pete du Pont took advantage of the opportunities for early campaigning available through two nonfederal PACs. One of these committees, GOPAC, was established in 1979 to make contributions to Republican challengers in state legislative races.[26] The other, called the National Leadership Council, was created to supplement GOPAC's efforts by raising monies to purchase computer equipment for local Republican parties.[27] These committees helped du Pont to meet grass-roots party members and political leaders, identify possible contributors, and recruit potential support. In 1985, he spent approximately two-thirds of his time traveling the country on behalf of GOPAC while at the same time preparing the way for his 1988 campaign.[28]

Because GOPAC and the National Leadership Council are involved solely in state and local political activities, they are subject to state rather than federal regulations. These committees therefore did not have to register with the FEC, are not subject to the contribution and expenditure limits of the FECA, are not limited to federally sanctioned sources when soliciting funds, and do not have to meet federal public disclosure requirements. It is thus impossible to determine the full extent of the committees' financial operations. In October 1985, however, GOPAC voluntarily released information summarizing its financial activities during the 1983-1984 election cycle.[29] The committee raised $2.5 million during this period and spent $2.3 million, including $235,450 in contributions to 390 candidates for state office and $210,050 to state Republican party committees.[30] In 1985, the committee reportedly shifted its financial operations to a "venture capital" approach. Instead of making contributions directly to candidates, it sought to spend $50,000 in each of fifty congressional districts where Republican candidates were not competitive to develop potential candidates and build a party base.[31] Information is not available as to whether the committee achieved its goal.

Besides these candidates, two other potential Republican contenders conducted activities through PACs in anticipation of a 1988 candidacy. Howard Baker, who decided against seeking reelection to the Senate in 1984 in order to concentrate on a presidential bid, took advantage of the Republican Majority Fund, a multicandidate committee he established in March 1980 after withdrawing from the presidential race.[32] Baker also established an exploratory committee, and as a result of the commission's decision in Advisory Opinion 1985-40, his Republican Majority Fund was limited in the amount of assistance it could give the exploratory committee in determining whether Baker should become a candidate. The PAC did, however, provide substantial assistance in the form of contributions to other candidates and payment of expenses for Baker's travel to party-related functions. In February 1987, as Baker was about to enter the race, President Reagan asked him to succeed Donald Regan as White House chief of staff. Baker accepted the president's offer and on February 27 declared that he would not seek the 1988 Republican nomination.[33]

Donald Rumsfeld also founded a PAC as part of the process of exploring a presidential candidacy. Rumsfeld, a former White House chief of staff and secretary of defense, was often mentioned publicly as a potential candidate and on December 23, 1985, he organized the Citizens for American Values PAC. During 1986 and the first six months of 1987, this PAC raised $1.17 million and spent $1.14 million. But in April 1987, Rumsfeld declared that he would not become a candidate. Thereafter the PAC's financial activity significantly declined. The committee raised only $5,500 and spent $11,600 during the last six months of 1987.[34]

Four of the eight contenders for the Democratic nomination established PACs, beginning with Richard Gephardt, who filed his Effective Government Committee with the FEC one month before the 1984 general election. Less than a month after the election, Paul Simon joined Gephardt by registering a committee called the Democracy Fund. In September 1985, Bruce Babbitt formed Americans for the National Interest and, in June 1986, Joseph Biden set up his Fund for '86.

Edward Kennedy, although he did not seek the 1988 nomination, was mentioned as a potential frontrunner early in the race and continued to conduct political activities through his Fund for a Democratic Majority. At the beginning of 1985, the PAC recruited Paul Tully, an operative in Kennedy's 1980 campaign and the political director of Mondale's 1984 campaign, to direct its operations.[35] The committee's activities at this time were directed in part toward broadening and solidifying a financial base in consideration of a possible presidential campaign.[36] But on December 19, 1985, Kennedy announced he would not be a candidate in 1988, and after the 1986 midterm elections he scaled down his PAC activities, reportedly to avoid depleting funds that could be given to other candidates, to concentrate on his own reelection, and to eliminate himself from any possible presidential draft movement.[37] The committee raised $1.29 million and spent $1.77 million before the senator announced his decision not to run.[38]

Another prominently mentioned Democratic possibility, New York Governor Mario Cuomo, also formed a PAC before the 1988 election. This committee, the Empire Leadership Fund, was set up to finance Cuomo's interstate travel, sponsor local forums for presidential candidates, and assist other candidates.[39] It was established in April 1987 amid speculation that Cuomo could still become a candidate despite his February 19 announcement that he would not seek the Democratic presidential nomination.[40] The committee raised $108,570 in 1987, but Cuomo did not alter his decision.[41] No additional funds were received in 1988.

Gary Hart did not form a PAC prior to the 1984 election and refused PAC contributions in his presidential campaign. In the early stages of the 1988 race he was widely acknowledged as the prospective Democratic frontrunner, but he maintained his anti-PAC stance and did not form such a committee to capitalize on his frontrunner status. Instead, Hart came up with a better idea: he established a tax-exempt, nonprofit foundation called the Center for a New Democracy, which opened its Washington office on May 1, 1985.[42] The avowed purpose of this foundation was to serve as a "think tank" for the creation of new policy ideas. In fulfillment of this end, it sponsored a series of seminars around the country during 1985 and 1986 with each seminar devoted to a particular policy issue. It also collected examples of "new" policies effective at the state and local level, as well as innovative federal proposals, and maintained a list of state and local officials receptive to these policies. According to the foundation's voluntarily-released reports, approximately $500,000 was raised in 1985 to support these activities, half of which came from ten individual contributions of $25,000 each. The group also received contributions of $5,000 or more from such corporations as United Technologies, Bank of America, Korean Airlines, Singapore Airlines, and American Express.[43]

Although a tax-exempt, nonprofit foundation is legally prohibited from providing direct or indirect assistance to candidates, it can be used to facilitate many of the precampaign activities that are possible with a PAC. The Center for a New Democracy provided Hart with a legal structure through which he could travel, develop policy initiatives, educate the public about policy issues, generate media attention, identify donors, and construct lists of potential supporters. This foundation also provided Hart with a number of significant capabilities not afforded by the PAC alternative. Contributions to a tax-exempt foundation are tax deductible to the donors, are subject to no contribution limits, and can be obtained from corporations and labor unions, which is not possible with a PAC. Because such a foundation is also a nonprofit organization, it enjoys preferential mailing rates, which provide substantial savings on large-scale mailings.[44] Furthermore, all receipts and expenditures need only be filed with the Internal Revenue Service and are not subject to public disclosure.[45] A foundation thus functions as a large-scale soft money fund that allows a prospective candidate to raise unlimited amounts of money relatively free of public scrutiny.

Hart was the first candidate to recognize the potential benefits of a tax-exempt foundation, but he was not alone in adopting this approach. Three other 1988 presidential aspirants followed Hart's example: Bruce Babbitt, who founded American Horizons; Pat Robertson, who formed the Freedom Council; and Jack Kemp, who established two separate foundations, the Fund for an American Renaissance and the Conservative Opportunity Society.[46] In each case, the prospective candidate's foundation was used to supplement the political activities already being conducted by the individual's political action committee.

Comprehensive data on the finances and activities of these tax-exempt organizations are not available because these foundations are not subject to full public disclosure requirements. The amounts raised by these groups can be estimated, however, from information gathered by the Center for Responsive Politics, which conducted a major study of tax-exempt organizations associated with prominent politicians in 1987.[47] The center examined these groups in part by reviewing Internal Revenue Service materials and Form 990 tax returns. This survey revealed that the foundations established by presidential aspirants raised a significant amount of money in the early years of the 1988 election cycle. Hart's Center for a New Democracy reported revenues of $854,000 for the period from its incorporation in 1985 through March of 1987. This was almost twice the sum reported by Babbitt's American Horizons, which raised $481,000 in 1985 and 1986. Kemp's Fund for an American Renaissance reported $608,000 in 1985-1986, a significant sum but less than half of the $1,577,380 reported by Robertson's Freedom Council for 1985 alone. Overall, the estimated total revenue of these four committees equals $3.52 million.[48]

Further knowledge of the role of these foundations in helping prospective candidates to circumvent the constraints of federal campaign finance laws can be obtained from voluntarily released information and journalistic accounts of their operations. For example,

Kemp's Fund for an American Renaissance (FAR) had raised $400,000 by October 1985 and his Conservative Opportunity Society (COS) reported a proposed budget of $200,000 to $500,000. These organizations sponsored policy seminars and funded travel by Kemp, including a trip to meet with European economic officials and political figures that cost COS $20,000. FAR financed a $40,000 documentary on urban revitalization, which Kemp narrated.[49] Robertson's Freedom Council reported $400,000 in expenditures to recruit precinct delegate candidates in Michigan, an amount said to represent only 15 to 18 percent of its national budget.[50] Individuals selected as precinct delegates in this 1986 election would later play a role in selecting Michigan's 1988 Republican National Convention delegates. The Freedom Council also conducted activities in Florida and North Carolina.[51] Babbitt's American Horizons had raised $100,000 by October 1985, with most of this sum coming from three contributions, two in the amount of $25,000 and one of $20,000.[52] This foundation, which was chaired by Babbitt and housed down the hall from his political action committee, conducted research for some of his major addresses and distributed speeches, Congressional testimony, and articles authored by Babbitt.[53] It thus functioned as a vehicle for informing potential supporters of Babbitt's policy views and opinions.

Reverend Jesse Jackson also established a nonprofit organization to facilitate his political activities prior to his 1988 candidacy. But his organization, the National Rainbow Coalition (NRC), acted more as an independent political operation than did the tax-exempt foundations created by other aspirants. The NRC was established in Washington in November 1984 to "energiz[e] other members of the Democratic Party to steer a course of social and economic justice."[54] The organization sought to fulfill this purpose by maintaining and expanding the political network developed by Jackson's 1984 campaign and by building on the support Jackson received in the 1984 Democratic primaries, where he won sixty-one congressional districts and earned 3.5 million votes.[55]

The NRC held several national leadership meetings in 1985 but failed to develop a strong organizational structure, partly due to a lack of financial resources after a March 1985 radiothon projected to generate $1 million in net revenues fell far short of its goal.[56] By early 1986, however, the coalition had developed a national political operation. In April 1986 the NRC staged a "national organizing convention" in Washington in which more than 750 delegates from forty-three states debated an organizational charter, operating procedures, and a policy agenda. One month later the coalition held another convention in Washington that included farmers bused in from

Nebraska and Wyoming, oil workers from Texas and Oklahoma, and meat packers from Minnesota, who at the time were in the midst of a bitter strike.[57] That these efforts were related to a potential 1988 Jackson candidacy was made clear at the time by Lamond Godwin, a key aide in Jackson's 1984 campaign, who noted that: "What comes out of this is intensive organizing for a national [NRC] convention in 1987, at which [Jackson] will either announce his candidacy or announce support for someone else. Between now and then, there will be very serious planning for another campaign."[58]

Thereafter the NRC sponsored an array of political activities including state and local grass-roots organizing, voter registration drives, get-out-the-vote efforts, and appearances by Jackson. These efforts were particularly targeted toward elections in which one of the candidates supported the coalition's policy agenda.[59] In 1987 the NRC relocated to Chicago; one report claimed this was done "to give his second presidential campaign a Midwest flavor."[60] Later that year, the plans set forth by Godwin were realized as Jackson announced his intention to run for the 1988 Democratic nomination at a meeting in Raleigh, North Carolina, that was billed as "the first biennial convention" of the Rainbow Coalition.[61]

Jackson also prepared the way for his second bid for the presidential nomination by forming an exploratory committee that began to conduct testing activities early in 1987. By March it had opened an Iowa office, and a few weeks later, more than one hundred Black ministers and elected officials met in Memphis to begin developing a nationwide political operation.[62] In June, Richard Hatcher was named director of the Jackson exploratory committee and the committee engaged in testing-the-waters activities until it was converted into Jackson's authorized campaign committee when he decided to become a candidate.[63]

Ironically, Michael Dukakis, the winner of the 1988 Democratic nomination, did not establish a PAC or tax-exempt foundation. He and President Carter are the only individuals in the past decade to win their party's nomination without the aid of a PAC. But like Carter in 1980, Dukakis had access to other resources. On April 6, 1987, the Dukakis Gubernatorial Committee (a state-level political committee) filed a statement of organization with the FEC to facilitate a transfer of funds to the Dukakis for President Committee, the federal campaign committee authorized by Dukakis for his presidential nomination campaign.[64] The state committee transferred $380,000, part of which was raised after the 1986 election, to the federal committee in accordance with federal regulations providing for transfers between a candidate's previous and current campaign committee.[65] Perhaps more importantly, the gubernatorial committee transferred its contributor and supporter lists to Dukakis's presidential campaign. This provided the Dukakis campaign with a valuable asset, one that some candidates sought to develop by establishing PACs or tax-exempt foundations. These lists allowed Dukakis to build a strong fundraising base at minimum cost. He raised more money from his home state than any of his opponents raised from their own, and on one night in June 1987, he raised $2 million at a Boston fundraiser, considerably more than any other Massachusetts politician had ever raised at a single event.[66]

This discussion of Table 4.1 highlights the proliferation of candidate-sponsored PACs that has occurred in recent elections. Prior to the 1980 presidential campaign, four of the ten major candidates established multicandidate committees. Prior to the 1988 campaign, nine of the fourteen major candidates utilized PACs to advance their candidacy, or ten of the fourteen if du Pont is included. In addition, prospective candidates in 1988 discovered a new organization they could exploit for precandidacy campaigning: the tax-exempt, nonprofit organization. This vehicle completely frees candidates of federal campaign finance regulations and thus creates widespread opportunities for abuse. This potential for abuse led the House Subcommittee on Oversight in March 1987 to investigate the use of these foundations by political candidates and to conduct a full and comprehensive review of the tax rules applicable to the lobbying and political activities of tax-exempt organizations.[67] Congress, however, took no action on this matter, thus leaving the door open to similar efforts to subvert the law in the future.

THE TIMING OF PAC OPERATIONS

Table 4.1 further evidences the link between the formation of these PACs and prospective presidential campaigns by noting the date on which each of these committees was registered with the Federal Election Commission. If Reagan's Citizens for the Republic in 1984 and Dole's Campaign America in 1988 are excluded (because these committees were originally established in anticipation of the 1980 election), then all but one of the committees listed was established during the election cycle in which its sponsor became a candidate. The one exception, Kemp's Campaign for Prosperity, was registered in 1976 and began operating in 1978.[68] But even in this instance, the committee's financial activity increased dramatically when Kemp began to consider a possible future presidential candidacy. During the 1983-1984 and 1985-1986 election cycles, the committee's total receipts were fourteen times greater than the amount raised in the previous two election cycles.[69]

That these PACs are intended to serve as front organizations for presidential campaigns is also indicated by their short periods of operation. Ten of the PACs listed in Table 4.1 either terminated their operations or severely reduced their activities once their sponsor became a candidate for the office of president. Two of the 1980 committees ended their operations before the beginning of the primary campaigns. George Bush's Fund for a Limited Government terminated its operations on March 31, 1979, two months after Bush established a principal campaign committee and one month before he publicly announced his decision to become a candidate.[70] John Connally's Citizens Forum terminated its operations on June 30, 1979, five months after Connally formed a campaign committee and publicly declared his candidacy.[71] Dole's Campaign America remained active throughout the formal campaign period but raised only $9,500 from April 1979 to June 1980.[72]

Of the committees established by candidates in advance of the 1984 election, only Alan Cranston's Committee for a Democratic Consensus closed down before the nomination campaign began, ending its operations five months after Cranston announced his intention to run.[73] The PACs established by other Democratic contenders maintained operations throughout the primaries but severely reduced their activities. Mondale's Committee for the Future of America raised only $24,000 in 1984 and reported no receipts thereafter. In June 1986, it informed the commission that it had terminated its operations.[74] Glenn's National Council on Public Policy and Hollings's Citizens for a Competitive America also decreased their activity after the campaign, respectively raising only $24,000 and $7,300 during the 1985-1986 election cycle.[75]

Two of the committees established in anticipation of the 1988 race ended operations before the campaign began and one committee, Paul Simon's Democracy Fund, closed soon after the primary campaign commenced. Babbitt's Americans for the National Interest terminated operations in December 1986, two weeks before Babbitt registered his principal campaign committee.[76] Joseph Biden's Fund for '86 ended its activities only a few days before Biden formed his campaign committee.[77] Simon's Democracy Fund continued to operate after his declaration of candidacy. But the committee raised only $5,000 in the last six months of 1987 and terminated its operations in March 1988.[78] Alexander Haig's Committee for America also remained active after its sponsor became a candidate, but it received only $11,600 between December 1987 and October 1988.[79]

THE FINANCIAL ACTIVITY OF CANDIDATE PACs

Despite their short periods of operation, PACs associated with prospective presidential candidates raise and spend substantial amounts of money. Tables 4.2 through 4.7 present summaries of the financial activity of these committees in each of the last three elections. Two tables are provided for each election cycle, one summarizing PAC receipts and the other PAC expenditures. The totals noted are based on the amounts reported by each committee in its required financial reports and disclosed in the FEC's Committee Index of Disclosure Documents. The tables include all reported data on receipts and expenditures for the entire nomination campaign election cycle, beginning January 1 of the year following a presidential election and ending June 30 of the election year in which the committees' sponsors ran for office. Because the central contention of this analysis is that candidates establish multicandidate committees to assist their presidential nomination campaigns, only monies raised or spent before the conclusion of the presidential primary campaign are included. Funds spent after the completion of the prenomination campaign would have little, if any, effect on a candidate's success in winning his or her party's nomination.

Before we examine the details of particular elections, three general patterns should be noted. First, the amount raised and spent by candidate PACs increased dramatically during the 1980s. The four candidate PACs active before the 1980 election raised about $6 million. The nine PACs organized at the federal level prior to the 1988 election raised more than $25 million. The expenditures of these committees normally matched their receipts; none of the groups sought to amass funds for future use.

Second, the most financially successful PACs were those associated with individuals who were well known or considered to be the early leaders among potential candidates. Well-known aspirants used these committees to achieve a substantial resource advantage over their lesser-known challengers. Particularly noteworthy are the sums raised by the PACs created by Reagan in 1980, Mondale in 1984, and Bush in 1988. The data show that these eventual nominees gained a substantial head start over their prospective opponents as a result of their respective PAC fundraising efforts.

Finally, the data reveal that most of the financial activity conducted by these groups occurs in the first two years of a presidential election cycle, or long before the candidates establish formal campaign committees. On average, these committees raised about 70 percent of their monies before the midterm elections. The level of financial activity then steeply declines as the election year approaches. If the fundamental purpose of these organizations were to assist the party, one would think that such assistance would be just as important in presidential years as in the midterm contests.

The 1980 Election

During the 1980 election cycle, the four PACs sponsored by candidates reported $6.11 million in aggregate receipts, as noted in Table 4.2. Seventy percent of this amount was raised during the first two years of the election cycle. Twenty-two percent of the committees' aggregate contributions ($1.32 million) were received in 1977 and 48 percent ($2.96 million) in 1978. An additional $1.28 million, or 21 percent of total revenues, was received in 1979. Only Reagan's PAC, Citizens for the Republic, continued to solicit contributions during the election year.

Reagan's Citizens for the Republic (CFTR) was responsible for the largest proportion of aggregate receipts, raising $4.9 million, or 80 percent of the aggregate amount reported by these committees. CFTR raised approximately $3.1 million, or 64 percent of its total revenue, in the first two years of the election cycle and another $1.24 million, or 25 percent of its total revenue, in 1979. These figures do not include the $1.6 million in leftover campaign funds from Reagan's 1976 race that

TABLE 4.2
Receipts of Candidate-Sponsored PACs, 1980 Election Cycle (thousand $)

PAC	1977	1978	1979	1980[a]	Total
Campaign America	0.0	205.2	33.9	0.0	239.1
Citizens for the Republic	1,094.8	2,019.7	1,239.3	549.7	4,903.5
Fund for a Limited Government	48.4	188.7	3.1	0.0	240.2
John Connally Citizens Forum	177.7	545.3	4.7	0.0	727.7
Annual total	1,320.9	2,958.9	1,281.0	549.7	6,110.5

[a]Amounts reported through June 30.

Source: Data based on receipts reported by each committee in Federal Election Commission, Committee Index of Disclosure Documents (C Index), 1977-1980, computer printouts, n.d.

served as the PAC's initial capital. These transferred monies represented about $1 million in net PAC receipts because the committee had to repay $581,000 to the U.S. Treasury after the FEC determined that this amount represented public matching funds that could not be transferred to a multicandidate committee.[80] When the net amount of the campaign transfer is added to the sum raised by the PAC after its formation, the committee's total revenues equal about $5.9 million.

CFTR's revenues greatly exceeded the funds raised by other candidate-sponsored PACs. John Connally's Citizens Forum, which was second to Reagan's PAC in fundraising, reported $727,000 in receipts, or one-eighth of CFTR's total. Bush's Fund for a Limited Government and Dole's Campaign America raised relatively small amounts compared to their competitors. The total receipts of each committee were less than a third of the amount generated by Connally's PAC and less than 5 percent of Reagan's total. Reagan thus achieved a financial edge of more than $5 million over his prospective opponents as a result of his PAC's financial activities.

As noted in Table 4.3, these committees disbursed approximately $7.48 million, an amount $1.4 million greater than their total receipts. This excess spending was made possible in large part by the surplus campaign funds available to Reagan's committee. CFTR spent approximately $6.9 million, nearly $2 million more than its total contributions. Dole's Campaign America also spent more than it

TABLE 4.3
Expenditures of Candidate-Sponsored PACs, 1980 Election Cycle (thousand $)

PAC	1977	1978	1979	1980[a]	Total
Campaign America	0.0	197.5	41.4	0.0	238.9
Citizens for the Republic	1,781.4	2,727.7	1,272.6	491.1	6,272.8
Fund for a Limited Government	5.2	222.3	12.7	0.0	240.2
John Connally Citizens Forum	45.1	673.8	8.8	0.0	727.7
Annual total	1,831.7	3,821.3	1,335.5	491.1	7,479.6

[a]Amounts reported through June 30.

Source: Data based on expenditures reported by each committee in Federal Election Commission, Committee Index of Disclosure Documents (C Index), 1977-1980, computer printouts, n.d.

raised. This committee reported $13,000 in excess spending. The other two committees spent an amount equal to their total receipts.

Spending patterns generally followed revenue patterns. Seventy-five percent of all expenditures were made in the first two years of the election cycle. An aggregate $1.83 million was disbursed in 1977 and $3.8 million in 1978, which represented 24 percent and 51 percent of total reported spending, respectively. An additional $1.33 million, or 18 percent of total spending, was disbursed in 1979. CFTR was the only committee to disburse funds in 1980, spending $491,200.

The 1984 Election

During the 1984 election cycle, candidate-sponsored PACs reported $7.2 million in aggregate receipts (see Table 4.4), an increase of 18 percent over 1980. But there were five committees active in 1984 as compared to four in 1980. The average amount received by each committee in 1984 actually declined slightly from $1.53 million in 1980 to $1.44 million. These figures do not account for funds received by Kennedy's Fund for a Democratic Majority because Kennedy never entered the race. This committee raised $2.3 million before he announced that he would not become a candidate. If these contributions are included in the aggregate amount, the total raised by these committees is $9.5 million, an increase of 56 percent over 1980.

As in the 1980 election cycle, most of these contributions (67 percent) were raised well in advance of the election. Twenty-four percent of the committees' aggregate contributions ($1.74 million) were received in 1981 and 44 percent ($3.13 million) in 1982. Nineteen percent of total revenues ($1.47 million) were raised in 1983 and only 10 percent ($868,700) in 1984. Most of the 1984 monies were generated by Reagan's Citizens for the Republic, which raised $840,700 during the election year.

Reagan's PAC again led all committees in fundraising. This is not surprising given the well-established donor base the PAC had developed after more than four years of continuous operation. CFTR raised approximately $4.27 million, or 59 percent of the aggregate receipts reported by the five candidate-sponsored committees. Sixty-one percent of this amount ($2.4 million) was received during the first two years of the election cycle. CFTR's 1984 revenues were therefore slightly lower than its 1980 proceeds, but its role was not as crucial in 1984 because Reagan had the advantages of the incumbency and faced no serious challenge for the party's nomination. Even so, $4 million is a hefty sum, especially when compared to the revenues of his Democratic counterparts.

TABLE 4.4
Receipts of Candidate-Sponsored PACs, 1984 Election Cycle (thousand $)

PAC	1981	1982	1983	1984[a]	Total
Citizens for a Competitive America	0.0	198.2	32.1	15.7	246.0
Citizens for the Republic	1,049.7	1,366.0	1,013.0	840.8	4,269.5
Committee for a Democratic Consensus	8.0	7.4	52.0	0.0	67.4
Committee for the Future of America	678.5	1,511.8	294.5	10.2	2,495.0
National Council on Public Policy	0.0	49.8	80.0	2.0	131.8
Annual total	1,736.2	3,133.2	1,471.6	868.7	7,209.7

[a]Amounts reported through June 30.

Source: Data based on receipts reported by each committee in Federal Election Commission, Committee Index of Disclosure Documents (C Index), 1981-1984, computer printouts, n.d.

The second most successful committee with respect to fundraising was Walter Mondale's Committee for the Future of America (CFA). This PAC raised $2.49 million, which was only 58 percent of CFTR's total but ten times more than its nearest Democratic counterpart. Like Reagan's committee, CFA began raising funds early. It received 88 percent of its total revenues during the first two years of the election cycle, raising $678,500 in 1981 and $1.51 million in 1982. Mondale's main challengers—Glenn's National Council on Public Policy, Hollings's Citizens for a Competitive America, and Cranston's Committee for a Democratic Consensus—organized later than CFA and initiated fundraising efforts well after CFA had begun soliciting donations. The only other committee to begin raising money in 1981 was Cranston's Committee for a Democratic Consensus, and it produced a meager $8,000 in that year. Overall, these three committees had aggregate receipts of $445,100, less than one-fifth of Mondale's total.

As noted in Table 4.5, the five committees active in the 1984 election cycle spent approximately $6.96 million, which was $250,000 less than they received and $520,000 less than the amount spent by the four committees active in 1980. Spending in the 1984 cycle generally followed the patterns established in 1980. Most expenditures were made early in the election cycle and tended to correspond to revenue

TABLE 4.5
Expenditures of Candidate-Sponsored PACs, 1984 Election Cycle (thousand $)

PAC	1981	1982	1983	1984[a]	Total
Citizens for a Competitive America	0.0	149.1	66.5	11.4	227.0
Citizens for the Republic	927.8	1,552.8	906.2	659.1	4,045.9
Comm. for a Democratic Consensus	5.1	9.5	57.4	0.0	72.0
Comm. for the Future of America	399.2	1,771.1	314.7	6.8	2,491.8
National Council on Public Policy	0.0	37.5	78.1	7.2	122.8
Annual total	1,332.1	3,520.0	1,422.9	684.5	6,959.5

[a]Amounts reported through June 30.

Source: Data based on expenditures reported by each committee in Federal Election Commission, Committee Index of Disclosure Documents (C Index), 1981-1984, computer printouts, n.d.

patterns. Seventy percent of aggregate expenditures were made in the first two years as compared to 75 percent in 1980. An aggregate $1.33 million was disbursed in 1981 and $3.52 million in 1982, which represented 19 percent and 51 percent of total spending. As in 1980, CFTR was responsible for most of the election-year expenditures, spending $659,100, or 96 percent of all expenditures made in 1984. Cranston's Committee for a Democratic Consensus was the only PAC to spend more than it received during the cycle, spending $4,600 more than it raised.

The decline in spending from 1980 was primarily a result of the lower level of expenditures made by Reagan's Citizens for the Republic. CFTR spent approximately $4 million, $220,000 less than it received and $2.9 million less than it disbursed in 1980. This reduced level of spending probably reflects the fact that Reagan was uncontested. Yet it dwarfed the sums spent by his prospective opponents.

The other committees disbursed $2.9 million, or 42 percent of the total funds expended. Mondale's CFA was responsible for 86 percent of these expenditures, spending $2.49 million, or a few thousand dollars less than it received. Hollings's Citizens for a Competitive America, Glenn's National Council on Public Policy, and Cranston's Committee for a Democratic Consensus spent significantly less than CFA, as would be expected given their modest resources. Thus, in 1984 Mondale succeeded in using a PAC as Reagan had in 1980. He outraised and outspent his competitors in the initial stage of the presidential contest, thereby achieving a significant financial lead prior to the beginning of the formal selection process.

The 1988 Election

The financial activity of candidate-sponsored PACs in the 1980 and 1984 election cycles, although substantial, is relatively insignificant when compared to the enormous sums generated in anticipation of the 1988 nomination contest. The nine federal committees active in the 1988 election cycle raised $25.25 million (see Table 4.6), twice the amount raised by the nine committees active in the two previous cycles and 250 percent more than the amount raised in 1984. The average amount received by each committee was $2.8 million, nearly double the $1.44 million average of the 1984 committees.

What is even more astounding is that these figures do not represent all of the funds spent through precampaign organizations in advance of the 1988 election. For example, they do not include the monies raised by the committees associated with Pete du Pont. Because GOPAC and the National Leadership Council are not active in federal elections, they are not subject to federal public disclosure procedures. Nor do they include the $3.52 million raised by tax-exempt foundations sponsored by presidential aspirants. These organizations are also exempt from FEC regulations since their activities fall under the jurisdiction of the Internal Revenue Service.

The figures also omit the monies raised by Baker's Republican Majority Fund (RMF), Rumsfeld's Citizens for American Values PAC (CAV), Kennedy's Fund for a Democratic Majority (FDM), and Cuomo's Empire Leadership Fund (ELF) because these individuals never entered the race. RMF raised $1.62 million, CAV $1.17 million, and FDM $1.29 million before their sponsors announced that they would not become candidates. ELF raised $108,570 before the speculation concerning a possible Cuomo candidacy subsided.[81] If these sums are included in the calculation of aggregate receipts, the total amount raised through PACs rises to $29.97 million. If the monies generated by tax-exempt organizations are added, the total reaches about $32.5 million. The amount of money raised by organizations other than authorized campaign committees was therefore four or five times greater than the similar amounts received in either the 1980 or 1984 campaign.

The revenue pattern of PACs active in the 1988 cycle was similar to earlier patterns, with one major exception: the level of early

TABLE 4.6
Receipts of Candidate-Sponsored PACs, 1988 Election Cycle (thousand $)

PAC	1985	1986	1987	1988[a]	Total
Americans for the Natl. Interest	52.2	104.3	0.0	0.0	156.5
Campaign America	418.0	2,929.4	2,417.7	380.6	6,145.7
Campaign for Prosperity	1,171.7	2,057.9	695.0	199.5	4,124.1
Comm. for America	0.0	650.7	418.4	11.6	1,080.7
Comm. for Freedom	161.3	399.3	76.8	75.2	712.6
The Democracy Fund	161.9	262.9	30.5	10.5	465.8
Effective Government Committee	361.5	722.5	89.4	52.8	1,226.2
Fund for America's Future	3,993.0	5,380.0	1,231.2	601.6	11,205.8
Fund for '86	0.0	132.3	0.9	0.0	133.2
Annual total	6,319.6	12,639.3	4,959.9	1,331.8	25,250.6

[a]Amounts reported through June 30.

Source: Data based on receipts reported by each committee in Federal Election Commission, Committee Index of Disclosure Documents (C Index), 1985-1988, computer printouts, n.d.

fundraising was greater than that of previous elections. Seventy-five percent of all funds ($18.9 million) were solicited in the first two years of the election cycle as compared to 70 percent in 1980 and 67 percent in 1984. The number of committees engaged in early fundraising also increased. Five of the nine committees began receiving funds in the second quarter of 1985 (the cycle's first year), compared to one committee in 1977 and three in 1984.[82]

The unprecedented level of financial activity in the 1988 election cycle was largely due to the fundraising efforts of PACs sponsored by candidates seeking the Republican nomination. Ninety-two percent of the aggregate funds raised in this cycle were generated by the five committees established by Republican contenders. Four of these committees raised more than $1 million. Of the PACs sponsored by Democratic candidates, only Gephardt's Effective Government Committee achieved this mark. The PAC primarily responsible for the increase in aggregate receipts was Bush's FAF, which raised a staggering $11.2 million. FAF's receipts constituted 44 percent of the total monies raised during the cycle. The second wealthiest committee,

Dole's Campaign America, raised $6.14 million, or 55 percent of FAF's total. Kemp's Campaign for Prosperity raised $4.12 million, a sum equivalent to the amount raised in the 1984 cycle by Citizens for the Republic, the leading fundraiser four years earlier. Haig's Committee for America, which did not begin soliciting contributions until 1986, also surpassed the $1 million mark, raising approximately $1.08 million. The only Republican-backed committee to raise less than $1 million was Robertson's Committee for Freedom, which raised $712,600. But the fundraising efforts of this committee were supplemented by the activities of Robertson's tax-exempt foundation.

This summary of the monies received by Republican-sponsored PACs indicates that three committees were primarily responsible for the enormous sum generated in the 1988 cycle. Bush's Fund for America's Future, Dole's Campaign America, and Kemp's Campaign for Prosperity raised $21.46 million, 85 percent of the total amount received by the 1988 committees. The success of these PACs is a result of the stature and previous experience of their sponsors. Bush, Dole, and Kemp were better known in the early stages of the campaign than the other individuals who sponsored PACs. Bush was the incumbent vice president. Dole was the Republican Senate majority leader and had formerly been a candidate for vice president and a contender for the 1980 presidential nomination. Kemp was less well known but he had achieved some prominence as cosponsor of the Kemp-Roth tax bill and as a leader of the party's conservative wing. In addition, these three individuals were perceived to be the most viable candidates early in the race. By mid-1985, they (and Howard Baker) were ranked in public opinion polls as the top contenders for the Republican nomination. They continued to lead the Republican field throughout 1986 and 1987.[83] Lastly, all three were familiar with PAC operations and had sponsored PACs prior to the 1988 election cycle. Bush had used a PAC before his 1980 presidential bid and benefited from the list of contributors developed by his 1980 campaign. Dole and Kemp relied on committees that had been active for years. This experience gave them a head start over the committees formed by their competitors and allowed them to raise $5.8 million in 1985 compared to $737,000 for the six other candidate-sponsored PACs.

PACs sponsored by Democratic candidates raised $1.98 million, less than 10 percent of the Republican PAC total. Gephardt's Effective Government Committee, which was the first committee organized by a Democratic hopeful in the 1988 cycle, raised 62 percent of these funds. This committee raised $1.22 million, two-and-a-half times more than its nearest counterpart, Simon's Democracy Fund, which raised $465,800. The other two committees established by Democrats,

Babbitt's Americans for the National Interest and Biden's Fund for '86, began soliciting contributions well after their competitors and were not as successful. Babbitt's PAC received only $156,500, but these funds were supplemented by the monies raised by American Horizons, Babbitt's tax-exempt foundation. Biden's committee was the last to be organized and raised only $133,200, or $1.1 million less than Gephardt's committee.

PAC spending in the 1988 cycle was similar to previous cycles, although the amount spent was unprecedented, as would be expected given the committees' aggregate receipts. The nine committees disbursed about $25.2 million (see Table 4.7), $25,000 less than they received. Only one committee spent more than it raised during the four-year period. Dole's Campaign America raised $6.14 million but spent $6.54 million, a difference of $400,000. The other eight committees disbursed approximately $18.7 million, $425,000 less than they received. Campaign America was able to spend more than it raised because it entered the 1988 election cycle with a surplus of approximately $450,000.[84] These funds,which were raised during a previous election cycle, are not included in the amounts listed in Table 4.6.

TABLE 4.7
Expenditures of Candidate-Sponsored PACs, 1988 Election Cycle (thousand $)

PAC	1985	1986	1987	1988[a]	Total
Americans for the Natl. Interest	45.7	110.6	0.0	0.0	156.3
Campaign America	390.4	2,859.1	2,917.0	378.3	6,544.8
Campaign for Prosperity	1,198.9	2,048.8	679.6	233.7	4,161.0
Comm. for America	0.0	599.7	465.3	10.0	1,075.0
Comm. for Freedom	56.3	514.6	67.5	45.8	684.2
The Democracy Fund	135.2	278.4	37.5	14.5	465.6
Effective Government Committee	317.7	750.5	102.1	53.4	1,223.7
Fund for America's Future	1,545.9	7,656.6	1,291.6	287.6	10,781.7
Fund for '86	0.0	121.2	12.0	0.0	133.2
Annual total	3,690.1	14,939.5	5,572.6	1,023.3	25,225.5

[a]Amounts reported through June 30.

Source: Data based on expenditures reported by each committee in Federal Election Commission, Committee Index of Disclosure Documents (C Index), 1985-1988, computer printouts, n.d.

Once again the committees spent monies as they were received, with some minor variance due to the excess spending by Dole's PAC. Seventy-four percent of the committees' total expenditures were made in the first two years of the election cycle. The comparable amounts in the two earlier cycles were 75 percent and 70 percent. The committees disbursed an aggregate $3.69 million in 1985 and $14.9 million in 1986, which represented 15 percent and 59 percent of total spending. Most of the committees continued to spend money during the election year just as they continued to solicit contributions. Although the percentage of funds spent during this period was lower than the percentage in 1980 and 1984, the total amount spent nearly equaled the combined total of the two previous election years.

THE 1992 ELECTION

The initial stage of the 1992 election cycle reflected the basic patterns established in the campaigns of the 1980s. A number of poten-tial presidential aspirants organized PAC operations and began the tasks associated with the beginnings of a presidential campaign.[85] George Bush, however, chose not to maintain his PAC operation in anticipation of the 1992 campaign. The Fund for America's Future remained active after Bush was elected president, but it ceased its fundraising efforts. The PAC spent about $43,000 in 1989 and 1990 before terminating its operations on June 4, 1990, transferring the $137,000 remaining in its account to the Republican National State Elections Committee for use in state and local elections.[86]

The PAC's termination report does not explain why it chose to end its operations. One reason may be that Bush no longer needed the committee to build a political and financial organization. Including his 1980 experience, Bush had spent twelve consecutive years running for president or serving as vice president and thus had developed an extensive nationwide financial and political base. Yet he still could have used the PAC to maintain his organization, as Reagan did during his first term in office. This approach, however, would have made it more difficult for Bush to assist his party in Congress, who were engaged at the time in a heated debate on a campaign finance reform package. A cornerstone of the Republican position on this issue was the need for legislation that severely restricted or, preferably, eliminated the role of PACs in financing congressional campaigns. Bush supported this reform and in his 1991 State of the Union address urged Congress to "totally eliminate political action committees."[87] It would have been difficult for the president to defend this proposal if he had continued to maintain his PAC operation.

Perhaps most prominent among the individuals who decided to form a PAC in anticipation of the 1992 election was the Reverend Jesse Jackson, who had failed to exploit the PAC option prior to his 1984 and 1988 candidacies. In June 1988, while still technically a candidate for the Democratic presidential nomination (Dukakis had received enough delegate support to secure the nomination, but the national convention was still a month away), Jackson announced that he would form a PAC to serve as the "basis for his activities beyond the 1988 election."[88] He further noted, according to political reporter Bernard Weintraub, that the PAC "would not only serve as an operational base but, for the first time, would also provide money to candidates aligned with [him] and set the stage for him to increase his political influence around the country among . . . 'progressive' candidates."[89] The committee filed with the FEC on June 30, 1988, under the name Keep Hope Alive PAC, and Steven Cobble, a member of Jackson's presidential campaign staff, became the group's executive director.

Keep Hope Alive PAC quickly began to raise money, organize a staff, and undertake various political activities. By mid-1989 the committee reported receipts of approximately $280,000. Much of this money was used as seed money to develop a national direct mail effort and lists of supporters.[90] By the end of 1989 the committee had raised approximately $561,000 and spent $513,000. It raised an additional $211,000 in 1990, while spending about $244,000.[91] Of these amounts, the committee contributed approximately $8,000 by mid-1989 to candidates for public office (most of whom were involved in mayoral and local judgeship races in Mississippi, Texas, and New Jersey) and donated an additional $7,025 to Democratic candidates for federal office in 1990.[92]

Jackson also maintained his affiliation with the National Rainbow Coalition, an independent, nonprofit group that was created before the 1988 election. By 1989 the organization had a full-time staff of seventeen and an annual budget of approximately $1 million, which was raised through direct mail solicitations and individual contributions.[93] Although the group's nonprofit status limits the types of political activities it may pursue, it is involved in a wide range of activities that could benefit a presidential campaign. For example, an offshoot of the organization, the Citizenship Education Fund, researches voter registration issues and helps direct voter registration drives around the country. The coalition also conducts canvasing drives to determine what issues the public may want the group to address.[94] In February 1989 the coalition took a more direct action with respect to a possible presidential candidacy and formed a subsidiary organization in Iowa. The organizers of the group stressed that its purpose "was more than just the start of Jesse Jackson's 1992 campaign for President" and was actually to help "empower" people at the state and local level. An advertisement in the group's convention booklet, however, read "Only 1,078 days before caucus. See you in '92!"[95]

Richard Gephardt also helped to keep his options for a 1992 candidacy open by maintaining the PAC he founded prior to the 1988 election. His Effective Government Committee raised about $280,000 in 1989 and $571,000 in 1990. The committee spent $240,000 in 1989 and $616,000 in advance of the midterm election.[96] A significant portion of these funds were spent in the form of contributions to candidates for federal office. During the 1989-1990 congressional election cycle, Gephardt's committee made donations to seventy-four Democratic candidates, which included four Senate contenders and seventy House candidates.[97] These contributions totaled $252,000, or approximately 30 percent of the sum raised by the committee during this period. This active giving largely reflected Gephardt's being selected as House Majority Leader in 1989; he used the PAC to help fellow party members. The political goodwill developed through these gifts, of course, would also benefit Gephardt if he were to run for the presidency in the future.

Mario Cuomo was also in position to begin a precampaign political operation in the initial stage of the 1992 race. The Empire Leadership Fund, a PAC formed in advance of the 1988 election, continued to operate after the election and could have served as a vehicle for promoting Cuomo's presidential prospects. But the fund was relatively inactive as Cuomo's political supporters concentrated their efforts on his 1990 gubernatorial reelection campaign. The fund raised no additional monies in 1989 and spent only $12,700. In August 1990 it terminated its activities and transferred the $55,000 remaining in its account to the New York State Democratic Committee.[98]

Cuomo's reelection committee, however, was very active during this period, raising close to $8.4 million. After the election, the committee held a surplus of approximately $3.8 million.[99] Cuomo was thus positioned to jump-start a presidential campaign. If he decided to enter the 1992 race, he could transfer the extensive donor list created by his reelection committee and any monies from his gubernatorial campaign that met federal contribution limits to a presidential committee and thus "hit the ground running" in the same way that Michael Dukakis had in 1987.

Another potential aspirant with a political organization in the earliest days of the 1992 election cycle was Congresswoman Patricia

Schroeder. Schroeder explored the possibility of a presidential bid in 1987, and after deciding against a candidacy, she converted her exploratory organization into a "political organization" named the Fund for the Future, which described itself as an "organization associated with a public official and certain views on public policy."[100] The committee began 1988 with over $880,000 in receipts generated by the exploratory committee and raised an additional $62,000 in 1988 and $119,000 in 1989. The group spent about $609,000 during this period.[101]

The Fund for the Future reported no contributions to federal candidates in the 1988 and 1990 elections. The committee did, however, conduct a direct mail fundraising effort and helped defray the costs of Schroeder's travel. This travel was largely for the purpose of delivering speeches and attending meetings in conjunction with Schroeder's efforts to promote a progressive issue agenda and educate the public about the policy needs in such areas as childcare and health care. By May 1989, Schroeder had traveled to thirty-two cities in seventeen states, including three separate trips to New Hampshire.[102] In mid-1991, however, the fund decided to terminate its operations and requested permission from the Federal Election Commission to transfer the $467,000 left in its account to Schroeder's 1992 congressional campaign committee. The commission approved this request with the proviso that the monies transferred would be subject to the provisions of federal law.[103]

Senator Bill Bradley of New Jersey, another official prominently mentioned as a possible 1992 contender, was also well positioned for a presidential bid in the earliest stage of the election cycle. Since the mid-1980s Bradley has been associated with the Fair Tax Foundation, a tax-exempt, nonprofit organization that sponsors policy forums and other public education efforts on issues associated with government tax policy.[104] This group thus provided Bradley with a vehicle similar to Gary Hart's Center for a New Democracy that could be used to sponsor his travel and public appearances and develop a list of potential campaign donors. During 1989 and 1990, however, Bradley concentrated on his reelection campaign. In doing so, he devoted substantial time to fundraising, soliciting more than $9 million by April 1990 and developing a nationwide donor base in the process.[105] He, like Cuomo, thus developed a financial base that could be used to initiate presidential fundraising effort.

These early Democratic efforts to pave the way for a possible presidential candidacy never reached the levels achieved in the 1988 campaign largely because of several extraordinary political circumstances. In general, one can assume that the scope and intensity of the campaign politicking prior to the 1992 election would not have equaled that of 1988 under any normal circumstances because the Democratic nominee would in all likelihood be facing an incumbent president. This prospect usually leads potential challengers to approach a race more cautiously, especially if the incumbent is a popular leader. And this was certainly the case with President Bush. Throughout his first eighteen months in office, Bush enjoyed notably high approval ratings in public opinion polls. During most of this period the percentage of the public that approved of the president's performance stood at more than 60 percent.[106] After the invasion of Panama late in 1989, public approval of the president's performance rose even higher, reaching 80 percent in January 1990, a mark exceeded in the Gallup Poll only once since World War II, that being in the poll conducted after the 1961 Bay of Pigs invasion.[107]

The president's popularity discouraged widespread Democratic politicking, and the dramatic events surrounding the August 1990 invasion of Kuwait by Iraq and the following war in the Gulf produced an abrupt chilling effect with respect to presidential campaigning. No Democrat was willing to pursue open campaigning while the nation was engulfed in this crisis. During this period many prominently mentioned potential candidates were also absorbed in their own reelection campaigns. Given the uncertainty regarding the outcome of events and their effect on the president's political support, no aspirant wanted to follow Gary Hart's 1988 approach and forsake a reelection bid to devote time to presidential politicking. Mario Cuomo, Bill Bradley, Richard Gephardt, Al Gore, Patricia Schroeder, and Governor Bill Clinton of Arkansas therefore concentrated their efforts on their 1990 reelection campaigns, in some cases promising not to seek the 1992 nomination if reelected.[108] Jackson also became more involved in nonpresidential politics, campaigning on behalf of D.C. statehood and winning selection to serve as one of D.C.'s "shadow senators" to promote the cause of statehood.

The outcome of the Gulf War left potential Democratic challengers facing the prospect of a steep uphill battle in 1992 as Bush's popularity soared again in early 1991, rising above the 80 percent mark from mid-February to early April.[109] Moreover, potential aspirants also had to weigh the consequences of mounting a national campaign in a relatively short period of time. Having failed to take advantage of the early window of opportunity to begin a campaign, Democratic hopefuls had to decide whether to try and jump-start a campaign less than ten months before the Iowa caucus or wait until 1996 when the climate might be more favorable to a Democratic bid. At this time it appeared that a Democrat who chose to wait would not have to face an incumbent president (because it was widely assumed that Bush was likely to be reelected). By deciding to wait, a candidate would also have three or four years to prepare for a campaign and could pursue the sorts of precampaign politicking that had become common in past elections. Predictably, many prominently mentioned potential candidates chose to sit out the 1992 contest. As a result, on May 1, 1991, less than ten months before the Iowa caucus, former senator Paul Tsongas of Massachusetts was the only Democrat to have decided to enter the race.

The 1992 election cycle, therefore, has not followed the patterns established in the 1980s. It is likely, however, that this will prove to be an aberration and that early campaigning will again play a significant role in the politics of 1996. The 1992 experience is the result of a rather unique set of political circumstances; it is not the result of a change in the nominating process or in the decisions made by candidates as to how to best conduct a presidential campaign. Barring a Democratic victory in 1992 or some other unforeseen circumstance, both parties will once again have hotly contested nomination campaigns in the 1996 election cycle. This is likely to encourage some aspirants, especially lesser-known contenders, to begin campaigning long before the first primary. In addition, the factors that induced candidates throughout the 1980s to begin campaigning early will continue to influence candidate strategies. Unless the rules governing campaign finance are dramatically reformed, presidential hopefuls will still have to contend with the conflicting pressures generated by the fixed contribution limit, the provisions of the public matching funds program, and the ceilings on state and aggregate spending. These aspirants will also have to confront the organizational and financial demands that accompany a front-loaded delegate selection process and rising campaign costs. In attempting to address these pressures, candidates will once again have to consider the potential advantages of a PAC operation or tax-exempt organization. The strategic environment of the nominating process will thus continue to highlight the benefits of a precandidacy PAC and induce some candidates to circumvent the limits of federal law.

CONCLUSION

The formation of a multicandidate PAC in the early years of a presidential election cycle became a common practice among presidential aspirants in the 1980s. Although these PACs assist other candidates and engage in party-building activities, they are established primarily to serve as front organizations for their sponsors' prospective campaign committees. This practice violates the original purpose of this type of committee, which was to provide labor unions, corporations, and organized groups with a structure through which they could participate legally in federal elections. It also challenges the legal prohibition against using a PAC as an authorized campaign committee.[110] But PACs have proven to be an effective vehicle for early campaigning. As a result, they have flourished.

The analysis presented in this chapter indicates four ways in which the efficacy of federal regulations has been undermined by the growth of precandidacy PACs. First, an increasing number of candidates are establishing PACs in anticipation of a presidential campaign. Second, these committees are raising and spending increasingly large sums of money outside of the limits imposed on candidates. Third, the use of PACs generates significant resource inequities among contenders for the presidential nomination. Finally, the trend toward PAC sponsorship in the early years of an election cycle increases the pressure to expand the length of a presidential campaign, thus contributing to further attempts to stretch the limits of the law.

In each of the last three election cycles, an increasing number of individuals have initiated a presidential campaign or attempted to initiate one by forming a political action committee. Prior to the 1980 election, four of the ten major candidates employed this alternative. Before the 1988 election, ten of the fourteen major candidates (du Pont included) exploited this option. In addition, four potential 1988 candidates (Baker, Rumsfeld, Kennedy, and Cuomo) were associated with PACs and used their resources, at least in part, to promote a potential future candidacy. Although PACs were not intended to serve this role, candidates form these committees with this express purpose in mind.

That presidential politics rather than party-building is the motivating force behind the formation of these committees is indicated by their periods of operation. The committees are usually established in the first eighteen months of a presidential election cycle. Once they have served their purpose (i.e., served as an "unofficial" campaign operation), they usually end their activities. Most of the committees are dormant once the formal primary campaign begins and end their operations shortly thereafter. The few that remain active well after a nomination contest are usually sponsored by individuals who have not foreclosed the possibility of a future presidential bid or who hold an elective office that could also benefit from a PAC affiliation. If the primary purpose of these committees were to assist other candidates and the party, they would probably not be characterized by such short periods of operation.

The second conclusion to be drawn from the data in this chapter is that the proliferation of candidate-sponsored PACs has been accompanied by a sizable increase in their financial activity. Prospective candidates have unabashedly employed these organizations to raise and spend millions of dollars outside the limits imposed on candidate campaign committees. Overall, these PACs have raised and spent more than $38 million in the last three election cycles. They raised $6.11 million in the 1980 cycle and $7.21 million in the 1984 cycle, an increase of 18 percent. In the 1988 cycle, the revenues generated by these committees totaled $25.25 million, an increase of 250 percent over 1984. In each of these periods, the committees spent about what they received, although actual spending in the 1980 cycle exceeded receipts by $1.3 million due to the surplus funds available to Reagan's Citizens for the Republic.

This growth in PAC revenues is significant even when adjusted for inflation, as noted in Table 4.8. These data document the real increase that has occurred since 1980, although they also indicate a decline in real revenues in the 1984 cycle. Real receipts fell from $5.20 million in the 1980 cycle to $4.25 million in 1984, an 18 percent decrease. The adjusted average receipts of each committee fell from $1.3 million to $850,200, a 35 percent decline. This reduction was primarily due to the comparatively modest sum raised by Citizens for the Republic (CFTR) during Reagan's first term. With Reagan uncontested for the nomination, CFTR raised an adjusted $2.50 million, approximately 40 percent less than its adjusted 1980 total of $4.14 million. The other 1984 committees partially offset this reduction by raising an adjusted $1.74 million, or 64 percent more than CFTR's 1980 counterparts.

Adjusted receipts, like actual receipts, increased considerably in the 1988 cycle. The PACs sponsored by candidates in this cycle generated an adjusted $13.0 million in total receipts, a real increase of 150 percent over the 1980 total and 207 percent more than the 1984 total. The average adjusted receipts of each committee rose to $1.45 million, a real increase of 11 percent over the 1980 average and 70 percent more than the 1984 average.

Table 4.9 provides summary data on PAC expenditures for the three election cycles under consideration. Generally, PAC expenditures have increased in conjunction with PAC receipts, with the committees spending slightly less than the total amount of money received. The one exception to this pattern is the level of spending in the 1980 cycle. In this period, adjusted expenditures exceeded adjusted receipts by $1.23 million. This additional spending was due to the $1.6 million in surplus funds available to Citizens for the Republic from Reagan's 1976 campaign committee. Furthermore, this excess spending, when

TABLE 4.8
Adjusted Receipts of Candidate-Sponsored PACs, 1980-1988 (thousand $)

Election Cycle	Actual Receipts	Adjusted Receipts[a]	No. of PACs	Adjusted Average Receipts/Committee[a]
1980	6,110.5	5,206.7	4	1,301.7
1984	7,209.7	4,251.0	5	850.2
1988	25,250.6	13,035.4	9	1,448.4

[a]Figures in 1976 dollars. Amounts noted based on the total receipts for these committees adjusted on a per annum basis for increases in the Consumer Price Index with 1976 as the base year (1976=100). Adjusted revenues for 1988 calculated on the basis of the unadjusted Consumer Price Index (1967=100) for June 1988.

TABLE 4.9
Adjusted Expenditures of Candidate-Sponsored PACs, 1980-1988 (thousand $)

Election Cycle	Actual Spending	Adjusted Spending[a]	No. of PACs	Adjusted Average Spending/Committee[a]
1980	7,479.6	6,441.2	4	1,610.3
1984	6,959.5	4,097.5	5	819.5
1988	25,225.5	12,995.7	9	1,444.0

[a]Figures in 1976 dollars. Amounts noted based on the total expenditures by these committees adjusted on a per annum basis for increases in the Consumer Price Index with 1976 as the base year (1976=100). Adjusted expenditures for 1988 calculated on the basis of the unadjusted Consumer Price Index (1967=100) for June 1988.

combined with CFTR's low level of spending in the 1984 cycle (the committee spent $220,000 less than it received), accounts for the large difference in adjusted expenditures between the 1980 and 1984 election cycles. Real spending in the 1984 cycle declined by $2.34 million from the previous cycle, a 36 percent decrease. In this same period, real revenues declined only 18 percent. But expenditures increased sharply in 1988. Candidate-sponsored PACs spent an adjusted $12.99 million during this cycle, an increase of 102 percent over 1980 spending and 217 percent more than in 1984.

The data in Tables 4.8 and 4.9 demonstrate that PAC sponsors have been extremely successful in using their committees to avoid the contribution and expenditure limits applicable to federal campaigns. These committees have raised and spent more than $38 million in the last three elections without having to allocate these monies to their sponsors' campaign committees. Moreover, this sum underestimates the amount of loophole spending conducted by candidates prior to declaring their candidacies. It does not include funds raised for nonfederal accounts that are not reported to the Federal Election Commission. Nor does it include nonallocable funds raised through organizations other than PACs, such as tax-exempt foundations. But even without accounting for these monies, the financial activity conducted by candidate-sponsored PACs has been extensive, highlighting the threat the committees pose to the efficacy of federal regulations.

A third conclusion is that these committees foster and accentuate resource inequities among candidates. One of the purposes of the federal campaign finance laws is to improve the equity of resources available to candidates. The statutes establish limits on contributions and expenditures in order to promote greater equity in the amount of money that each candidate can raise and spend. The use of PACs by prospective candidates undermines this goal.

Presidential hopefuls who establish PACs have a comparative resource advantage over their opponents who choose not to violate the intent of the law. Because the funds they raise or spend through the PAC are not allocable to their campaign committees, the financial activity of the PAC does not count against the limits applicable to their campaigns. PAC sponsors may thus raise and expend funds that may benefit their individual candidacies without limiting the resources available to their campaigns. This provides them with a substantial advantage over their competitors who lack similar resources.

The use of PACs also fosters inequities among the candidates who sponsor these committees. In each of the three election cycles in which candidates have established PACs, the committee sponsored by the better-known candidate has raised a significantly greater amount than the committees formed by his opponents. In the first three years of the 1980 election cycle, Reagan's Citizens for the Republic raised $4.35 million. This sum exceeded the amount raised by the second most successful fundraiser, John Connally's Citizens Forum, by $3.62 million and surpassed the amount raised by the least successful committee, Dole's Campaign America, by $4.11 million. In the first three years of the 1984 cycle, Mondale's Committee for the Future of America raised $2.48 million. This sum was $2.25 million more than the amount received by the second most successful committee, Hollings's Citizens for a Competitive America, and $2.41 million more than the least successful committee, Cranston's Committee for a Democratic Consensus. In the first three years of the most recent cycle, Bush's Fund for America's Future raised $10.6 million, $4.84 million more than Dole's Campaign America and $9.96 million more than Robertson's Committee for Freedom, the least successful committee. Among the Democrats, Gephardt's Effective Government Committee raised $1.17 million, $718,100 more than Simon's Democracy Fund and $1.04 million more than Biden's Fund for '86. The disparites revealed by these data clearly demonstrate the resource inequities that candidate-sponsored PACs have generated in recent elections.

A final conclusion is that PACs have served to increase the pressure placed on candidates to extend the length of their campaigns. Prospective candidates organize PACs in the initial year of an election cycle in order to maximize the potential resource advantage and opportunities for political activity that these organizations afford. PACs allow presidential aspirants to begin campaigning early, thereby accommodating the pressures created by presidential campaign finance regulations and the front-loading of the delegate selection process. In turn, the use of these committees has intensified the pressure placed on candidates to begin their campaigns early. Candidates who fail to capitalize on the opportunities afforded by PAC sponsorship face a potentially insurmountable organizational and financial disadvantage once the formal campaign period begins. Consequently, most candidates now establish PACs as their first step toward becoming a formal candidate. Those who refuse to establish PACs have thus been forced to consider other means of advancing their candidacies in the early stages of an election in order to maintain their relative prospects for success.

In the 1988 nomination contest, Gary Hart resolved this need by creating a tax-exempt, nonprofit foundation through which he conducted many activities that could later benefit his presidential campaign. Three other candidates soon followed Hart's lead and established foundations of their own. These tax-exempt organizations wholly undermine the goals of campaign finance reform. They are subject to no public disclosure laws. They are allowed to accept contributions from sources prohibited by federal law. And they can engage in unlimited fundraising and spending. These foundations thus pose a greater threat to the efficacy of federal campaign finance statutes than candidate-sponsored PACs. It is likely that potential candidates will employ these tax-exempt organizations in the future in their continuing quest to avoid the restrictions imposed on candidate committees. So one organizational loophole used to exploit the law has bred another designed to evade it altogether.

5

The Financial Advantages
of PAC Sponsorship

Presidential aspirants, eager to advance their candidacies and establish a foundation for their nomination campaigns, have increasingly relied on PACs to fulfill their objectives. As noted in the previous chapters, a PAC provides a prospective candidate with an organizational structure through which he or she can initiate fundraising and political activities without becoming a formal candidate. Because a PAC is legally distinct from a candidate's campaign committee and governed by different regulations, it offers its sponsor a number of financial, political, and strategic advantages that could not be achieved through an exploratory committee or authorized campaign committee. Consequently, the number of candidates sponsoring PACs has grown, fundamentally changing the way in which presidential candidates pursue their quest for the nomination.

Presidential hopefuls and their advisers have developed innovative and ingenious methods for realizing a PAC's potential. They have become increasingly adept at exploiting the unique opportunities afforded by a PAC to gain financial benefits and circumvent the limits of the law. Besides employing PACs to raise and spend money beyond federal limits, prospective candidates have used PACs for other financial advantages, including the solicitation of large contributions and soft money funds from sources banned under federal law, the use of undisclosed financial accounts, and the means to make contributions to other candidates. These advantages are the focus of the analysis in this chapter.

OVERVIEW

Presidential aspirants establish PACs in order to enhance their public visibility and begin the process of developing support for their prospective nomination campaigns. They especially want to begin the difficult and time-consuming task of developing the broad-based financial support needed to sustain a national campaign. A multicandidate PAC is an effective and popular vehicle for achieving this goal because it can help an individual fulfill this objective regardless of his or her prospects for the nomination in the early stages of a presidential race. Whether a presumed frontrunner or relatively unknown dark horse, an individual can improve the financial prospects for his or her campaign by capitalizing on the financial possibilities offered by a precandidacy PAC.

Well-known individuals or highly regarded presidential prospects, such as Reagan in 1980 and 1984, Mondale in 1984, and Bush and Dole in 1988, can use a PAC to raise large amounts of money from their established base of financial supporters. By concentrating on the solicitation of large contributions, these PACs can raise significant amounts of money in a relatively short period of time and use these funds as seed money for further fundraising activities designed to expand their financial base. Funds received by the PAC can also be used to make contributions to a large number of federal candidates. These contributions help to build political support for the PAC's sponsor in addition to assisting a party's candidates in congressional elections.

A relatively unknown candidate can use a PAC to establish a base of financial support. But unlike well-known candidates, who usually tend to raise PAC funds on the strength of their personal political appeal, lesser-known candidates usually emphasize the individuals whom they hope to help through their PACs in soliciting funds. These lesser-known candidates, at least initially, are likely to be more successful raising money if they are soliciting funds on behalf of someone else, for example, an incumbent member of Congress or a popular statewide candidate. By promoting the role of their PACs in helping other candidates, they look to build potential support for themselves among candidates and their supporters. Well-known candidates share this motive. But this aspect of a PAC operation is not as crucial to their financial success as it is for a relatively unknown presidential hopeful.

Presidential aspirants establish PACs in part because of the unique financial opportunities these committees provide. Since the federal regulations governing PACs differ from those imposed on candidate exploratory committees and authorized campaign committees, there are a number of financial practices that are either prohibited for candidate committees but allowed for a PAC or allowed for both types of committee but for practical purposes only conducted through a PAC. By establishing a PAC, a prospective candidate creates a vehicle with the ability to conduct activities that could not or would not be performed by a campaign committee. Most important among these are the ability to solicit large contributions, the ability to solicit funds from sources banned by federal law, and the capacity to make substantial donations to other candidates.

Because a PAC is subject to different contribution limits than a candidate committee, it provides a potential candidate with access to individual contributions larger than those available to an authorized campaign committee. Over the course of a presidential election cycle, a PAC can receive up to $20,000 from an individual, an amount twenty times greater than the maximum amount that can be given to a candidate's primary campaign. Prospective candidates have therefore employed PACs to solicit contributions in excess of $1,000, a practice that would not be permitted in their campaigns. Their success in soliciting such large gifts accounts for the massive sums raised by committees active during the 1988 election cycle.

A PAC can also establish soft money accounts, that is, accounts that can receive contributions for nonfederal political activities such as state and local elections or party-building activities. These accounts are governed by state and local campaign finance regulations, which are usually less restrictive than federal proscriptions. A presidential exploratory committee or campaign committee is prohibited from establishing such accounts because they are by definition only concerned with federal elections. A candidate-sponsored PAC, however, can establish a soft money account to supplement the financial activities it conducts on the federal level and gain access to funding sources that campaign committees may not legally solicit. This tactic is legal so long as the funds are received and expended in accordance with state and local law. These nonfederal accounts thus provide a means for receiving contributions in excess of the limits imposed by federal law or from sources banned by federal law, such as labor unions and corporations.

A final benefit obtained by forming a PAC is the capacity to make a substantial number of contributions to other candidates. This advantage is a unique feature of PAC sponsorship as a matter of practice rather than law. Federal regulations allow candidate campaign committees to contribute to other candidates; but campaign committees, especially in presidential elections, rarely, if ever, exercise this option. Every contribution made by a presidential candidate's campaign committee to the committee of another candidate depletes the resources available to his or her own nomination campaign. Presidential candidates, therefore, are unwilling to spend their funds in this way. A primary purpose of a PAC, however, is to make contributions to candidate committees. Furthermore, a PAC can contribute $5,000 per election to a federal candidate whereas a candidate's authorized committee is limited to a maximum of $1,000 per election. These donations constitute a primary means by which a PAC can fulfill its party-building responsibilities. Donations are also a means by which a presidential aspirant can build potential support among other candidates without having to expend valuable campaign resources.

ACCESS TO LARGE CONTRIBUTIONS

Every candidate who establishes a PAC hopes to capitalize on one of its primary assets, its ability to accept large contributions, which can be defined as contributions that exceed the amount legally permitted in a presidential campaign. A PAC can solicit up to $5,000 per year from an individual donor or up to $20,000 over the course of an election cycle; a primary campaign committee is limited to a maximum individual contribution of $1,000. A PAC thus allows a prospective candidate to circumvent one of the goals of federal campaign finance statutes, which is to restrict the amount an individual may donate to a particular candidate.

This access to large contributions also facilitates the purpose, not intended by the reforms, for which presidential hopefuls establish these committees: to serve as front organizations for their presidential campaigns. If a PAC is to be effective in this role, it must acquire the financial resources needed to fund the wide range of activities this purpose entails. It must therefore raise substantial amounts of money quickly because most of these committees are operative for only a short period of time. This end can best be accomplished if a committee focuses on large contributions as the basis for its fundraising.

The extent to which candidates exploit the potential for large contributions offered by a PAC is indicated in Table 5.1. This table documents the number of large contributions received by the PACs sponsored by presidential candidates in the 1988 election cycle. It summarizes the number of contributions in the amount of $1,000 or more received by each committee and divides them according to the size of the contribution. It notes the number of $1,000 contributions each PAC received (the maximum amount that could be given to a presidential candidate) and the number of large contributions each committee received in excess of this amount based on one of three categories: contributions given in the amount of $1,001 to $2,500, contributions of

TABLE 5.1
Large Contributions to Candidate-Sponsored PACs, 1985-1988

PAC	*$1,000*	*$1,001-2,500*	*$2,501-4,999*	*$5,000*
		Amount of Contribution		
Fund for America's				
Future (Bush - R)	1,994	572	95	1,186
Campaign America (Dole - R)	819	200	57	451
Campaign for Prosperity				
(Kemp - R)	809	78	34	215
Committee for America				
(Haig - R)	294	45	11	87
Effective Government				
Committee (Gephardt - D)	134	78	15	61
Committee for Freedom				
(Robertson - R)	105	22	5	48
The Democracy Fund				
(Simon - D)	54	26	3	14
Americans for the National				
Interest (Babbitt - D)	10	6	1	21
Fund for '86 (Biden - D)	34	0	0	16
Totals	4,253	1,027	221	2,099
Republicans	4,021	917	202	1,987
Democrats	232	110	19	112

Source: Based on the contributions disclosed in Federal Election Commission, Selected List of Receipts and Expenditures (G Index), 1985-1988, computer printouts, n.d.

$2,501 to $4,999, and contributions of $5,000, the maximum amount permitted by federal law. The data presented are based on the contributions filed by each committee in their reports to the Federal Election Commission and disclosed in the commission's *Selected List of Receipts and Expenditures*, which details all contributions to a PAC in excess of $500.

Table 5.1 clearly demonstrates that presidential candidates have successfully used PACs to solicit large contributions and thus circumvent the contribution limits imposed on their campaigns. During the 1988 election cycle, the nine committees associated with presidential candidates received 7,600 contributions of $1,000 or more. Of this total, 3,347 contributions, or 44 percent, were in amounts greater than $1,000.

The committees received 1,027 contributions of $1,001 to $2,500, 221 contributions of $2,501 to $4,999, and 2,099 maximum contributions of $5,000. None of these 3,347 contributions would be considered legal if given to a candidate's campaign committee. These data also suggest that candidate PACs emphasize $5,000 contributions when soliciting large donations. The committees solicited 2,099 contributions of $5,000 compared to 1,248 contributions in amounts ranging from $1,001 to $4,999, or approximately five maximum contributions for every three in amounts over $1,000. These maximum contributions constitute about 28 percent of all donations of $1,000 or more received by candidate PACs and 63 percent of all contributions received in excess of $1,000.

Although every PAC received some large contributions, committees associated with Republican hopefuls were much more successful in this regard than those associated with their Democratic counterparts. The five Republican committees (Bush's Fund for America's Future, Dole's Campaign America, Kemp's Campaign for Prosperity, Haig's Committee for America, and Robertson's Committee for Freedom) generated 7,127 contributions of $1,000 or more, or 93.7 percent of all such contributions received by candidate-sponsored PACs during the 1988 cycle. The four Democratic committees (Gephardt's Effective Government Committee, Simon's Democracy Fund, Babbitt's Americans for the National Interest, and Biden's Fund for '86) generated only 473 large contributions, or approximately one for every fifteen received by their potential Republican opponents. The disparity in the number of $5,000 contributions received by each group was even greater, with Democratic committees raising a "mere" 112 maximum contributions compared to 1,987 for the Republican committees, or approximately one for every eighteen received by their possible opponents.

This Republican advantage was mostly due to the success of the committees sponsored by then-Vice President George Bush and Senate Majority Leader Robert Dole, who were considered to be the early frontrunners for the Republican nomination and who had PAC experience prior to the beginning of the election cycle, and the committee associated with Congressman Jack Kemp, another aspirant with previous PAC experience. Bush's Fund for America's Future (FAF) greatly outdistanced all competitors in the quest for large donations. This committee received 3,847 contributions of $1,000 or more, or 50.6 percent of the total achieved by all candidate-sponsored committees and more than twice as many as its closest competitor. It solicited 1,994 contributions of $1,000 and 1,853 contributions of more than $1,000, including an impressive 1,186 contributions of $5,000. The next most successful PAC, Dole's Campaign America, received 819 donations of $1,000 (41.1 percent of FAF's total) and 708 large contributions, including 451 maximum contributions, or slightly more than one-third of FAF's total. Kemp's Campaign for Prosperity, the third most successful committee, raised a similar number of $1,000 donations but only half as many large contributions as Campaign America.

The other committees sponsored by Republicans, the Committee for America and the Committee for Freedom, raised significantly fewer large contributions than the three leading committees. Haig's Committee for America generated 294 $1,000 donations and 143 in excess of $1,000, including 87 contributions of $5,000; Robertson's Committee for Freedom received 105 checks for $1,000 and only 75 large contributions, but 48 of these were for the maximum allowable amount. The relatively modest success of these committees was probably due to the fact that their respective sponsors, Haig and Robertson, were largely unknown. It may also be due to other circumstances affecting the performance of these committees. Haig was the last Republican candidate to establish a PAC, registering a committee almost a year after Bush did. (For dates on which prospective candidates registered their political action committees, see Table 4.1.) His committee was therefore operating for less than two years before he became a candidate. Robertson supplemented his PAC activities with a tax-exempt foundation, the Freedom Council, which could solicit contributions in unlimited amounts; he therefore did not need to rely solely on his PAC as a receptacle for large donations.

All of the Democratic committees were sponsored by relatively unknown presidential prospects because Gary Hart, the clear early frontrunner, eschewed the PAC option. With the exception of Gephardt's Effective Government Committee, these PACS were less successful than their Republican counterparts in soliciting large contributions. The Effective Government Committee led the Democratic PACs with 61 contributions of $5,000 and 154 total contributions in excess of $1,000. It also raised 134 contributions of $1,000. The committee thus surpassed Robertson's PAC and raised a few more large contributions than Haig's (although Haig's PAC raised more maximum contributions than Gephardt's and more than twice as many $1,000 contributions). But its total number of large contributions was relatively small compared to the totals achieved by the leading Republican committees.

Gephardt's Effective Government Committee (EFG) fared well in comparison to committees sponsored by other Democrats. EFG solicited three times as many large contributions as its nearest competitor, Simon's Democracy Fund. This committee raised 43 large contributions and only 14 maximum donations, or less than a quarter of EFG's total. It also trailed Gephardt's committee in $1,000 contributions, receiving only 54 donations in this amount as opposed to 134 for EFG. The other Democratic committees, Babbitt's Americans for the National Interest and Biden's Fund for '86, generated few large contributions.

These figures from Table 5.1 highlight the number of contributions candidate PACs accept in excess of the amount permitted their campaigns, but they fail to reveal the true extent to which these committees are used to thwart campaign contribution limits. Because the purpose of this table is simply to detail the number of large contributions received by each PAC during the 1988 election cycle, it provides no accounting of the aggregate amounts donated by particular contributors. Unlike the contribution limits for campaign committees, which are based on the amount given in an election cycle, the contribution limits applicable to PACs are determined on an annual basis. An individual contributor can thus give more than $5,000 to a PAC by making multiple donations. The extent to which PACs exploit this possibility can be determined by examining the contributions of the 2,099 individuals who contributed the maximum amount during the 1988 cycle on an annual basis. The number of individuals donating $5,000 in two different years (for an aggregate contribution of $10,000), three different years ($15,000), or all four years of the election cycle ($20,000) could thus be determined. The results of this analysis are contained in Table 5.2.

Table 5.2 indicates that candidate PACs have solicited large sums from a small group of wealthy donors. During the 1988 election cycle, 318 individuals gave $5,000 to a candidate-sponsored multicandidate committee in more than one year. Of these, 228 contributed this amount twice for a total of $10,000, 68 in three years for $15,000, and 22 in every year of the election cycle for an aggregate contribution of $20,000, the maximum allowable amount. Overall, these wealthy donors were responsible for 748, or 36 percent, of the 2,099 maximum contributions received by these committees. They contributed a total of $3.74 million, or 15 percent of the total revenues generated by candidate-sponsored PACs prior to the 1988 election.

As might be expected, Bush's Fund for America's Future had the greatest number of multiple contributors. This committee received an aggregate individual donation of at least $10,000 from 206 individuals, including 22 who gave the full $20,000 allowed by law. It was followed by Dole's Campaign America, which received contributions of $10,000 or more from 46 contributors, including 4 who gave $20,000, and Kemp's Campaign for Prosperity, which successfully resolicited 39 of its $5,000 donors, including 2 who donated the maximum $20,000. The other committees active during the cycle failed to attract a $20,000 donation, but most received aggregate individual contributions of $10,000 or more.

TABLE 5.2
Large Contributors to Candidate-Sponsored PACs, 1985-1988

| PAC | Amount of Contribution | | | |
	$10,000	$15,000	$20,000	Total
Fund for America's				
Future	141	49	16	206
Campaign America	33	9	4	46
Campaign for Prosperity	29	8	2	39
Effective Government				
Committee	8	1	0	9
Committee for America	7	0	0	7
Committee for Freedom	7	0	0	7
The Democracy Fund	3	1	0	4
Americans for the National				
Interest	0	0	0	0
Fund for '86	0	0	0	0
Totals	228	68	22	318

Source: Based on an analysis of $5,000 contributors as disclosed in Federal Election Commission, Selected List of Receipts and Expenditures (G Index), 1985-1988, computer printouts, n.d.

In the case of Haig's Committee for America, the 7 donors who gave a total of $10,000 apiece actually contributed the maximum legal amount since the committee actively solicited funds for only two years.[1] The only committees that did not enjoy the largesse of multiple donors were Biden's Fund for '86 and Babbitt's Americans for the National Interest. But this apparent failure was due to lack of opportunity rather than lack of desire. Biden's committee was operative for less than a year; thus it could not legally resolicit its big donors. Babbit's committee was active for only fifteen months and his tax-exempt foundation, American Horizons, provided supporters with another receptacle for large donations. This organization received at least two individual contributions of $25,000 and another for $20,000.[2]

Perhaps the best indicator of the emphasis placed on large contributions and their importance to the financial success of a candidate-sponsored PAC is the amounts of money raised through these contributions. These sums are presented in Tables 5.3 and 5.4. Table 5.3 details the amounts raised by each committee from contributions in excess of $1,000 and disaggregates these sums into three categories based on the size of the contribution received. Table 5.4 then compares the committees' large contribution receipts to their total revenues in order to determine the extent to which these receipts account for the funds raised by each PAC. These analyses indicate that candidate PACs rely on wealthy donors for a large portion of their financial resources and that the ability to generate large contributions is an important factor in explaining a committee's financial success.

During the 1988 election cycle, candidate PACs raised $25.25 million, approximately $13.5 million of which was received in contributions of more than $1,000. The committees raised approximately $2.17 million in contributions of $1,001-2,500; $777,000 in contributions of $2,501-$4,999; and $10.5 million in contributions of $5,000 (see Table 5.3). Large contributions were thus responsible for more than half (53.3 percent) of the total revenues solicited by the committees. An additional $4.25 million was solicited in $1,000 contributions. When this amount is added to the monies received through large contributions, the sum is $17.7 million, or 70 percent of the committees' total revenues from all sources.

Bush's Fund for America's Future solicited most of the money received through large contributions. The committee raised $7.5 million from its broad base of wealthy donors, or 55.7 percent of the aggregate amount generated by all nine committees. Almost 80 percent of this $7.5 million ($5.93 million) was raised in contributions of $5,000. FAF also received $1.99 million in $1,000 donations. The committee thus derived two-thirds of its $11.2 million in total revenues from large contributions and an additional 17.8 percent from $1,000 donors.

Two other PACs raised substantial amounts from wealthy contributors, although neither approached FAF's large-donor income. The second most successful committee, Dole's Campaign America, raised $2.87 million in large contributions, or approximately $4.64 million less than FAF. Kemp's Campaign for Prosperity, which finished third in large-donor receipts, raised approximately $1.35 million, or $6.15 million less than FAF. Indeed, Bush's PAC was so successful in garnering large donations that its $7.5 million in large-donor receipts exceeded the total revenues of the five candidate PACs active during the 1984 election cycle by over $400,000.

The Fund for America's Future's high percentage of large donor-based funds is also noteworthy, especially given the PAC's substantial revenues. Although all of the committees based their fundraising on large contributions (every PAC received at least a third of its income from this source), none of the other well-financed committees achieved FAF's percentage (see Table 5.4). Dole's Campaign America raised 46.7 percent of its revenues through large donations; Kemp's Campaign for Prosperity raised 32.8 percent; and Gephardt's Effective Government

TABLE 5.3
Candidate PAC Receipts from Large Contributions, 1985-1988 (rounded to nearest $100)

| PAC | Amount Received | | | | Total Receipts |
	Contributions of $1,001-$2,500	Contributions of $2,501-$4,999	Contributions of $5,000	
Fund for America's Future	1,239,900	341,000	5,930,000		7,510,900
Campaign America	424,400	190,500	2,255,000		2,869,900
Campaign for Prosperity	152,100	126,300	1,075,000		1,353,400
Committee for America	93,800	39,100	435,000		567,900
Effective Government Committee	147,100	46,700	305,000		498,800
Committee for Freedom	43,900	17,700	240,000		301,600
The Democracy Fund	59,200	12,000	90,000		161,200
Americans for the Natl. Interest	13,300	4,000	105,000		122,300
Fund for '86	0	0	80,000		80,000
Total	2,173,700	777,300	10,515,000		13,466,000

Source: Based on the contributions disclosed in Federal Election Commission, Selected List of Receipts and Expenditures (G Index), 1985-1988, Computer Printouts, n.d.

Committee raised 40.7 percent. The only committee to surpass FAF's percentage was Babbitt's Americans for the National Interest, but this was a function of the committee's relatively small total revenues.

These figures illustrate the efficiency with which the Fund for America's Future capitalized on the revenue potential of large contributions. By focusing its fundraising efforts on the solicitation of large contributions, it developed a broad base of wealthy contributors, each of whom contributed an average of $4,000, and thus raised more than two-thirds of its unprecedented total revenues. More importantly, the committee's success in soliciting large donations resulted in an enormous resource advantage over the PACs sponsored by Bush's closest competitors. FAF raised $5.06 million more than Dole's Campaign America, $4.64 million of which was due to the difference in the amounts received from large donors. FAF raised $7.08 million more than Kemp's Campaign for Prosperity, $6.15 million of which resulted from the difference in large-donor receipts. The disparity in revenues from large contributions thus accounts for 92 percent of Bush's financial advantage over Dole and 87 percent of his advantage over Kemp.

This analysis implies that well-known candidates obtain the greatest benefits from the large contributions made possible by a precandidacy PAC. These individuals can take advantage of the less restrictive contribution limits governing PACs to raise substantial amounts of money from their broad base of financial supporters. But the data in Table 5.4 indicate that large contributions also play a significant role in the financing of committees sponsored by lesser-known candidates. Although these PACs do not amass large sums from these donations (as compared to the committees established by better-known presidential aspirants), the ability to solicit contributions of more than $1,000 provides them with a means of raising the seed money needed to initiate the financial and political activities that can help advance their fledgling candidacies. This analysis also demonstrates how prospective candidates, by taking advantage of the Federal Election Campaign Act's (FECA) less restrictive contribution limits for multicandidate political committees, used their PACs prior to the 1988 election to solicit contributions that would be illegal if given to their campaign committees. This purpose can also be achieved by exploiting a PAC's ability to establish nonfederal accounts or subsidiary committees on the state or local level. Because a PAC is not by definition solely concerned with federal elections (as is a presidential candidate's authorized campaign committee), it may raise and expend funds for nonfederal political activities such as state election campaigns or state and local party-building. These funds are usually drawn from a PAC's federal bank account(s), which is subject to the

TABLE 5.4
Percent of Total Candidate PAC Receipts from Large ($1,001-$5,000)
Contributions,1985-1988 (rounded to nearest hundred $)

PAC	Total Receipts	Receipts from Large Contributions	% of Total Receipts
Americans for the National Interest	156,500	122,300	78.1
Fund for America's Future	11,205,800	7,510,900	67.0
Fund for '86	133,200	80,000	60.1
Committee for America	1,080,700	567,900	52.5
Campaign America	6,145,700	2,869,900	46.7
Committee for Freedom	712,600	301,600	42.3
Effective Government Committee	1,226,200	498,800	40.7
The Democracy Fund	465,800	161,200	34.6
Campaign for Prosperity	4,124,100	1,353,400	32.8
Total	25,250,600	13,466,000	53.3

Source: Based on the data in Tables 4.6 and 5.3.

provisions of federal law. But a PAC may choose to employ other legal structures for its nonfederal activities, for example, a separate bank account(s) or a subsidiary committee registered in a particular state. These structures, so long as they are used only for non-federal political activities, are governed by state and local elections laws rather than federal regulations. They may therefore receive contributions that are prohibited by the FECA because the regulations in many states are less stringent than those established by Congress. These soft money contributions are another unique benefit of a precandidacy PAC and can be an important source of extralegal revenue for presidential aspirants seeking to avoid the constraints of federal law.

SOFT MONEY

"Soft money" is a popular umbrella term for describing "any political money not regulated by federal law."[3] It is used to refer to the monies raised by individuals, interest groups, political action committees, and national, state, and local party committees that are exempt from federal contribution and expenditure limits as a result of the provisions of the FECA amendments of 1979. But Herbert Alexander, in a recent study of the role of soft money in campaign finance, identifies a number of other types of unregulated money permitted in federal elections. Accordingly, he defines soft money as "money raised from sources outside the restraints of federal law but spent on activities intended to affect federal election outcomes."[4] This definition encompasses the soft money solicited by candidate-sponsored PACs, which consists of contributions received in non-FECA regulated funds that are spent, at least in part, on activities designed to assist an impending presidential candidacy.

Most observers of campaign financing claim that the widespread use of soft money by PACs and other political organizations emerged as a result of the FECA amendments of 1979.[5] Prior to the adoption of these reforms, the Federal Election Commission permitted party committees active in federal and nonfederal elections to establish separate federal and nonfederal bank accounts.[6] It also allowed these committees to allocate administrative expenses between federal and nonfederal accounts based on the proportion of funds spent on each type of election or on another "reasonable basis."[7] But all federal election-related activity had to be financed from a party committee's federal account, which could only receive funds permitted under the FECA.

Although the 1979 legislation is commonly cited as the source of the soft money explosion, Brooks Jackson, a journalist who specializes in campaign finance, has recently noted that the soft money loophole actually was created by a Federal Election Commission advisory opinion issued in 1978. In this decision, the commission allowed the Kansas Republican party to use corporate and union funds to finance a voter drive to benefit both state and federal candidates. Although corporate and union contributions are prohibited in federal contests, such donations are permissible under Kansas law. The commission therefore ruled that contributions from these sources could be used for voter drives and other activities that would help to develop the state's party organization as well as assist candidates.[8]

The 1979 amendments reinforced this decision and helped to operationalize the use of soft money in presidential elections by loosening the act's restrictions on contributions and expenditures. The amendments changed the law's definitions of "contribution" and "expenditure" to exclude monies used to conduct specific activities designed to promote grass-roots participation in presidential and other federal election campaigns. These activities include the preparation and distribution of slate cards, sample ballots, and other listings of three or more candidates by state and local party committees; the production of grass-roots campaign materials such as pins, bumper stickers, brochures, and posters; and the costs associated with voter registration and turnout drives conducted by state or local party committees on behalf of their party's presidential ticket.[9] The law thus created a new realm of unlimited spending in presidential campaigns.

National party committee and presidential campaign staff members quickly recognized the financial possibilities offered by these exemptions and began to work with state and local party committees to raise unrestricted funds to finance exempted activities. The monies raised, which amounted to more than $10 million in each of the last three presidential elections, were then used by state and local party committees to supplement the public monies available to presidential nominees under the FECA.[10] These coordinated efforts to "funnel" unrestricted contributions to state and local party committees thus opened the floodgates to the receipt and expenditure of millions of dollars beyond the limits proscribed for presidential campaigns.

The 1979 amendments made no specific provision for the use of nonfederal soft money accounts by nonparty political committees. The use of separate nonfederal accounts by PACs is therefore a result of the ambiguities of federal law rather than its particular sanctions. Facing no prohibition against the use of such accounts, PACs soon began to employ them in various ways to supplement their federal political activities. In one instance, noted by Alexander, a PAC requested an advisory opinion ruling regarding the possibility of establishing a separate account to collect non-FECA-regulated funds to pay for activities unrelated to federal election campaigns. The PAC, organized by the New Mexico Voter Freeze, sought to use soft money contributions to finance its educational and lobbying activities and related operating costs. But the advisory opinion request was withdrawn before the commission could render its decision. One source, however, indicated that the commission's staff attorneys had drafted a response that would have approved the request.[11]

That political action committees, particularly those sponsored by presidential aspirants, have responded to the ambiguities of the law by creating soft money, accounts is not surprising given the compelling financial opportunities these structures create. Because such accounts are governed by more permissive state and local regulations, they provide a means of completely avoiding the contribution limits of federal law. Nonfederal accounts may receive contributions in excess of the amount permitted by federal statutes, solicit funds from sources long prohibited from participating in federal elections, and donate large sums to state and local candidates. They can also operate in relative secrecy because most state disclosure laws lack the rigorous requirements for public disclosure established at the federal level. Indeed, given the tremendous benefits that can be attained through the use of these accounts, what is surprising is that some candidate-sponsored PACs have failed to exploit this option.

A PAC accrues three basic advantages by establishing a nonfederal, or soft money, account. First, it can solicit contributions that are illegal under federal law. A PAC can solicit soft money donations in amounts greater than $5,000 per year because at least sixteen states place no restrictions on individual contributions. It can also raise unlimited amounts for nonfederal purposes from individuals who have already given the maximum amount permitted under the FECA. In addition, a PAC can solicit unlimited amounts from labor unions and corporations, despite long-standing federal bans on labor and corporate contributions to federal candidates, because most states allow these organizations to participate financially in political campaigns.[12] Only ten states prohibit labor union contributions, and twenty states ban corporate donations. Sixteen states allow these organizations to give unlimited amounts to state and local candidates or political committees. A soft money account therefore provides a PAC with a nearly unfettered ability to solicit funds and a virtually unlimited fundraising potential.

Another advantage of a nonfederal account is the freer reign it gives a PAC in making contributions to candidates and elected officials. As with contributions to a PAC, contributions from a PAC are usually less stringently regulated by state as compared to federal laws. Whereas federal law limits PAC contributions to political candidates to $5,000 per election, twenty-nine states place no limit on the amount a PAC may contribute to state and local candidates and three others allow unlimited contributions with but a few exceptions. A PAC can therefore use a nonfederal account to channel large sums of money to state and local politicians who may one day be asked to support a PAC sponsor's bid for the presidency.

Finally, a soft money account allows a PAC to conduct financial activities with little accountability. Although all state campaign finance laws have some form of reporting requirement, the information required of candidates varies from state to state, as do filing deadlines, and disclosure provisions are not uniformly enforced. In addition, only twenty-two states publish aggregate data on receipts and expenditures. As a result, these state disclosure requirements are generally ineffective. Often the only means of determining whether a PAC is using soft money in a state is to conduct a thorough comparison of federal reports with those filed in a state election office. Such an approach, however, is infeasible on a fifty-state basis. Even if this approach were practical, the information obtained would contain numerous inaccuracies due to the laxity of some states' disclosure laws and enforcement procedures. Achieving an accurate estimate of unregulated financial activity is difficult even when soft money is included in federal reports filed with the Federal Election Commission (for example, when a political committee discloses the proportion of funds used for nonfederal purposes in allocating funds between a federal and nonfederal account), because there is no single formula for allocating expenses between federal and nonfederal activities.[13]

These disclosure problems make it impossible to determine precisely the amount of soft money raised and spent by candidate-sponsored PACs. No comprehensive, or even uniform, data are available regarding contributions to nonfederal accounts, the sums disbursed through these accounts, or the politicians who receive donations from these funds. This lack of information in itself suggests the value of a soft money fund to a prospective candidate: it provides a means of raising money from federally prohibited sources with little fear of public scrutiny. Indeed, these accounts sometimes function so deep in the shadows of campaign finance regulations that it is often difficult to determine whether a PAC is using them at all. For example, Herbert Alexander and Brian Haggerty credit Mondale's pre-1984 campaign PAC, the Committee for the Future of America, with adding this "new dimension to presidential PAC fund raising."[14] But Elizabeth Drew reports that, prior to the 1980 election, Reagan's Citizens for the Republic raised soft money in the form of corporate contributions, which it spent in "the state of California and elsewhere."[15] She further notes that this PAC gave an unknown amount of corporate money to state parties in 1982.[16]

Although the full extent of the finance activity of PACs remains unknown, some information on the nonfederal accounts of presidential candidate PACs is available from voluntarily released reports and other accounts. The best insight is obtained from information released by Mondale's Committee for the Future of America (CFA) in July 1984. This committee was apparently the only candidate-sponsored PAC other than Reagan's Citizens for the Republic to employ soft money accounts during the 1984 election cycle. Reagan's PAC never issued a public summary of its nonfederal activities. But after a Washington, D.C., business magazine revealed the existence of CFA's nonfederal accounts,[17] the committee publicly released an eleven-page memorandum detailing their structure and receipts.

CFA established what amounted to four state and local sub-committees, CFA State and Local I, II, III, IV, which were designed to accommodate variations in state elections laws.[18] The four committees raised a total of $395,000, nearly all of which would have been illegal if given to the PAC's federal account. They received $150,475 in corporate contributions, $160,275 from labor unions, and $84,250 in mostly large contributions from individuals and groups that had already contributed the maximum legal amount under federal law to CFA's main account.[19]

At least a quarter of the funds accepted by CFA's nonfederal committees were raised through large contributions. The committees received one contribution of $20,000 and another of $10,000 from individuals who had already given $5,000 to the PAC's federal account. They also received a number of large corporate donations, including $10,000 from Aviva Enterprises, a San Francisco toy company, and $5,000 each from seven other corporations. The largest labor union gift was the $25,000 donated by the Los Angeles Committee on Political Education (AFL-CIO). It was followed by a $15,000 contribution from the United Food and Commercial Workers of Region 13.[20]

Of the $395,000 in total soft money revenue, only $101,813 was given to state and local campaigns. This included a contribution of $18,000 to the California gubernatorial campaign of Los Angeles mayor Tom Bradley, who later became a leading Black supporter in Mondale's presidential campaign.[21] The remaining funds were used to finance the state and local committees' operating costs and subsidize some of the federal committee's obligations. For example, state committee funds paid for some of the travel expenses, hotel bills, and a portion of the staff salaries and consultant fees incurred by the federal PAC. These payments were based on an undisclosed formula for determining federal and nonfederal allocations.[22]

Further understanding of the use of soft money accounts by candidate-sponsored PACs is provided by a recent study by Teresa Riordan of Common Cause.[23] Her investigation of disclosure reports filed in key presidential primary states revealed that at least three of the PACs supported by presidential candidates during the 1988 election cycle employed nonfederal accounts. Biden's Fund for '86 and Dole's Campaign America each formed at least one nonfederal account and Kemp's Campaign for Prosperity had two, Campaign for Prosperity-Iowa and Campaign for Prosperity-New Hampshire.[24] That Kemp's committee chose to locate its non-federal subsidiaries in Iowa and New Hampshire indicates that considerations other than party-building were the motivating factor in the establishment of these soft money funds.

Riordan was unable to determine the amount of financial activity conducted through these four soft money accounts. None of the committees were willing to divulge how much they raised in soft money or identify who contributed to these accounts. Nor could this information be obtained from state disclosure reports. For example, in Iowa, elections laws only require that out-of-state PACs disclose the amounts they contribute to individual candidates; they do not require disclosure of a committee's other expenditures, receipts, or sources of contributions. The information that is available, however, indicates one way in which prospective candidates use nonfederal funds to assist their future campaigns.

Each of the PACs that accepted soft money contributions used these funds to make donations to state and local candidates in Iowa or New Hampshire. Biden's Fund for '86 gave $43,516 to state candidates in Iowa from its nonfederal account.[25] Dole's Campaign America gave approximately $32,000 to state candidates in Iowa, $13,344 of which came from its nonfederal account.[26] The amount of soft money donated to candidates by the Campaign for Prosperity's Iowa subsidiary is less easy to determine. The reports of the state elections office record only a $5,000 contribution to Republican gubernatorial candidate Terry Branstad. Reports filed independently by state legislators document at least another $10,800 in contributions to legislative candidates. The PAC's federal account showed additional donations of approximately $7,000 to state candidates in Iowa. The PAC's other nonfederal account, Campaign for Prosperity-New Hampshire, contributed at least $5,287 to candidates in that state.[27]

These examples of PAC soft money activity demonstrate the advantages that prospective candidates achieve when they pursue the opportunities offered by this loophole. PAC sponsors can solicit extralegal, unlimited contributions for nonfederal accounts and use the funds received for almost any purpose. The available data on soft money suggest that one of the primary purposes for which these funds are used is to make contributions to state and local candidates. PAC sponsors hope that these donations, in addition to helping their fellow party members, will assist their individual bids for the presidency by inducing those who receive financial assistance to support their benefactor's presidential campaign and convince their supporters to do the same.

In particular, each PAC sponsor hopes that his or her committee's largesse will generate a base of political support in those states that hold crucial early presidential primary contests. This more focused strategic approach seems to have been the operative principle governing the use of soft money funds by candidates seeking the 1988 nomination. The nonfederal accounts formed by Kemp's Campaign for Prosperity were established for the sole purpose of channeling funds into Iowa and New Hampshire. Biden and Dole also focused soft money spending in these states. As Riordan notes, these committees gave significant amounts to candidates in Iowa or New Hampshire but donated little or nothing to candidates in neighboring states such as Kansas or Vermont.[28] She therefore concludes that these "PAC activities seem inextricably linked with campaign activities."[29]

CONTRIBUTIONS TO FEDERAL CANDIDATES

One of the reasons a presidential hopeful would choose to establish a PAC rather than a tax-exempt foundation before becoming a candidate is that a PAC can perform a wider range of political activities.   In particular, a PAC may make direct contributions to candidates whereas a tax-exempt foundation may not.   Indeed, donating funds to other candidates is the fundamental purpose envisioned for a PAC by the federal campaign finance regulations.

Under the provisions of federal law, a tax-exempt foundation may solicit contributions in unlimited amounts from individuals and corporations and does not have to report or disclose these donations in accordance with the requirements of the FECA. It therefore may accept unrestricted donations similar to the soft money contributions that a PAC can receive through a nonfederal account, although contributors to a foundation may generally deduct their donations from their taxes and PAC donors may not.[30] But as specified in section 501(c)(3) of the Internal Revenue Code, a foundation must operate exclusively for educational purposes if it is to retain its tax-exempt status; it may not participate in or intervene in any political campaigns on behalf of any candidate for public office.[31]   This type of organization is thus prohibited from making contributions to political candidates.

A multicandidate PAC, however, may contribute up to $5,000 per election to a candidate for federal office. It may therefore donate up to $10,000 to individuals nominated for federal office because federal regulations consider a primary and a general election to be separate elections (a PAC may donate up to $15,000 in the event of a special or runoff election).   In comparison, a candidate's authorized campaign committee may contribute only up to $1,000 per election to a federal candidate or a total of $2,000 to nominees.[32] Federal regulations thus encourage the formation of PACs by individuals interested in providing financial assistance to federal candidates.

The advantage PACs offer prospective presidential candidates with respect to contributions is even greater in practice than that established by the regulations because these individuals rarely, if ever, make contributions to other candidates from their own campaign committee monies.   For example, the nominees in the last two presidential elections (Reagan, Mondale, Bush, and Dukakis) contributed a total of $1,000 to other federal candidates despite aggregate receipts of more than $100 million.[33] A precandidacy PAC thus provides a presidential aspirant with an unparalleled ability to assist other candidates financially, which in turn can enhance the prospects for his or her nomination by building potential support among those who receive PAC contributions.

The extent to which candidate-sponsored PACs contribute funds to federal candidates can be determined by examining disclosure reports filed with the Federal Election Commission. Federal reporting procedures require that PACs disclose all contributions to federal candidates.[34] The commission then compiles the contributions to federal candidates reported by each PAC on the basis of a two-year congressional election cycle and discloses them in its *Committee Index of Candidates Supported/Opposed*. The information contained in this index is summarized in Tables 5.5 through 5.8. Tables 5.5, 5.6, and 5.7 respectively detail the number and amount of contributions made by candidate-sponsored PACs during each of the last three presidential election cycles. Table 5.8 summarizes these data on a percentage basis according to congressional election cycles in order to determine the distribution of PAC contributions between the first and second halves of the presidential election period.

Tables 5.5 through 5.7 indicate that presidential aspirants have effectively used PACs to channel millions of dollars to hundreds of federal candidates. They also reveal a number of trends or patterns in candidate PAC giving. The total amount given to federal candidates has increased in every presidential election cycle included in this analysis. This illustrates the growing use of this tactic to build support for a potential candidacy. It also reflects, to a certain extent, the general increase in candidate PAC spending, a claim that is further supported by the fact that the best-financed committees are the largest donors to federal campaigns. PACs generally tend to spend more in contributions when they have more available to spend. The data additionally indicate that PAC giving is increasingly concentrated in the first two years of a presidential election cycle. Whether determined on the basis of the total number of contributions or the total amount contributed, the proportion of PAC giving that takes place in advance of the midterm elections has grown.

Despite these increases, the data also demonstrate that the amounts of direct financial assistance awarded by PACs constitute a small fraction of total PAC spending. Moreover, the percentage of total spending accounted for by PAC donations declined significantly in the 1988 cycle. This suggests that candidate-sponsored PACs, although

TABLE 5.5
Contributions by Candidate-Sponsored PACs, 1977-1980[a]

PAC	No. of Contributions			Total Amount Contributed ($)			% of PAC's Spending
	1977-1978	1979-1980	Total	1977-1978	1979-1980	Total	
Campaign America	15	0[b]	15	9,704	0	9,704	4.1
Citizens for the Republic	266	127	393	431,586	242,800	674,386	10.7
Fund for a Limited Government	58	0[c]	58	36,163	0	36,163	15.0
John Connally Citizens Forum	63	0[d]	63	76,427[e]	0	76,427	10.5
Totals	402	127	529	553,880	242,800	796,680	10.6

[a]Figures reflect contributions to federal candidates through the 1980 general election.
[b]Dole's Campaign America remained active through the 1980 election but essentially ceased operations after March 1979. From April 1979 to June 1980, the committee raised only $9,500.
[c]Bush's Fund for a Limited Government ceased operations as of March 31, 1979.
[d]John Connally's Citizens Forum ceased operations as of June 30, 1979.
[e]In the 1977-1978 election cycle, the John Connally Citizens Forum contributed $77,427 to sixty-three candidates for federal office. This amount included a contribution of $1,111 to David Crane, a Republican candidate for Congress in Indiana's Sixth District. In 1982 Crane's committee returned $1,000 to the PAC, so this amount is not included in the sum noted here.

Source: Data based on contributions reported by each committee in the Federal Election Commission's Committee Index of Candidates Supported/Opposed (D Index), 1977-1980, Computer printouts, n.d.

TABLE 5.6
Contributions by Candidate-Sponsored PACs, 1981-1984[a]

PAC	No. of Contributions			Total Amount Contributed ($)			% of PAC's Spending
	1981-1982	1983-1984	Total	1981-1982	1983-1984	Total	
Citizens for a Competitive America	6	12[b]	18	6,000	17,400	23,400	10.3
Citizens for the Republic	116	117	233	471,367	762,320	1,233,687	30.5
Committee for a Democratic Consensus	1	2[c]	3	122	6,500	6,622	9.2
Comm. for the Future of America	180	0	180	228,251[d]	0	228,251	9.2
Natl. Council on Public Policy	54	24[e]	78	20,388	30,294	50,682	41.3
Totals	357	155	512	726,128	816,514	1,542,642	22.2
Democrats[f]	241	38	279	254,761	54,194	308,955	10.6

[a]Figures reflect contributions to federal candidates through the 1984 general election.
[b]Includes a contribution of $5,000 to Hollings's presidential campaign committee.
[c]Includes a contribution of $1,500 to Cranston's senate campaign committee. This PAC disbanded after filing its 1983 midterm financial report.
[d]In the 1981-1982 election cycle, the Committee for the Future of America contributed $288,326 to 180 candidates for federal office. This amount included a contribution of $5,074 to Representative Philip Burton of California's Fifth District. This contribution exceeded the legal limit of $5,000. In 1983, Burton's campaign committee returned $75 to the PAC in order to comply with the law. This amount is not included in the sum noted here.
[e]Includes a contribution of $5,000 to Glenn's presidential campaign committee.
[f]Total without Citizens for the Republic.

Source: Data based on contributions reported by each committee in Federal Election Commission Committee Index of Candidates Supported/Opposed (D Index), 1981-1984, computer printouts, n.d.

TABLE 5.7
Contributions by Candidate-Sponsored PACs, 1985-1988[a]

PAC	No. of Contributions			Total Amount Contributed ($)			% of PAC's Spending
	1985-1986	1987-1988	Total	1985-1986	1987-1988	Total	
Americans for the National Interest	15	0[b]	15	40,600	0[b]	40,600	26.0
Campaign America	103[c]	26[d]	129	294,422	61,950	356,372	5.4
Campaign for Prosperity	104[e]	24	128	130,315	30,600	160,915	3.9
Comm. for America	20	3	23	11,325	3,500	14,825	1.4
Comm. for Freedom	19	2	21	32,693	5,100	37,793	5.5
The Democracy Fund	60	7[f]	67	68,973	7,413	76,386	16.4
Effective Government Committee	59	1	60	58,096	1,000	59,096	4.8
Fund for America's Future	278	30	308	813,917	30,444	844,361	7.8
Fund for '86	20	0[g]	20	19,655	0[g]	19,655	14.8
Totals	678	93	771	1,469,996	140,007	1,610,003	6.4
Democrats	154	8	162	187,324	8,413	195,737	9.9
Republicans	524	85	609	1,282,672	131,594	1,414,266	6.1

[a]Figures reflect contributions to federal candidates through the 1988 general election.

[b]Babbitt's Americans for the National Interest disbanded in December 1986, two weeks before Babbitt registered his authorized campaign committee.

[c]Does not include a contribution of $600 to Senator Robert Packwood (R-OR), which was returned.

[d]Does not include a contribution of $1,000 to Bill Calvert, a Republican candidate for Congress in Oklahoma's First District.

[e]Does not include a contribution of $250 to Congressman Robert Dornan (R-CA), which was returned.

[f]Includes a contribution of $4,000 to Simon's senate campaign committee.

[g]Biden's Fund for '86 disbanded in February 1987, a few days before Biden registered his authorized campaign committee.

Source: Data based on contributions reported by each committee in Federal Election Commission Committee Index of Candidates Supported/Opposed (D Index), 1986-1988, computer printouts, n.d.

concerned with using their resources to assist party candidates (which every PAC sponsor claims is the purpose for organizing a committee), devote the bulk of their resources to other purposes.

PACs sponsored by presidential hopefuls contributed approximately $3.95 million to federal candidates over the course of the last three presidential election cycles. The four committees established in advance of the 1980 election disbursed 529 contributions to federal candidates, totaling $796,680 (see Table 5.5). The committees gave $553,880 in 402 donations to 1978 midterm election candidates and another $242,800 in 127 donations to candidates seeking office in 1980. About 85 percent of the total amount contributed, or $674,386, was contributed by Reagan's Citizens for the Republic.

The five committees active before the 1984 election made slightly fewer donations (512) than the 1980 committees but gave $1,542,642 to federal candidates, nearly twice the amount contributed in the 1980 cycle (see Table 5.6). The committees gave $726,128 in 357 contributions to 1982 midterm election candidates and $816,514 in 155 contributions to candidates seeking office in 1984. Reagan's Citizens for the Republic again led all committees in candidate assistance, disbursing almost 80 percent, or $1.23 million, of the total amount awarded during the cycle. The only other committee to spend a significant amount helping other candidates was Mondale's Committee for the Future of America, which donated $228,251 to those seeking federal office.

The nine committees operative during the 1988 cycle made 771 contributions, an increase of approximately 50 percent over the number made in previous cycles (see Table 5.7). The total amount awarded, however, did not increase proportionately. The nine committees spent $1,610,003 in candidate contributions, an increase of $67,361, or 4.3 percent, over the amount disbursed by the five 1984 committees. The amount donated, therefore, increased only marginally despite substantial giving by a number of the committees. Bush, the largest 1988 donor, gave $844,361 to federal candidates. This sum exceeded the amount spent by every other previous candidate-backed committee, with the exception of Reagan's 1984 PAC, which could afford to be generous because he was essentially unopposed in his quest for renomination. Dole's Campaign America also donated a relatively large amount, $356,372, and Kemp's Campaign for Prosperity gave away $160,915. But neither these efforts nor the greater number of active committees served to increase substantially the aggregate amount donated by PACs in 1988 as compared to the previous cycle.

In each election cycle, the PAC that raised the most money also gave the most money to federal candidates. Moreover, the sums contributed by other committees suggest a direct relationship between a PAC's ability to raise money and its willingness to provide financial support to federal candidates.[35] This relationship is clear in the 1980 cycle. Reagan's Citizens for the Republic was the wealthiest committee and donated the largest amount; John Connally's Citizens Forum raised the second largest sum and gave the second largest amount; Bush's Fund for a Limited Government raised and gave the third largest sum; and Dole's Campaign America raised and contributed the smallest amount. This pattern held true in the 1984 cycle with one exception. Glenn's National Council on Public Policy raised less than Hollings's Citizens for a Competitive America but contributed $27,282 more to federal candidates. Otherwise, the order of PACs in terms of giving followed the order of these committees when ranked on the basis of receipts. In the 1988 cycle, the top three committees in terms of total receipts were also the top three donors to federal candidates. But the financial practices of the other committees deviated from the pattern. For example, Simon's Democracy Fund raised less than Gephardt's Effective Government Committee but spent $17,290 more in contributions. Babbitt's Americans for the National Interest raised less than Haig's Committee for America and Robertson's Committee for Freedom but was more generous to federal candidates than either of these committees. The data therefore show that, in most instances, the greater a PAC's total receipts, the greater the amount of its contributions.

PAC donations also follow fundraising patterns in that most contributions are issued during the first two years of a presidential election cycle. As noted in the previous chapter, candidate-sponsored PACs raise most of their money in the early years of a presidential election cycle. In the 1980 cycle, these committees received 70 percent of their funds during the first two years of the cycle; in 1984, 67 percent; and in 1988, 75 percent. The figures in Table 5.8 demonstrate that candidate PACs also make most of their contributions during the initial two years of a presidential cycle.

The committees active in the 1980 cycle made 76 percent of their contributions and disbursed 69.5 percent of the total monies contributed in 1977 and 1978. During the corresponding period in the 1984 cycle, the committees issued a slightly smaller portion of their contributions (69.7 percent) and disbursed only 47 percent of the total amount they gave to candidates. Both figures, however, are largely the result of the atypical contribution pattern of Reagan's Citizens for the Republic. This committee, which was probably more concerned with party-building and candidate assistance than other presidential PACs because Reagan was basically unchallenged, evenly distributed its contributions between the 1981-1982 and 1983-1984 congressional

TABLE 5.8
Distribution of Contributions by Candidate-Sponsored PACs

Presidential Election Cycle		% of Total Contributions to Candidates		% of Total Funds Contributed	
		1st 2 Years	2nd 2 Years	1st 2 Years	2nd 2 Years
1980		76.0	24.0	69.5	30.5
1984	(w/CFTR)[a]	69.7	30.3	47.0	53.0
	(w/o CFTR)	86.0	14.0	82.0	18.0
1988		87.9	12.1	91.3	8.7

[a]Citizens for the Republic, the PAC originally chaired by Ronald Reagan and the only committee associated with a Republican candidate in the 1984 cycle.

Source: Based on data in Tables 5.5, 5.6, and 5.7.

election cycles and distributed only 38.2 percent of the total amount it awarded to candidates during the first two-year period. The other 1984 committees placed greater emphasis on early giving. These PACs, which were all sponsored by individuals seeking the Democratic presidential nomination, made 86 percent of their contributions and spent 82 percent of their total funds contributed in 1981 and 1982. The 1988 committees allocated their donations in similar proportions. They made 87.9 percent of their contributions and spent 91.3 percent of the monies given to candidates during the first two years of the 1988 presidential cycle. The data in Table 5.8 thus indicate that, absent Reagan's 1984 committee, candidate-sponsored PACs have concentrated their giving in such a way that most of their donations are made in the midterm congressional election cycle. In addition, the data reveal that this emphasis has increased in recent election cycles.

The ostensible purpose for which PACs contribute funds is to help build the party by assisting its candidates. But if this were the sole motive informing a PAC's largesse, its donations would probably not be so heavily apportioned to candidates in midterm elections. After all, the Democratic and Republican parties presumably need assistance in presidential election years as well. Candidate PACs emphasize midterm donations because their objective in assisting candidates is largely to build support for their respective sponsors' future campaigns. PAC organizers consider the ability to make contributions to be one of their most effective means of generating future support, because it is one of the few ways they can directly assist candidates and elected offi- cials. Although simply donating funds to a candidate does not in itself usually secure an endorsement, a PAC's contributions are considered to be an important part of the recruitment process.

Insofar as direct financial assistance is a factor in generating political support, those who sponsor the most financially successful PACs are positioned to garner the most support because they are the largest contributors to federal candidates. Sponsors of well-financed PACs thus obtain a valuable political asset by using their committee to channel funds to other politicians. The extent of the advantage that can be achieved is suggested by the data in Tables 5.5 through 5.7. In the 1980 cycle, Reagan's Citizens for the Republic made 393 contributions, more than six times as many as its nearest competitors, John Connally's Citizens Forum and Bush's Fund for a Limited Government. In the 1984 cycle, Mondale's Committee for the Future of America awarded 180 contributions, more than twice the number made by Glenn's National Council on Public Policy, the next largest Democratic donor. In the most recent cycle, Bush's Fund for America's Future distributed 308 contributions, more than twice the number of its closest competition, Dole's Campaign America and Kemp's Campaign for Prosperity. On the Democratic side, Simon's Democracy Fund made 67 contributions and Gephardt's Effective Government Committee made 60, which was at least three times the number of contributions offered by Biden's Fund for '86 and Babbitt's Americans for the National Interest. The best-financed PACs thus make a significantly greater number of contributions than their competitors, which gives their sponsors a meaningful advantage in recruiting campaign support. And although this analysis does not document the actual support PAC sponsors ultimately receive as a result of their committees' donations, it is logical to assume that these contributions help to build potential support by generating goodwill between an aspirant and fellow party members. PAC gifts can thus help an aspirant to develop a relationship with other candidates or can help to secure the support of officials who are already predisposed to support a PAC sponsor's candidacy.

One final characteristic of PAC giving evidenced by Tables 5.5 through 5.7 is that the money disbursed in contributions constitutes a small proportion of PAC spending. Although assisting candidates is supposed to be the primary purpose for which these committees are formed, their aggregate donations since 1977 ($3.95 million) represent only 10.2 percent of their aggregate expenditures ($38.57 million). Of the eighteen PACs formed by presidential candidates over the last three election cycles, nine spent less than 10 percent of their funds in direct contributions and only four (two in each of the last two cycles) devoted more than 15 percent of their spending to this activity. During the 1984 cycle, Glenn's National Council on Public Policy disbursed 41.3

percent of its expenditures in contributions (the largest percentage achieved to date by a candidate PAC) and Reagan's Citizens for the Republic devoted 30.5 percent of its spending to candidate donations. During the 1988 cycle, Babbitt's Americans for the National Interest made 26 percent of its total expenditures in contributions and Simon's Democracy Fund spent 16.4 percent of its total in this way.

PACs are not required by federal law to allocate a certain portion of their receipts or expenditures to political contributions. Federal regulations simply require that a PAC donate funds to at least five candidates in order to qualify as a multicandidate committee and thus become eligible for the higher contribution limits established for this type of committee.[36] The small percentage of funds spent on contributions by candidate PACs does not therefore directly violate the regulations governing these committees or serve to subvert federal law. But it does indicate that these committees devote most of their resources to other purposes and do not conduct their activities in a manner designed to maximize their grants to federal candidates.

Why candidate PACs devote such a small percentage of their spending to candidate donations is partly explained by their particular status under federal guidelines. These committees are organized as what are commonly termed "nonconnected" PACs. That is, they are PACs established independently by groups other than labor unions, corporations, or trade associations. PACs established by the latter organizations are legally viewed as being affiliated with these organizations and technically function as "separate segregated funds" of these organizations. They are essentially political committees established by their sponsoring organizations (specified in the law as a corporation, labor union, membership organization, cooperative, corporation without capital stock, or a trade associaton) to conduct political activities on behalf of their sponsors in accordance with federal guidelines. This type of committee was sanctioned by the FECA to provide these organizations with a means of participating in federal elections without abolishing the long-standing federal prohibitions against their direct financial participation in federal campaigns.[37]

The major difference between an affiliated, or "connected," separate segregated fund and a "nonconnected" PAC is that the sponsoring organization of a separate segregated fund may legally absorb some of the fund's administrative costs and pay for them out of union or corporate treasury funds.[38] A nonconnected PAC, however, has to finance all of its costs out of the monies it raises through contributions. In addition, a separate segregated fund begins its operations with an identifiable donor base (for example, its union's members or its company's employees), but a nonconnected PAC is established with no such "guaranteed" base of donors. As a result, nonconnected PACs, such as those sponsored by presidential aspirants, tend to have higher administrative and fundraising costs than other types of PACs and thus tend to give a smaller percentage of their revenues to other candidates.[39]

But the nonconnected status of candidate-sponsored PACs does not completely explain the meager portion of funds committed to candidates by these organizations. After all, Glenn's 1984 committee managed to apportion 41.3 percent of its spending to other candidates, and Reagan's PAC, during the same cycle, disbursed 30.5 percent of its expenditures in candidate donations. Moreover, these committees accomplished this end not only without a sponsoring organization that could finance some of their expenses but also without defraying some of their costs by establishing a tax-exempt foundation or, in Glenn's case, a nonfederal soft money account. These committees therefore demonstrate that a candidate PAC could, if it so desired, share a significant portion of its funds with other candidates. Apparently, most prospective candidates would rather use a PAC's resources for other activities.

Furthermore, the nonconnected status of the presidential PACs does not explain the dramatic decline in the portion of funds spent on contributions in the most recent cycle. During the 1980 cycle, the percentage of aggregate PAC spending accounted for by contributions was 10.6 percent. This figure rose to 22.2 percent in the 1984 cycle, although the increase was the result of the high level of donations awarded by Reagan's Citizens for the Republic. If this committee's donations are excluded from the calculations so that only committees sponsored by Democratic aspirants (who faced a competitive nomination contest) are considered, the percentage of spending accounted for by contributions is 10.6 percent, the same percentage as in the 1980 cycle.

The committees active in the 1988 cycle devoted only 6.4 percent of their spending to candidate contributions. This share was less than a third of the percentage donated by the 1984 committees and less than two-thirds of the percentage donated by the 1980 committees or the 1984 Democratic PACs. Committees sponsored by Republican hopefuls committed a mere 6.1 percent of their spending to candidate contributions. Democratic committees gave away a slightly higher percentage than their Republican counterparts, 9.9 percent, but still fell below the average percentage achieved in previous cycles. As a result, the total amount contributed by the five Republican committees alone in the 1988 cycle was nearly $130,000 less than the amount contributed by the five committees active prior to the 1984 election. Yet, overall, these five 1988 committees spent more than three times as much as their 1984 counterparts.

These figures indicate that, despite unprecedented revenues, the

PACs active in advance of the 1988 election adopted a rather miserly approach toward sharing their bounty with other candidates. Although PAC receipts increased by more than 260 percent between 1984 and 1988 (from approximately $6.96 million to $25.25 million), PAC contributions increased by a mere 4.4 percent (from $1.54 million to $1.61 million) and actually declined as a percentage of total spending. Thus, although prospective candidates rely on PACs as a means of channeling funds to other candidates, most of the funds they raise are expended for other purposes.

CONCLUSION

Because the federal regulations governing multicandidate PACs are less restrictive than those established for authorized campaign committees, a PAC offers a presidential aspirant unique financial opportunities. The creation of a PAC in the precampaign period provides an individual with the ability to engage in activities that would not be permitted if undertaken through a campaign committee. In particular, a PAC allows a prospective candidate to accept individual contributions in excess of the maximum amount allowed in a presidential campaign, solicit unrestricted soft money funds, and make contributions to a large number of candidates. The analysis presented in this chapter indicates the extent to which presidential candidates have capitalized on these opportunities in hopes of advancing the prospects of their nomination campaigns.

One of the primary advantages of a PAC is its ability to solicit individual contributions in excess of the $1,000 limit established for presidential campaigns. A prospective candidate may use a PAC to solicit up to $5,000 a year from an individual donor, or up to $20,000 over the course of a presidential election cycle. Those who give funds to a candidate's PAC remain eligible to contribute up to $1,000 to his or her campaign committee so long as the PAC is organized and operated independently of any future campaign organization.

A precandidacy PAC thus allows a potential candidate to initiate fundraising activities and identify possible donors to his or her campaign. More importantly, it provides a means of maximizing the revenue potential of identified supporters by allowing a candidate to accept large donations from these individuals before his or her campaign committee is established. Prospective candidates who adopt this approach can raise millions of dollars in the early years of a presidential election cycle without violating the contribution limits applicable to presidential campaigns.

The role of these large contributions in candidate PAC financing is illustrated by the fundraising activities of the committees active in advance of the 1988 election. These committees aggressively pursued the opportunities afforded by the regulations, raising more than half of their $25.25 million in total revenue in contributions of more than $1,000. They were especially successful in soliciting funds from wealthy individuals who each gave at least $10,000 to one of the candidate-backed committees. Every committee accepted contributions that would have been illegal if given to a presidential campaign and every sponsor, regardless of his prospects, benefited from these generous donations. Lesser-known candidates relied on large donations from a relative handful of supporters to raise the seed money needed to launch their prospective bids for the nomination and finance their precampaign political activities. Better-known candidates or potential frontrunners, who had broader bases of financial support, raised millions of dollars from large donors and thereby gained a substantial resource advantage over possible opponents.

Some candidates, however, are not satisfied with the larger amounts they can solicit through PACs under federal law. They therefore seek to expand their access to large donations by taking advantage of another unique feature of a multicandidate PAC, its ability to use nonfederal, soft money accounts. This type of account provides a committee with an essentially unrestricted ability to raise funds so long as the monies received are used solely for nonfederal political activities. PACs that establish these accounts, as did three of the committees sponsored by 1988 candidates, may solicit individual contributions in unlimited amounts and accept unregulated contributions from sources banned from participating in federal elections, such as labor unions and corporations. In addition, they can conduct these activities in almost total secrecy because most states lack stringent public disclosure laws requiring that PACs submit a complete accounting of their contributors and the amounts of their donations.

A soft money account thus provides a presidential PAC with an important resource and a way of conducting financial activities free of federal constraints. It also offers other strategic benefits. First, the money raised through a nonfederal account serves to increase any resource advantage over potential opponents that a candidate PAC achieves through its federal fundraising efforts. This is especially true for those opponents who follow the intent of campaign finance laws and employ no preformal campaign organizations before declaring their candidacy. Second, by using its soft money to make contributions to state and local politicians, a PAC can expand the potential support for its sponsor's impending campaign. In particular, a PAC may be used to build support in key presidential primary states, such as Iowa and New Hampshire, and thus assist its sponsor's prospects in these crucial early contests.

Yet, despite the benefits of a soft money account, few candidate-sponsored PACs to date have pursued this option. Only five of the eighteen PACs formed by candidates in the last three election cycles are known to have used soft money funds: Reagan's Citizens for the Republic, Mondale's Committee for the Future of America, Dole's Campaign America, Kemp's Campaign for Prosperity, and Biden's Fund for '86. With the exception of Biden's PAC, these committees were sponsored by well-known individuals who were considered to be viable contenders for their party's nomination. Their nonfederal accounts thus provided them with a means of increasing the resource advantage they had already developed through their federal accounts. Why so many PACs have failed to capitalize on this opportunity is not clear. Perhaps their hesitancy is due to the legal ambiguities surrounding the use of nonfederal accounts by nonparty committees. Or there may be a learning curve involved in the more technical niceties of PAC financing, with some candidates having mastered all of the rules of the game better than others. Whatever the reason, the advantages that accrue from a soft money fund are such that future candidate PACs are likely to make greater use of this option.

Finally, prospective candidates also establish PACs so that they may contribute funds to a large number of candidates. Although campaign funds may be used legally for this purpose, a PAC may donate larger sums than an authorized campaign committee, and candidates have been unwilling to share their campaign funds with others because to do so would reduce the resources available to their own campaigns. As a result, candidates in the last three election cycles have relied on their PACs to channel millions of dollars to hundreds of federal candidates.

Although presidential hopefuls use their PACs to offer gifts to other candidates, they expend a relatively small share of their funds in this way. Although the aggregate amount given to candidates has increased in each of the last three cycles, the percentage of spending devoted to this function has declined. Consequently, the amount given to candidates during the 1988 presidential election cycle increased only marginally, even though revenues increased dramatically. In other words, candidate PACs spend an increasingly large percentage of their funds on activities other than candidate assistance, which suggests that this purpose is not the primary reason for which these committees are organized.

6

The Shadow Campaign

The campaign finance laws specifically prohibit a candidate from designating a PAC as an authorized campaign committee. The statutory purpose of a PAC is to serve as a vehicle for raising and spending funds to assist candidates and party organizations; it is not to serve as a formal campaign organization for a particular candidate. Nor is it to serve as an informal campaign committee. Although a PAC may assist a candidate by contributing funds or financing campaign-related activities, this participation is limited. The regulations state that any funds spent by a PAC on activities that directly benefit a candidate must be reported as a qualified campaign contribution or expenditure that is subject to the legal limits established for federal elections (unless the assistance is in the form of an independent expenditure). The law also discourages precampaign politicking by a prospective candidate through a PAC. Any monies spent by a PAC on activities considered to be indicative of a formal candidacy on the part of a PAC sponsor or other individual must be reported as campaign expenditures if that individual decides to run for federal office and are subject to campaign contribution and spending limits. The law thus attempts to ensure that a candidate cannot avoid the contribution and spending limits by financing campaign activities through a PAC.

These regulations have done little to deter presidential aspirants from using their PACs as front organizations for their nomination campaigns. Instead candidates have taken advantage of the technical provisions set forth in the administrative rulings implementing these guidelines to carry out an extensive amount of unregulated campaigning. The key to their success in circumventing the law has been the rather narrow standards adopted by the Federal Election Commission to determine whether a PAC's activities are indicative of a formal candidacy on the part of its sponsor. Under the provisions of recent advisory opinions and commission regulations, a PAC's activities do not affect its sponsor's legal status as a noncandidate as long as the committee does not (1) use general public political advertising to publicize its sponsor's intention to campaign for federal office; (2) undertake activities designed to amass campaign funds that would be spent after its sponsor becomes a candidate; (3) make written or oral statements that refer to its sponsor as a candidate for a particular office; (4) conduct activities in close proximity to the election or over a protracted period of time; or (5) take action to qualify him or her for the ballot under state law.[1]

Given these simple guidelines, a prospective candidate can easily spend millions of PAC dollars on campaign-related activities without engaging in an activity that would trigger a ruling that the aspirant is a legally qualified candidate, which would make the PAC's expenditures subject to the financial limits imposed on a candidate's campaign committee. By aggressively pursuing the actions permitted under these guidelines, a presidential hopeful can essentially use a PAC to finance the basic components of a nomination campaign. Provided that the PAC avoids any mention of its sponsor as a candidate or prospective challenger for a particular office, this committee can carry out almost every task essential to a campaign operation with the possible exception of media advertising, the creation of a financial war chest, and activities such as petition drives that would qualify its sponsor for the presidential ballot in particular states.

This chapter describes the ingenious methods by which presidential aspirants take advantage of the regulations to conduct shadow campaigns through precandidacy PACs. These shadow campaigns are an essential part of the modern nominating process because they represent the means by which presidential candidates have resolved the strategic problem of accomplishing the early campaigning required by recent reforms without violating the expenditure ceilings imposed on their campaign committees. Specifically, this chapter details how prospective candidates use PACs to accomplish three fundamental tasks: the formation of a campaign organization, the development of a fundraising program, and the creation of a base of political support.

A PAC provides a presidential aspirant with a means of recruiting the individuals who will form the nucleus of a future campaign organization. A PAC can hire staff members and retain the services of political consultants to assist it with its work. These individuals are often employed with the understanding that they will be offered a role in the committee sponsor's future campaign organization if he or she decides to run for office. A PAC can therefore essentially be used as a vehicle for recruiting and temporarily employing the core of a campaign staff. It can also be used to identify prospective members of state and local campaign organizations. A PAC can establish state subsidiaries or steering committees consisting of elected officials, party activists, and other political operatives. Once a candidate establishes a formal campaign committee, the individuals serving on these committees may be asked to serve on campaign steering committees or offered some other key role in a state organization. By encouraging the formation of state or local PAC committees, a prospective candidate can establish the basic structure for a fifty-state political operation, which would provide his or her campaign with a valuable organizational advantage.

A potential candidate can also gain a significant head start on campaign fundraising by establishing a precandidacy PAC. Although a PAC may not solicit campaign contributions, it may solicit funds for its own purposes through appeals that highlight a prospective candidate's name and committee affiliation. Those who respond to such appeals represent potential future campaign donors because they are likely to respond to later appeals from the candidate soliciting campaign gifts. In order to tap this source of revenue, a candidate's campaign committee simply has to rent or purchase the donor list created by the PAC.

A PAC's donor list is a highly valuable campaign asset. It facilitates early fundraising success, which can help to establish an individual's viability as a candidate and provide a substantial financial advantage over the competition in the early stages of a nomination contest. It also significantly reduces a campaign's fundraising costs and the amount of time needed to develop a fundraising program. Furthermore, it enhances a candidate's ability to qualify for matching funds early in the race, which can result in a sizable financial lead in the crucial first stage of the delegate selection process. A candidate who receives a large number of matchable contributions in the year before a presidential primary election will receive a large matching fund payment when the first public funds are disbursed on January 1 of the election year. In some cases, the amount of the subsidy received by a candidate may exceed that given to his or her opponents by millions of dollars. A candidate who successfully raises matchable contributions early will therefore be better prepared to meet the resource demands generated by the front-loading of the delegate selection process and be in a position to outspend opponents in the initial primaries.

A potential candidate can also accrue tangible political benefits from a precandidacy PAC. As a representative of a PAC, a presidential aspirant may travel around the country, meet public opinion leaders and political activists, make public appearances, and assist state and local politicians and party organizations. A PAC may also be used to conduct political activities that, in effect, begin the process of recruiting delegate candidates and delegate support. These activities can expand a candidate's political network, improve his or her public name recognition, increase the anticipated level of political support for his or her candidacy, and result in future delegate commitments. More simply, a PAC may be used to accomplish many of the political objectives established by campaign strategists at the outset of a race. And it can do so at no cost to the campaign.

DEVELOPING A CAMPAIGN ORGANIZATION

A PAC may not overtly build a campaign organization or hire personnel with an express guarantee that they will also be employed by the PAC sponsor's future campaign committee without jeopardizing its sponsor's legal status as a noncandidate. But it may engage in activities that effectively accomplish these ends. A PAC may hire political operatives and consultants to help it plan and conduct its operations. It may also form state subsidiaries or steering committees and recruit volunteers to assist its staff in implementing committee programs. When an aspirant registers his or her formal campaign committee, these individuals can be shifted from the PAC's payroll to the campaign's payroll or be asked to assist the campaign in some voluntary capacity. A PAC is thus used to recruit and employ a shadow campaign staff while remaining legally unaffiliated with its sponsor's campaign committee.

Bush's Fund for America's Future (FAF) represents the best example of how a PAC is used to establish the foundation of a campaign organization. From the outset, this committee's structure closely resembled the organizational schema of a presidential campaign in its initial phase. By May of 1986, the committee had a nationwide staff of approximately fifty persons and an average monthly payroll of about $60,000.[2] Half of the staff worked in the committee's Washington office, including the committee's chairman, Lee Atwater, who served as the deputy campaign manager of the 1984 Reagan-Bush Committee; its executive director, William Maxwell, a former executive director of the Republican National Committee; and its political director, Helen Cameron, who ran voter registration efforts for the 1984 Reagan-Bush campaign. The fund also hired a staff of three researchers and a number of consultants, including Fred Bush, a specialist in major donor fundraising; Odell, Roper and Associates, a well-known direct mail firm; Craig Shirley, a consultant who works with youth and conservative groups; Roy Hale, an accounting specialist; and Jan Baran, a federal election law expert who formerly served as executive assistant to the chair of the Federal Election Commission.[3]

FAF's political operation was coordinated by four Washington-based regional political directors, each of whom was responsible for one of four geographic areas (the South, the Southwest and grain-belt states, the West, and the Northeast and Midwest).[4] These individuals worked with staff members hired by the committee to work in specific states and with volunteers recruited by the PAC to help carry out its activities in states and localities. In particular, FAF established political operations in states that would hold crucial delegate selection contests in the 1988 election. In Michigan, where the 1986 precinct delegate elections were considered to be the first major political contest of the 1988 Republican nomination campaign, the committee hired a staff of fourteen and recruited a large corps of volunteers.[5] FAF also hired full-time staff in Iowa and New Hampshire.[6] These individuals, in addition to helping build the party, laid the groundwork for Bush's campaign organizations in these states.

One of the tasks FAF assigned to its political staff was the formation of state steering committees. A state steering committee is a group of prominent citizens, elected officials, party leaders, and political activists who agree to serve as a PAC's public representatives. Their role is usually to assist a PAC by offering advice, serving as public spokespersons, raising funds, recruiting volunteers, and making appearances on the committee's behalf.

The formation of steering committees creates political opportunities that can be of great benefit to a presidential campaign. A steering committee provides an aspirant with a pretense for pursuing early public endorsements from political leaders and other activists who act as opinion leaders for members of their own constituencies and the electorate at large. That these individuals are willing to serve on a committee is often perceived to be an indication of a prospective candidate's organizational ability and potential political support. One reason why a candidate-sponsored PAC establishes these committees, therefore, is to promote the perception that its sponsor has broad political support in a state. Another reason is to generate early press coverage of a sponsor's activities. The public unveiling of a steering committee usually occurs at a press conference. If not, members of the press are informed by some other means, such as a press release. This normally generates at least localized press coverage, which can improve a sponsor's local name recognition and draw attention to the individuals who have agreed to offer their support.

The Fund for America's Future was evidently aware of the potential advantages of state steering committees. On January 22, 1986, the committee asked the Federal Election Commission for its opinion as to whether it could expend funds on certain activities without allocating the costs to any potential future campaign by then-Vice President Bush.[7] One of the activities specifically noted was the establishment and operation of steering committees "to involve local party officials, leaders, and officeholders in the work of the Fund, and to provide them with an opportunity to advise and consult with the Fund concerning contributions to Republican candidates."[8] The commission ruled that the fund could operate steering committees and that any expenditures related to its activities would not be allocable to a future Bush campaign provided that the committees did not promote Bush's potential candidacy by forming a campaign organization, by participating in the delegate selection process on his behalf, or by requiring that an individual support his potential future candidacy in order to receive assistance from the fund.[9]

Upon receiving the commission's decision, Bush's PAC began to form a number of steering committees. These organizations, which were formed in accordance with the commission's restrictions, included members from every state[10] and were designed to fulfill campaign-related objectives. FAF organized a national steering committee consisting of individuals who had supported Bush's 1980 campaign, long-time party regulars, and supporters of President Reagan.[11] This committee was created to demonstrate Bush's widespread appeal and highlight his support among those faithful to Reagan. In October 1985, in anticipation of Michigan's 1986 precinct delegate elections, Bush named four leading Republican party figures, including two Republican national committee members, as co-chairs of his PAC in that state. FAF also announced a steering committee of 658 members, which had expanded to about 1,800 members by May 1986.[12] This group provided Bush with an extensive political network that symbolized his political strength in the state. More importantly, it served as the foundation for his political operation in the precinct delegate contests, which claimed to have recruited 4,800 of the 9,000 Republicans who filed for precinct delegate slots.[13]

In addition to establishing steering committees to advance Bush's prospects, FAF also used them to undermine the candidacies of prospective rivals. For example, early in 1986, the PAC unveiled its New York Congressional Steering Committee, which included fourteen of the state's fifteen Republican House members. The only Republican member of Congress omitted from this group was Jack Kemp, one of Bush's leading prospective opponents. The expressed purpose of this group was to serve as a vehicle for electing Republican candidates in the 1986 elections. But its implicit purpose was to raise questions about the viability of a Kemp candidacy by emphasizing Kemp's weakness in his home state.[14]

When considered as a whole, the staff and organization established by FAF had all the "earmarks of a presidential campaign in miniature."[15] It included the personnel needed to raise funds from large and small donors, develop national and state political structures, recruit volunteers, engage in policy research, implement political outreach programs to general and specialized constituencies, conduct direct mail programs, and monitor compliance with federal regulations and procedures. About all the committee could not do was solicit campaign commitments directly and engage in activities that were blatantly campaign-related, such as qualifying Bush for a state primary ballot. The PAC's staffing and recruitment activities thus provided Bush with a shadow campaign organization, which was prepared to undertake campaign responsibilities as soon as Bush declared his candidacy. That this was the intended purpose of the FAF's organizational efforts was noted by Paul Taylor, a Washington political reporter who claimed that Bush and his PAC staff recruited individuals "with winks and nods" that "made it clear they want[ed] recruits for 1986 to stick around for the [nomination campaign] in 1988."[16]

The other 1988 candidate PAC sponsors also relied on their committees to begin developing a campaign organization. These committees undertook most of the activities conducted by Bush's PAC, although on a much smaller scale. Kemp's Campaign for Prosperity, for example, had only five persons on its payroll and retained the services of five consultants.[17] Yet even this limited operation offered Kemp important campaign-related advantages. He hired John Maxwell, a seasoned Iowa-born campaign organizer and former aide to Iowa Senators Roger Jepsen and Charles Grassley, as his PAC's executive director.[18] Maxwell helped develop a national political network and played a particularly important role in advancing Kemp's candidacy in Iowa, where he had well-established political contacts. Kemp's organizational efforts were also advanced by a number of state-level committees created under the auspices of his PAC. The committee established subsidiary structures designed to engender political support in Iowa and New Hampshire. In Michigan, Kemp established a political network through a state-level PAC, the Michigan Opportunity Society, which was chaired by W. Clark Durant III, a former chair of the federal Legal Services Corporation and a member of a prominent family in Michigan's conservative political circles.[19] The PAC also hired two direct mail consultants who helped the committee build a broad base of potential campaign contributors.

Bush, therefore, was not the only 1988 candidate to rely on a PAC to get a head start on the development of a campaign organization. Nor was he the first. The staff of Mondale's preelection PAC, for example, was "indistinguishable" from his initial 1984 campaign operation, which included fourteen of the PAC's seventeen employees.[20] But no other candidate has matched Bush in developing so extensive an organization or at least one so visible.[21] Bush's Fund for America's Future therefore stands as a model for future presidential hopefuls of how to subvert federal law and establish a campaign organization through a precandidacy PAC.

DEVELOPING A FUNDRAISING PROGRAM

Presidential aspirants also sponsor PACs in order to begin a campaign fundraising program. In most cases, this is the primary objective a prospective candidate hopes to achieve by establishing a multicandidate committee. A PAC can benefit a campaign fundraising program in two ways: it can increase a candidate's base of financial support and develop a valuable campaign asset, a list of likely campaign donors. By accomplishing these ends, a PAC can improve a candidate's prospects of early fundraising success, increase his or her ability to generate matching funds, and significantly reduce campaign fundraising costs. It therefore alleviates the conflicting financial demands imposed on presidential candidates by the campaign finance system and delegate selection process. It facilitates the early fundraising required by the system but does so without affecting the amount a candidate may legally spend on a nomination campaign.

Because of the contribution limits established by the Federal Election Campaign Act, a campaign must be financed through small contributions. A presidential candidate must solicit thousands of contributions in order to raise the millions of dollars needed to mount a competitive campaign. This is a time-consuming task, especially for those candidates who begin their campaigns with a limited base of financial support. Even prospective frontrunners with well-established donor bases must begin raising funds early if they are to generate the sums needed to meet the financial demands of the nomination process.

Presidential candidates employ a number of fundraising approaches in their efforts to solicit the large number of small donations needed to finance their campaigns. But the primary vehicle for achieving this objective is direct mail. Direct mail is a fundraising tool that provides its users with an ability to make direct, personalized, targeted appeals to pretested audiences.[22] When used effectively, a single solicitation can generate thousands of contributions, with an average donation in the amount of twenty to thirty dollars. No other fundraising device can solicit tens of thousands of donors so efficiently. Consequently, direct mail is considered to be a necessary component of a presidential fundraising program, and all candidates employ it in some form.

The major drawback in direct mail fundraising is the time and expense involved in the creation of a well-developed "house" list of likely donors, which is the key to the success of this technique. A "house" list is a list of "proven donors, who, having contributed once [to a candidate or organization] are believed good possibilities for additional donations."[23] These individuals constitute the foundation of a direct mail program. They are the targets of repeated mailings during the course of a campaign, each of which is normally very profitable because individuals who contribute once to a candidate will usually give again when resolicited.[24] A well-developed house list is thus an invaluable resource to a campaign.

To create a house list, a campaign must first conduct a number of "prospect" mailings. A "prospect" mailing is a "general, mass mailing to suspected potential campaign donors—based on some characteristics or qualities thought likely to make them susceptible to a candidate's appeal for funds."[25] These mailings are used to identify the donors who become part of a campaign's house list. To conduct such a mailing, a campaign must rent or purchase lists of potential contributors and construct a prospecting list (or hire a direct mail firm to perform this task for it). This list generally must include "a universe of 1 million potential givers" before a mailing program "is thought to have a reasonable chance of success."[26] The campaign must then pay the costs of preparing and sending the letters, which can range from thirty cents to three dollars per letter, depending on the preparation and contents of the mailing.[27] These costs are often not recovered in the initial mailings because, on average, only 1.5 to 2.0 percent of those solicited respond to prospecting appeals.[28] These mailings therefore "frequently lose money or manage to pay for themselves with a wafer-thin profit."[29] Those that do realize a profit generally cost fifteen dollars for every eighteen dollars raised in contributions and thus produce a low net return.[30] But these costs are accepted because the fundamental purpose of these mailings is to identify donors rather than earn a profit. Any net income received from such a mailing is viewed as a bonus and is commonly reinvested in additional prospecting. This additional prospecting is needed because an adequate number of donors is rarely identified in a single mailing. Generally, about five mailings are needed to build a sizable list. Prospecting is therefore "a lengthy and arduous process" that can take a year or more to complete.[31]

 The amount of money and time required to build a house list extensive enough to raise the sums needed by a presidential campaign can be discerned from estimates based on model direct mail programs. One such program is presented in political scientist Larry Sabato's 1981 study of political consultants. Sabato notes that the creation of a house list of 200,000 donors capable of producing $2 million in net income would require five prospect mailings and two interim house list mailings at a total cost of approximately $2.02 million.[32] In 1985, direct mail consultant Roger Craver presented another model that estimated that the creation of a house list of 22,000 donors capable of raising approximately $400,000 would require five prospect mailings conducted over an eleven-month period at a gross cost of $525,000 or a net loss of $41,000.[33] To generate a net income of approximately $400,000 would require fourteen mailings to persons on the house list over a fifteen-month period at a gross cost of $118,500.[34]

These examples indicate that a candidate who is willing to invest the necessary time and money to create a productive house list can realize a substantial amount of income in return for the investment. Unlike prospect mailings, house list mailings have high rates of return that average around 10 percent and may range as high as 20 percent.[35] As a result, these solicitations produce an average of ten dollars in contributions for every one dollar spent.[36] And these returns are effectively doubled in a presidential campaign because most of these donations would be matched with public funds. More importantly, a house list can be resolicited on a regular basis and maintain its high rate of return. It thus serves as a reliable source of income throughout a campaign. It is therefore "not uncommon for an organization to realize up to a 300 percent return on its original investment in a full, three-year direct mail development program."[37]

Given these costs and benefits, direct mail fundraising is often viewed as a mixed blessing by presidential campaign fundraisers. On the one hand, it is an effective vehicle for raising small donations that qualify for public matching funds. As such, it is an important source of campaign revenue. But it is also an expensive and time-consuming technique. A presidential campaign generally lacks the time needed to realize the full income potential of a direct mail program, especially when it has to initiate a program from scratch. Even if a campaign had the time, the costs associated with such an effort would consume a major portion of a campaign's ceiling-exempt fundraising expenditures, leaving a limited amount for other fundraising activities and perhaps requiring the allocation of some fundraising expenses against the campaign's overall spending limit.

Because of these drawbacks, a presidential campaign is, as Sabato notes, "not very well suited to direct mail," despite its financial benefits.[38] But many presidential aspirants have discovered that a precandidacy PAC is. A PAC can be used to initiate a direct mail program and build a house list of likely donors for its sponsor's presidential campaign committee. To do so, the committee simply performs the tasks normally undertaken in a direct mail fundraising program, taking care to ensure that its sponsor is somehow highlighted in the appeals. Then, when its sponsor has established a formal campaign committee, the PAC rents or sells its donor list to that committee, which can in turn solicit campaign contributions from the PAC donors. Because these individuals have already responded to an appeal from the candidate made on behalf of the PAC, it is highly probable that they will respond to similar appeals for donations to his or her campaign. In this way, a PAC can easily be used to develop the foundation of a campaign fundraising program.

This tactic is possible because federal law permits a candidate to solicit a list developed by a PAC or other organization provided that the list is obtained in accordance with federal guidelines. Under the Federal Election Commission's current interpretation of the law, a political committee can rent its donor list to a candidate, in which case the candidate must simply report the cost as a fundraising expense. Or a PAC can sell its list to a candidate without reporting it as a contribution if the list is sold at the "usual and normal charge" (which generally amounts to less than 1 percent of the cost of building the list). If it sells the list at a price greater than market value, the difference between the market value and the sale price represents a contribution from the candidate to the PAC and must be reported as such. Conversely, if the list is sold for less than market value, the difference must be reported as a contribution from the PAC to the candidate and would be subject to the contribution limits established for presidential elections.[39] A candidate can also acquire a PAC's donor list by exchanging names from a list compiled by his or her campaign for those gathered by a PAC. If the lists are of equal value, which normally means that an equal number of names are exchanged, this transaction is not considered to be a contribution on the part of either party. Three-way or multiparty exchanges are also allowed, if the lists are of corresponding value. Finally, a candidate can obtain a PAC's donor list indirectly by purchasing it from a third party that has rights to the list.[40]

The commission's position on mailing list transfers has encouraged presidential aspirants to use PACs to develop donor lists for their campaigns. By 1980, Ronald Reagan's Citizens for the Republic had constructed a list of 300,000 donors, all of whom were likely contributors to Reagan's campaign. Walter Mondale began his 1984 nomination campaign with a list of 25,000 prospective donors that was developed by his Committee for the Future of America. Similarly, Jack Kemp relied on his Campaign for Prosperity to identify 75,000 to 100,000 donors, a number that equaled the number of potential donors on Bush's fundraising lists.[41]

These PACs had to spend enormous amounts of money on direct mail in order to develop these lists. Reagan's Citizens for the Republic spent heavily on direct mail fundraising prior to the 1980 campaign. Mondale's Committee for the Future of America spent about 40 percent of its total budget, or nearly $1 million, building its list.[42] Kemp's Campaign for Prosperity spent 30 to 40 percent of its budget, or approximately $1.25 million to $1.66 million based on the committee's total expenditures, on direct mail.[43]

Because the committees incurred these expenses before their sponsors became formal candidates, these costs were not allocable to their sponsors' respective campaigns. And because the commission only requires the payment of the "usual and normal charge" for the purchase of a list, the campaign committees established by these candidates were able to acquire the lists for a mere fraction of the amount it cost to build them. For example, Mondale's campaign committee gained access to his precandidacy PAC's donor list apparently by paying a small fee through a third party that brokered the sale. This "hidden" transaction was reported by Bill Hogan and Alan Green, the journalists who uncovered the PAC's soft money accounts.[44]

Even before Mondale announced his candidacy . . . his top advisers planned the presidential campaign's secret use of the PAC's 25,000-name contributor list, which had been compiled over two years at a cost of nearly $1 million. To keep it secret, they routed payments through Targeted Communications Corporation, a direct-mail consulting firm based in Falls Church, Virginia. Because Targeted Communications had been retained by both Mondale's PAC (the "left hand") and his presidential committee (the "right hand"), it was the ideal conduit for shielding financial handshakes from public view.

Even though the Mondale for President Committee used the PAC's fundraising list in early 1983, there was no way for outsiders to know it. In its report to the Federal Election Commission for the last half of 1983, Mondale's PAC showed an undated payment of $2,002 from Targeted Communications that it described as "direct mail list income." It made no reference at all to the Mondale for President Committee.

By employing the same direct mail firm to raise funds for his PAC and his presidential committee, Mondale quietly acquired a valuable campaign fundraising list. As a result, his campaign immediately realized a two-year head start on the development of its fundraising program and reduced its prospective fundraising costs by almost a million dollars. Viewed from another perspective, the PAC's activities in effect increased the campaign's limit-exempt fundraising allowance by about a million dollars because the amount the campaign would have had to spend to develop a house mailing list could now be spent on other fundraising activities. Yet the total cost of all of these advantages was a mere $2,002. Mondale's experience thus indicates the savings that can be achieved by investing in a precandidacy PAC.

Other candidates have achieved similar benefits by using a PAC to initiate their fundraising efforts. Bush's campaign committee paid $275 to the Fund for America's Future on September 17, 1986, for a "list expense."[45] On February 18, 1987, the day before Bush officially registered his campaign committee with the Federal Election Commission, the committee paid an additional $590 to the Fund for America's Future for a "list expense" and $13,744 for the "purchase of equipment, list, and office supplies."[46] The total amount, $14,609, would fail to cover the cost of postage for a modest prospect mailing, not to mention the costs associated with the development of a direct mail operation. Bush thus saved his campaign several million dollars in fundraising costs. Similarly, Dole's campaign finance director, Kirk Clinkenbeard, reportedly estimated that "the development of donor lists by Campaign America, Dole's PAC, had saved the presidential campaign as much as $2 million" in fundraising costs.[47] Roger Stone, a consultant to Kemp's presidential committee, claimed that Kemp's campaign had also saved about $2 million as a result of the fundraising activities conducted by Kemp's PAC.[48] Pete du Pont also saved substantial amounts by relying on the donor lists developed by GOPAC and the National Leadership Council, the two nonfederal PACs with which he was associated prior to his 1988 candidacy. The precise amount spent by these committees on direct mail is unknown, but it certainly exceeded the token amount spent by du Pont's campaign committee to acquire their donor lists. The presidential committee paid $750 on June 30, 1986, to the National Leadership Council for the rental of its list and paid $527 and $1,750 to rent GOPAC's list.[49]

Besides saving valuable time and reducing a campaign's expenses, a PAC's fundraising efforts can increase a campaign's revenue prospects. A PAC's contributor list provides a candidate with a base of highly likely donors. Although all of these individuals may not donate money to a PAC sponsor's campaign committee, the fact that they have responded to appeals made by a candidate on behalf of a PAC or made by a PAC associated with a candidate means that they will probably respond to the sponsor's appeal for campaign contributions. A PAC's donor list therefore functions as the house list for its sponsor's campaign. As such, it improves a candidate's ability to raise funds early by ensuring high rates of return from direct mail solicitations. It also enhances a candidate's long-term financial prospects because the individuals who give money to a candidate's PAC and campaign usually become a permanent source of campaign income. A presidential committee can solicit these donors on a regular basis throughout the course of the nomination process and maintain high rates of return that can result in substantial amounts of net income.

The ability to raise funds early is especially important because the monies received are supplemented by public matching funds. A candidate who generates a large sum in matchable contributions in the year prior to an election receives a large sum of public money when the first payments are issued in January of the election year. This public subsidy is an indispensable source of campaign revenue and often determines whether a candidate will have the funds needed to wage a competitive campaign in the early delegate selection contests. Furthermore, it can provide the candidate who accumulates the largest sum in preelection year matching funds with an important strategic advantage. By exceeding the amount of public money accrued by other contenders, a candidate can virtually guarantee that he or she will enjoy a resource advantage in the initial stage of the delegate selection process.

The scope of the financial advantage that a candidate can achieve by relying on a PAC's donor list to gain a head start in the aggregation of matching funds is evidenced by Mondale's experience in 1984. Mondale registered his principal campaign committee with the Federal Election Commission on January 3, 1983, two days after the date on which a candidate could begin to receive contributions eligible for public matching subsidies.[50]   His committee began soliciting contributions immediately, relying on his PAC's contributor list as its initial base of prospective donors. Within forty-eight hours of its creation, the committee had fulfilled the eligibility requirements of the matching funds program, and by the end of the first quarter of 1983 it had raised $2.4 million in net income.[51] The campaign continued to raise funds successfully throughout 1983. When the first matching payments were issued by the Treasury in January 1984, Mondale received $4.34 million; John Glenn, $2.34 million; Alan Cranston, $1.48 million; Reubin Askew, $863,600; Gary Hart, $678,600; and Ernest Hollings, $678,400.[52] The initial installment of public money thus provided Mondale with a net financial gain of $2 million over Glenn and almost $3 million over Cranston. This financial advantage helped to solidify his position as the early frontrunner in the race and later helped him to endure the impressive and unexpected challenge posed by Gary Hart.[53]

Mondale's presidential campaign realized tangible benefits from his PAC's "noncampaign-related" fundraising activities. In addition to saving almost $1 million in start-up costs, the PAC identified a donor base that served as the foundation of the campaign's fundraising program. This foundation helped Mondale develop an early fundraising lead, which none of his opponents was able to overcome. This fundraising advantage was an important factor in Mondale's success in the primary campaign, although other factors such as the particular strategies employed in state contests were more significant in determining the election's final outcome.[54] But regardless of the influence of money on the results of the 1984 campaign, it is clear that Mondale's Committee for the Future of America served its intended purpose: it launched a fundraising operation capable of financing a successful presidential nomination campaign. And the evidence indicates that the efficacy of his PAC strategy was not lost on other candidates because most of the 1988 contenders adopted a similar approach in developing their fundraising programs.

DEVELOPING POLITICAL SUPPORT

A precandidacy PAC can also be used to develop a base of political support for a presidential campaign. A PAC provides a presidential aspirant with a means of financing national travel, meeting political leaders and party activists, making public appearances, and engaging in a wide range of other political activities. These "noncampaign-related" activities increase an aspirant's exposure to party members, provide countless opportunities for developing political contacts, and help to improve an individual's public name recognition. In other words, they allow a prospective candidate to develop the political network and potential political support needed to launch a presidential campaign.

A PAC can essentially fulfill all of the early political objectives of a presidential campaign because the Federal Election Commission allows a multicandidate committee to conduct most of the political activities usually associated with a presidential campaign. A PAC can arrange public appearances for its sponsor and staff, finance their travel, host political receptions, develop political outreach programs, form steering committees, and organize volunteer efforts. It can also undertake activities that are commonly excluded from a campaign's political program such as providing assistance to state and local candidates and party organizations and conducting political operations designed to influence nonfederal or party elections. A PAC is allowed to engage in these activities because they are considered to be appropriate to the task of party-building, a purpose sanctioned by federal regulations. This is the avowed purpose of every candidate-sponsored PAC. But these sponsors understand that PACs are also suited to the task of building a campaign. Consequently, the primary purpose for which these activities are undertaken is to obtain campaign-related benefits.

A presidential aspirant needs to develop a broad base of political support to be regarded as a viable candidate. To accomplish this, the prospective candidate must become acquainted with elected officials and other political opinion leaders throughout the country, increase his or her public exposure in states and localities, and develop personal relationships that can result in support for his or her candidacy. To begin this process, a presidential hopeful must devote months, if not years, to the simple task of initially meeting various individuals and groups. This task, in addition to being time-consuming, is expensive because it requires extensive travel and a substantial number of personal appearances.

Presidential aspirants have discovered that a precandidacy PAC is an effective vehicle for conducting the activities needed to develop a broad base of potential support. A PAC offers an almost unlimited ability to meet political leaders, appear at public gatherings, and travel throughout the country. As a PAC's primary representative or spokesperson, a potential candidate may attend all PAC-sponsored functions, whether hosted on a national, regional, statewide, or local basis. He or she may attend PAC meetings, participate in PAC-sponsored issues forums, appear at public events or press conferences, attend steering committee or volunteer meetings and events, and host committee receptions. A PAC sponsor may also attend functions related to a PAC's activities. These include events at which a PAC publicly presents a contribution to a candidate or party committee; events sponsored by candidates such as campaign fundraisers or rallies; national, state, or local party committee meetings; and issues forums or other policy-related events. In sum, a PAC provides its sponsor with numerous opportunities to meet political leaders, party members, political activists, and other members of the electorate.

By taking advantage of these opportunities, a potential candidate engages in a substantial amount of precampaign politicking. Walter Mondale, for example, traveled extensively and attended more than a hundred events under the auspices of his Committee for the Future of America. The PAC financed his travel to 42 of the 50 states.[55] In 1982 alone, he attended 41 events for Democratic candidates and party organizations and was personally active in 93 House, 15 Senate, and 19 gubernatorial election campaigns.[56] The PAC reported over $200,000 in travel expenses for Mondale and his staff. Of this amount, $139,330 was not allocated to any political campaign, which suggests that the purpose of these trips was not to attend an event in support of a particular candidate.[57] In addition, the PAC financed a three-day conference at the Wye Plantation on Maryland's Eastern Shore, at which more than a hundred Mondale supporters received strategy briefings.[58] The PAC also helped finance Mondale's political operation at the 1982 Democratic National Party Conference, a crucial early showcase for the individuals seeking the party's standard in 1984.

Richard Gephardt's Effective Government Committee serves as another example of how a PAC can be used to defray the costs of precampaign political travel. As a relatively unknown aspirant, Gephardt had to build a national political network virtually from scratch. He therefore relied on his PAC to finance trips designed to develop political contacts and increase his public exposure. He supplemented this travel with trips taken in his capacities as chairman of both the Democratic Leadership Council and House Democratic Caucus. As a result, he made more than 200 appearances in 30 states during 1985. By the end of November 1986, he had traveled to 38 states, visiting 8 of them more than 10 times apiece. Before each trip, Gephardt would receive a detailed memorandum prepared by William Romjue, the PAC's executive director, on the political geography of the state he was about to visit. Afterward, the PAC collected any names of contacts or potential supporters gathered during the trip and incorporated them into its political network.[59] The PAC particularly focused its efforts on the development of a political network in Iowa, because Gephardt would have to do well there if he hoped to become a viable contender for the party's nomination. The committee spent at least $750,000 on staff salaries and Gephardt's travel in this state, and Gephardt spent 40 days there between January 1986 and February 1987.[60] By the time of the caucus, Gephardt had spent 190 days in Iowa, and Iowa's Democrats rewarded his perseverance with a victory on election night.[61]

These examples, which are not atypical, illustrate how Mondale and Gephardt used their PACs to carry out the political outreach required in the early stages of a presidential campaign. Their committees subsidized their travel and sponsored their appearances at hundreds of political events. At each of these functions, Mondale and Gephardt met politically important individuals and groups, became acquainted with party regulars, and introduced themselves to potential voters. They also identified persons who would be willing to assist them if (or when) they decided to become candidates. Each, therefore, employed his PAC to develop an informal political network and build future campaign support, especially in the states that hold early primary contests.

This PAC-sponsored travel also allowed Mondale and Gephardt to fulfill other campaign-related objectives. They were able to improve their understanding of state and local politics, increase their knowledge of subnational political issues and policy concerns, and develop an awareness of the political dynamics that exist in different parts of the country. Their appearances generated press reports in the national and local media that helped to promote their presidential ambitions and increase their public name recognition. Their PAC-sponsored speaking engagements allowed them to develop and "pretest" possible campaign themes, speeches, and policy proposals. In sum, Mondale and Gephardt were able to engage in almost all of the political tasks required at the beginning of a presidential campaign. But by diligently maintaining the pretense of performing activities solely related to the PAC's avowed purpose of building the party and assisting its candidates, each of these candidates was able to complete these campaign-related tasks at no cost to his future campaign committee.

In addition to these informal methods of generating political support, an aspirant may utilize a PAC to create a more formal and structured group of supporters. As noted earlier in this chapter, a PAC may establish a formal political organization consisting of a central staff, subsidiary committees, and state or local volunteer operations. This organizational structure can be an effective vehicle for securing political commitments even before an individual becomes a candidate. Although an aspirant may not overtly solicit commitments of campaign support before declaring a formal candidacy, he or she can identify prospective supporters and attempt to secure their support by offering them a role in a PAC's operation such as a staff position, membership on a steering committee or policy advisory committee, or a formal volunteer responsibility. This was the approach employed by Bush's PAC prior to the 1988 campaign. Then, once a formal campaign committee is established, these individuals can be incorporated into the campaign's organizational structure.

In the interim period between the identification of a supporter and the formal beginning of the campaign, a PAC can maintain contact with its recruits and attempt to expand its base of support by establishing some type of ongoing communications program. The most common means of achieving this end, besides regular PAC meetings, is some form of PAC newsletter. Reagan's Citizens for the Republic began publishing a bimonthly newsletter in February 1977, less than a month after it was established. The newsletter featured information on PAC activities and articles written by Reagan on a variety of conservative issues. By December 1978, its circulation, which included PAC contributors and members of the press, approached 40,000.[62] Mondale's Committee for the Future of America also regularly published a newsletter. It included features such as "A Message from Walter Mondale," "Excerpts from Mondale Speeches," and "Mondale on the Issues."[63] The contents of these publications indicate that their purpose was largely to promote their sponsor's political views and issue positions. So they essentially were designed to serve as campaign literature, the only major substantive difference being that the newsletters made no specific mention of its sponsor's intention to run for office.

Presidential aspirants also seek to recruit campaign support by providing financial assistance to candidates and party organizations. This aid, in addition to building the party, promotes the development of favorable political relationships between a PAC's sponsor and those who receive PAC contributions. Every prospective candidate hopes that his generosity will induce the recipients of PAC assistance, and perhaps their supporters, to respond in kind by assisting him in his own bid for office. Or, at least, each hopes that these recipients will remain open to further attempts to solicit their support.

Prospective candidates pursue this objective through a variety of fundraising activities. Besides making direct contributions to a candidate or party committee, a PAC sponsor can solicit donations from other PACs or individuals on behalf of a candidate or party. He or she can draft or endorse a letter for use in a direct mail appeal or share a PAC's donor list with a candidate or party committee. Another common practice is to serve as the primary speaker or guest at a fundraising event arranged by a candidate or party organization. This latter option is probably the most effective means by which a presidential aspirant can help others raise funds, especially if he or she is a relatively well-known politician.

By acting as a surrogate or "main draw" at a fundraising event, a prospective candidate can help raise an amount of money well in excess of the amount a PAC can legally contribute under federal law. Whereas a PAC is limited to a donation of $5,000 per election to federal candidates, a fundraiser featuring a well-known aspirant can usually generate at least $25,000 to $100,000. A PAC sponsor can therefore provide substantial assistance to fellow party members by agreeing to appear at candidate fundraisers. This is especially true for nationally recognized politicians considered to be presidential frontrunners in the early years of a presidential election cycle. These individuals are usually in the greatest demand on the political dinner circuit. They therefore attract the largest audiences at the highest prices. Accordingly, they are capable of raising the largest sums of money, which translates into the most political capital for the race ahead.

The value of surrogate fundraising appearances and the relative advantage they offer a better-known candidate can be deduced from the experience of Jack Kemp and George Bush in the first years of the 1988 contest. Both of these candidates began raising funds for others early. For example, in 1985 Kemp made at least fifty-three fundraising appearances and Bush made thirty-seven.[64] By November 1986, Kemp had raised approximately $1.4 million for Republican candidates and party organizations, or more than ten times the amount his PAC had directly contributed to federal candidates. These appearances thus provided Kemp with a means of greatly enhancing his financial influence among party members.

Yet Kemp's total, although impressive, paled in comparison to the amount raised by Bush during this period. According to William Phillips, executive director of Bush's Fund for America's Future, the then-vice president's appearances were estimated to have raised approximately ten times more than Kemp's outings (or roughly $14 million). One event attended by Bush reportedly generated $350,000 for state senate candidates in Michigan.[65] When this sum is added to the more than $813,000 that Bush's PAC directly gave to federal candidates in advance of the 1986 elections, the advantage Bush enjoyed with regard to his financial influence, and the potential political capital generated by that advantage, become apparent. No one versed in the dynamics of presidential campaigns would argue that these efforts did not directly benefit Bush's bid for the Oval Office.

Surrogate fundraising appearances can thus be an efficient, as well as an effective, means of generating support. By attending events organized on behalf of a group of candidates, an aspirant can assist a number of candidates at one time, which maximizes the potential support that may result from each event. This approach also makes efficient use of an aspirant's time and promotes the efficient use of PAC funds because the costs associated with these appearances (usually travel and hotel expenses) constitute a fraction of the amount that a PAC would spend if it gave individual contributions to each of the candidates assisted by these appearances.

These PAC-sponsored fundraising activities are particularly important given the role of elected officials in the presidential nominations process. These individuals are perceived as leaders of political opinion and can sometimes influence the views of their loyal constituents. Their willingness to support a candidate is usually perceived by members of the press and others as an indicator of a candidate's political strength. Elected officials often fill visible positions in a campaign such as serving as honorary campaign chairs or as campaign advisers, and their public endorsements of a candidate can be a valuable asset in building political support for a candidacy. It is also more than likely that elected officials will be delegates to the national party conventions. A PAC's fundraising activities can thus help a prospective candidate accomplish the most important task in a presidential campaign, the recruitment of delegate support.

In recent conventions, a majority of the members of Congress, U.S. senators, and governors have been selected to serve as delegates to their party's nominating convention. This is especially true for Democratic officeholders since the Democratic National Committee, beginning with the 1984 election, established a special category of unpledged-party-leader and elected-official delegates that are popularly known as "superdelegates." In the late 1960s and early 1970s, the representation of these officials in the nominating convention had declined significantly. In order to reverse this trend, the 1984 Democratic National Committee's rules for delegate selection authorized the House Democratic Caucus and the Senate Democratic Conference to select up to three-fifths of their respective members to serve as national convention delegates. In addition, the state parties were authorized to select unpledged-party-leader and elected-official delegates with the proviso that each give priority consideration to the governor, followed in order by large-city mayors, statewide elected officials, state legislators, members of Congress not previously selected, and other state and local politicians and party leaders.[66] The party's 1988 delegate selection rules further increased the representation of elected officials by authorizing the House Democratic Caucus and the Senate Democratic Conference to select up to four-fifths of their respective members to serve as delegates and by ensuring that all Democratic governors would be delegates.[67] Accordingly, the percentage of Democratic senators chosen as delegates increased from 14 percent in 1980 to 56 percent in 1984 and 84 percent in 1988. The percentage of Democratic House members chosen as delegates increased from 14 percent in 1980 to 62 percent in 1984 and 87 percent in 1988. The percentage of governors increased from 74 percent in 1980 to 91 percent in 1984 and 100 percent in 1988.[68] So, under the current rules, a Democratic presidential aspirant can assume that at least 8 out of 10 of the party's members of Congress and all of its governors will be delegates.

Unlike the Democrats, the Republican party did not experience a significant decline in the participation of elected officials in its presidential nominating conventions during the late 1960s and 1970s. It therefore felt no pressure to adopt special delegate selection rules guaranteeing the representation of these groups, especially since members of Congress and governors have been well represented at recent conventions. In 1980, 68 percent of the Republican governors were selected as delegates; in 1984, 93 percent; and in 1988, 87 percent. The percentage of Republican House members chosen as delegates has increased in each of the last three elections, rising from 40 percent in 1980 to 53 percent in 1984 and 57 percent in 1988. Each of the last three conventions has also included a majority of the Republican senators, with 68 percent selected as delegates in 1980, 93 percent in 1984, and 87 percent in 1988.[69] A prospective Republican presidential candidate can therefore expect that at least half of the party's House members and most of its senators and governors will be delegates to the nominating convention.

The formation of a PAC thus provides a presidential aspirant with a valuable tool for recruiting potential delegate support. By relying on a PAC to make contributions or otherwise offer financial aid to federal and statewide candidates, a presidential hopeful can provide direct assistance to individuals who are likely to become delegates. For example, of the 278 congressional candidates to whom Bush's Fund for America's Future donated funds in 1985 and 1986, 98 were delegates to the 1988 convention. Of the 104 candidates receiving donations from

Kemp's Campaign for Prosperity in 1985 and 1986, 30 were eventually selected as delegates. On the Democratic side, 35 of the 60 congressional candidates who received a contribution from Simon's Democracy Fund in 1985 and 1986 were delegates in 1988. Gephardt's Effective Government Committee contributed funds to 59 candidates, including 21 delegates. Babbitt's Americans for the National Interest gave money to only 15 candidates in 1985 and 1986, but 10 of these individuals were chosen to be delegates in 1988.[70]

Although candidate-sponsored PACs may not necessarily make these contributions for the specific purpose of recruiting delegate support, their donations can certainly have this effect. Or at least they can serve as a means of developing relationships that can ultimately lead to delegate support. In either case, presidential aspirants are fully aware of these potential consequences and establish PACs in part to take advantage of this means of recruiting prospective delegates. But PAC sponsors never publicly acknowledge this possibility; rather, they emphasize the party-building aspects of their committees' largesse. After all, the Federal Election Commission considers these donations and the other political and fundraising activities that PACs conduct to be "noncampaign-related" because they are carried out in a manner that does not violate the criteria that have been established for determining a PAC sponsor's formal candidacy. If the commission accepts these actions as "noncampaign-related," why should a presidential aspirant suggest otherwise?

CONCLUSION

A presidential aspirant's PAC can undertake financial and political activities without being subject to the regulatory requirements imposed on presidential campaigns if these activities are not related to a future campaign. Otherwise, the funds raised and costs incurred in these efforts are allocable to the sponsor's future campaign committee and may be deemed to be indicative of a sponsor's formal candidacy, in which case the sponsor is subject to the full legal requirements mandated for federal candidates. This regulatory safeguard was designed to prevent candidates or prospective candidates from circumventing the law by encouraging committees other than their individual campaign committees to raise and spend money on their behalf. But the efficacy of this restraint has been undermined by the Federal Election Commission's standards for determining whether an activity is indicative of a candidacy or "campaign-related." Whereas the commission has adopted a broad interpretive stance with respect to the activities that a potential candidate's PAC may conduct, it has advanced a narrow interpretation of the law in defining the actions indicative of a formal candidacy. The guidelines promulgated by the commission set forth five simple criteria for determining whether a candidate's actions are campaign-related. So long as an individual or that person's PAC avoids these types of activity, that individual retains his or her legal status as a noncandidate and is free of the candidate provisions of federal law.

The restraints imposed by the commission are so limited in their scope that they have failed to inhibit prospective candidates from using PACs to conduct shadow campaigns for the presidency. In fact, PACs have proven to be an effective vehicle for accomplishing the early campaigning encouraged by the campaign finance laws and the front-loading of the delegate selection process. A PAC can be used to conduct virtually all of the activities usually required at the beginning of a presidential campaign. As a result, presidential hopefuls have increasingly relied on these committees to perform an array of campaign-related tasks.

Most PAC sponsors use their committees to recruit and develop an organizational framework for their future campaigns. A PAC can hire staff, retain consultants, create state and local subsidiaries, form steering committees, and recruit volunteers. It thus provides its sponsor with a means of soliciting early political commitments and recruiting the individuals who will play major roles in his or her campaign. Once a formal campaign committee is established, a candidate can easily convert the PAC's personnel into a campaign organization; the individuals simply have to resign from the PAC and be shifted to the campaign's payroll. By using a PAC in this way, a candidate can secure the services of key operatives early in the process at no cost to his or her campaign and can help ensure that the campaign committee "hits the ground running."

A prospective candidate can also realize tangible campaign benefits from a PAC's fundraising activities. A PAC can be used to develop a fundraising program, identify potential donors, and build a donor list that can serve as the basis of the campaign's direct mail program. In other words, it can conduct all of the tasks needed to launch a campaign fundraising effort. This is perhaps the most important campaign-related activity that a PAC can undertake. A committee that performs this task successfully provides its sponsor with a valuable campaign asset, a list of prospective campaign donors who can serve as a base for the campaign's fundraising operation. By relying on a PAC to create this list, a candidate can save at least a year in terms of the time needed to develop a direct mail fundraising program and can reduce anticipated fundraising costs by a sizable sum. This practice essentially allows a candidate to transfer the burdensome start-up costs of a direct mail program from his or her campaign committee to a PAC, which, in effect, increases the limit-exempt fundraising allowance available to the campaign committee because it frees up monies that would otherwise be spent developing an initial donor list. The extent of the advantage that can be achieved by exploiting this loophole is suggested by the experience of the 1988 candidates, some of whom estimate that their PACs' efforts saved their campaigns up to $2 million.

A PAC's fundraising efforts also directly affect a campaign's revenue prospects. By building a list of probable donors, a PAC enhances a candidate's ability to raise money early. This is particularly important given that many of the contributions received from these donors will qualify for federal matching subsidies. As a result, a candidate who effectively utilizes the PAC alternative can generate a substantial amount of money in the preelection year, which is necessary if a candidate hopes to wage a competitive campaign given the early resource demands of the current nominating process.

Finally, a PAC provides a prospective candidate with innumerable opportunities to engage in precampaign politicking. A PAC may stage events to increase its sponsor's public exposure or it may finance his or her travel to party functions, issue forums, or candidate events. It may also support its sponsor's appearances as the host or main speaker at fundraising events for state and local party committees or candidates or may allow its sponsor to present committee contributions in person to those it has decided to assist. These activities serve a number of campaign-related purposes. They allow an aspirant to meet with key party leaders and political activists, build political networks, test possible campaign themes or policy ideas, and improve his or her knowledge of the political landscape in different states and localities. The political relationships developed as a result of these appearances constitute a crucial step in the process of generating political support, securing campaign endorsements, and, in some instances, recruiting future delegate support.

Because they allow potential candidates to engage in most of the basic activities essential to the development of a national campaign, candidate-sponsored PACs have become a popular feature of the presidential nominations process. A PAC allows a candidate to build a campaign organization, develop a fundraising program, and generate political support. And all of these tasks can be conducted outside of the legal restraints imposed on presidential campaigns. Given the advantages that can be achieved through PAC sponsorship, it is not surprising that many candidates have taken advantage of this loophole. Unless the Federal Election Commission takes note of this new political reality and adjusts its regulations accordingly, future candidates will continue this practice, which will further undermine the integrity of the campaign finance system.

Candidate PACs and the Campaign Finance System

The Federal Election Campaign Act and its subsequent amendments constitute one of the most significant efforts to legislate political reform in American history. These statutes greatly expanded the role of the federal government in the regulation of political campaigns in order to cure the ills generated by a private system of financing elections. They required full public disclosure of all campaign funds, limited the size of political contributions, set strict ceilings on campaign spending, and established a program of public funding for presidential primary and general election campaigns. In addition, a new regulatory agency, the Federal Election Commission, was created to administer and enforce the law.

This restructuring of the presidential campaign finance system was adopted to fulfill an array of laudable purposes. The reforms require strict accountability and public disclosure of all campaign monies in order to encourage the creation of a more informed electorate. They are designed to decrease the emphasis on fundraising in presidential elections so that candidates can spend more time developing policy proposals and discussing their positions on issues of public concern. They also attempt to enhance the quality of representation in the electoral process by equalizing the amounts individuals may contribute to candidates and by reducing the financial barriers that might discourage candidates from pursuing a bid for the Oval Office. Finally, the regulations seek to minimize the effects of money on electoral outcomes and protect the integrity of the electoral process from the potentially corruptive influence of large contributions.

None of these goals have been achieved. Although candidates have taken some actions to comply with the law, they have generally adapted to the new regulatory environment in ways that were unforeseen at the time the Federal Election Campaign Act was adopted. Instead of accepting the limits imposed by the act and adjusting their strategies to conform to the financial parameters mandated by Congress, presidential aspirants have simply discovered ways to circumvent these limits. As a result, many of the problems that the reforms sought to eliminate remain. Campaign spending continues to rise at alarming rates. Large contributions from wealthy donors still constitute a major source of revenue in presidential elections. Candidates still employ surrogate organizations and undisclosed financial accounts to fund campaign activities in defiance of the law. And these practices have become more commonplace in recent elections as candidates improve their understanding of the advantages of a PAC and engage in bolder efforts to cope with regulations that increasingly fail to reflect political reality.

This desire to evade the law is a direct result of its effect on the strategic environment of presidential nomination campaigns. The regulations imposed conflicting pressures on candidates that complicated their strategic and operational planning. Some provisions of the law, such as the limit on contributions and the matching funds program, encouraged candidates to begin fundraising early because it takes a lengthy period of time to amass the large sums needed to finance a national campaign through the small donations mandated by the reforms. The law's spending ceilings, however, are designed to encourage candidates to limit the length of their campaigns and avoid the expenditure of large sums in the preelection year. Campaign strategists were therefore faced with the problem of determining how to raise the funds and complete the organizational tasks needed to launch a viable campaign without incurring significant costs that might restrict their ability to spend in the future.

Since the 1976 election, the first conducted under the new finance regulations, the strategic and operational pressures imposed on candidates have intensified as a result of a widening gap between the realities of the nominating process and the financial practices permitted by the regulations. Although the expenditure ceilings have risen in each election to account for inflation, these adjustments have only served to increase the problem. While candidates are allowed to spend more in each election, the amount they may solicit from a contributor has remained static at a maximum of $1,000. In order to spend the legally permissible amount, a candidate must raise more money from more individuals than in previous elections, which increases the cost of fundraising and the pressure to begin early. In addition, the costs of essential campaign services, especially television advertising, have grown at a rate that surpasses the rate of inflation. The spending limits therefore become less reflective of the real costs of campaigns with each new election. Furthermore, the ceilings fail to account for the concurrent procedural changes that have taken place in the presidential nominating process. Most importantly, the law has not been modified to account for the creation of a front-loaded delegate selection calendar. This change alone has dramatically increased the financial and organizational demands of a presidential campaign, compelling candidates to begin their efforts earlier and earlier in the preelection year, which heightens concern over the role of the spending limits and forces resource allocation decisions to the forefront of a candidate's strategic planning.

As the financial demands of a nomination campaign have skyrocketed, candidates and their fundraisers have also increasingly come to recognize the impracticality of the limit placed on individual donations. In real terms, the $1,000 maximum established in 1974 is now worth less than $450. In each subsequent election, inflation and the adjusting of spending limits combine to make the $1,000 gift less and less significant, thus artificially increasing a campaign's fundraising burden. Candidates know that there are thousands of donors who can and would donate more than $1,000 if they could do so without violating the law. If it were possible to accept these large donations, the costs and time associated with fundraising would be reduced substantially, as would the pressure to begin raising money very early in the election cycle. The regulations have thus encouraged candidates to seek out ways to evade the contribution limit so that they may exploit the largesse of wealthy individuals.

Although it may be possible to conduct a successful campaign within the regulations by strictly monitoring spending and carefully apportioning funds, many candidates have decided that the easiest method of resolving the strategic problems generated by modern reforms is to find ways to raise and spend money outside of the law. The most effective method discovered to date is to establish a precandidacy PAC to serve as a front organization for a presidential campaign committee.

Precandidacy PACs have become a common component of presidential campaign organizations because they allow an aspirant to conduct a wide range of campaign activities without triggering the regulations applicable to presidential candidates. A PAC can be used to identify and recruit the nucleus of a nationwide political operation, develop a fundraising program and list of potential campaign donors, and finance precandidacy travel and politicking. By aggressively pursuing these objectives, a prospective candidate can complete the basic organizational tasks and extensive early campaigning needed to launch a viable bid for the presidential nomination. And as long as this committee avoids the handful of specific activities and legal technicalities that the Federal Election Commission uses to determine whether an individual is a formal candidate for a particular office, none of the monies spent on these efforts have to be reported as campaign funds. A PAC thus provides an aspirant with a means of evading the contribution and spending limits imposed on federal candidates.

The potential strategic advantages that accompany the ability to raise and spend funds outside of the regulations provide candidates with a compelling incentive to take advantage of the PAC option. Indeed, the creation of such a committee is a logical response to the strategic problems generated by the campaign finance laws. It is therefore not surprising that the number of candidates sponsoring a PAC has increased in each of the last three election cycles. In the 1988 election, most of the major party candidates began their campaigns by forming a PAC. In addition, a number of potential challengers who decided not to run, including Mario Cuomo, Howard Baker, and Donald Rumsfeld, organized PACs as part of the process of keeping the possibility of seeking the nomination alive.

Although candidate-sponsored PACs are primarily an outcome of the restraints imposed on campaign committees, two other factors have stimulated the proliferation of these groups in recent elections. First, presidential aspirants have succumbed to a "keep-up-with-the-Joneses" mentality that encourages the formation of precandidacy PACs in an effort to remain competitive in the earliest stage of a presidential race. The decision by some aspirants to pursue the PAC option in order to minimize the effect of the spending limits and maximize the resources available to their campaigns has induced other aspirants to establish PACs of their own. Accordingly, PACs have been used most extensively in competitive nomination contests. Candidates who fail to adopt this alternative place themselves in a vulnerable strategic position that may seriously affect their electoral prospects. A candidate who abides by the intent of the law and does not create a PAC provides opponents with a head start and an opportunity to spend more on the race than the law allows. This may provide a PAC sponsor with a significant strategic advantage that may prove to be impossible to overcome. Few candidates have been willing to concede such an advantage to their prospective opponents. Consequently, in each subsequent election, past experience and the dynamics of the nominating contest have combined to produce an increasing number of precandidacy PAC operations.

Second, and perhaps more important, the Federal Election Commission has in effect legitimized this unanticipated use of a PAC organization. The commission's advisory opinion rulings in 1985 and 1986 sanctioned the formation of PACs by potential candidates and thereby opened the door to acts that facilitate widespread evasion of the law. Although the commission clearly noted in these decisions that PAC activities designed to promote an individual candidacy would subject a PAC's financial assistance to the regulations applicable to presidential campaigns, it set forth a very narrow definition of the types of activities that would indicate a formal candidacy on the part of a PAC sponsor. This outcome reflects the fact that the commission had to weigh competing objectives of the law in rendering these decisions. On the one hand, it had to try to enforce the ceilings on contributions and expenditures established for presidential elections and hold candidates accountable for all funds spent on campaign-related activities. On the other, it had to acknowledge the party-building aspects of PAC activities and the restraints imposed on its ability to regulate these organizations given the protections of the First Amendment. The result of this balancing act was a set of rulings that tried to restrict this kind of activity but failed to eliminate the PAC campaign option. Instead, these rulings have promoted the creation of these committees because they have essentially provided operating guidelines for those individuals who wish to use this type of committee as a vehicle for conducting an informal campaign operation.

The rise of precandidacy PACs highlights the failure of the most recent attempt to reform the campaign finance system. Instead of limiting the role of money and reducing the emphasis on fundraising in presidential elections, the reforms have inspired candidates to develop ingenious strategies that are designed to gain access to unregulated sources of revenue and to circumvent the major restraints imposed by the law. As a result, the campaign finance reforms have failed to achieve their central goals. More importantly, the development of this form of unregulated campaigning demonstrates the limits of the Federal Election Commission's ability to control political behavior. For, unlike other major loopholes in the system such as independent expenditures and soft money, the proliferation of precandidacy PACs is largely a result of the commission's regulatory decisions, which have served to stimulate rather than restrict this unintended outcome of the reforms. The candidate PAC phenomenon thus demonstrates the need for a fundamental revision of the current regulatory approach for the financing of presidential elections.

PACs AND THE OBJECTIVES OF THE
CAMPAIGN FINANCE REFORMS

Because candidate-sponsored PACs operate independent of the

regulations governing political campaigns, these committees have had a major impact on the effectiveness of the campaign finance reforms. The financial practices of these organizations violate the spirit of almost every major provision of the Federal Election Campaign Act. Candidates have used PACs to establish undisclosed bank accounts and engage in unaccountable financing, to solicit large contributions from wealthy donors and sources deemed illegal under federal law, and to spend unlimited amounts of money. These committees have therefore played a significant role in undermining the efficacy of campaign finance regulations.

One of the law's basic objectives is to reduce the potential for corruption and promote a more informed electorate by requiring full public disclosure of a candidate's finances. The law requires each candidate to register one central campaign committee, identify any subsidiary or affiliated committee(s), and provide regular reports detailing the monies raised and spent by the committee(s). These provisions seek to ensure that a candidate can be held strictly accountable for his or her finances and does not evade the contribution and spending limits by setting up multiple committees or secret "slush funds." More importantly, it seeks to promote a more informed electorate by making financial information available to the public so that individual voters can make more informed decisions when judging particular candidates.

Precandidacy PACs seriously undercut the law's attempt to ensure meaningful disclosure and a more informed citizenry. Because these committees are legally separate from their sponsors' formal campaign committee, the monies they raise and spend are not included in the reports on presidential campaign finance prepared by the Federal Election Commission and are therefore usually omitted from press accounts of the financial activities of presidential candidates. As a result, candidates in the last three elections have managed to avoid strict public scrutiny of more than $40 million in receipts and expenditures. This ability to conduct campaign-related financial activities without having to report these monies on campaign finance reports directly violates the intent of the public disclosure provisions of federal law.

Of course, candidate PACs are not wholly exempt from federal disclosure requirements; these committees, like campaign committees, are required to file financial disclosure reports with the commission. A reporter or individual citizen can examine these reports if interested in the financial activities of these groups. But it is often difficult to trace the links between these committees and their prospective candidate sponsors. Because these PACs can best serve the purposes for which they are established if they are deemed to be legally distinct entities from their sponsors' future campaign committees, presidential aspirants often refuse to acknowledge the relationship between their PACs and their future campaign organizations. The committees have vague or generic titles that do not include the name of the potential candidate and, in some cases, the presidential aspirant is excluded from the list of PAC officers that is filed with the commission. Although these actions usually amount to little more than transparent acts of subterfuge, they complicate the reporting process and reduce the accessibility of information, which is a key to full and meaningful disclosure.

Even when it is possible to trace the financial activities of these groups, the reports only include the funds raised or spent in conjunction with federal elections. Any soft money accounts established by a committee are not reported and, given the lack of stringent disclosure laws in most states, it is nearly impossible to determine whether these accounts exist or the amount of money that has been raised and spent in this manner. This lack of effective disclosure laws at the state level is particularly troublesome because a candidate may choose to conduct precampaign activities through a PAC that is solely concerned with state and local elections or party organizations, as in the case of GOPAC, the committee with which Republican Pete du Pont was associated prior to the 1988 election. A committee of this sort has no obligation to disclose its finances to the Federal Election Commission. It can therefore effectively conceal its financial activities from even the most determined investigators.

The Federal Election Campaign Act also attempts to reduce the potential for corruption and enhance the equity of the electoral process by equalizing the financial influence of individual citizens. The act limits the amount an individual can contribute to a federal candidate to $1,000 per election in order to eliminate the gross disparities that can result from political giving. By minimizing the possible disparities in financial participation, the law seeks to promote a more representative system that better reflects the fundamental principle of "one person, one vote." This also helps to ensure that individual citizens capable of donating large sums to candidates do not have an undue influence on electoral outcomes.

The limit on individual donations has become meaningless in the wake of the rise of precandidacy PACs. An individual can contribute up to $5,000 per year to a prospective candidate's PAC and, because this committee is legally separate from any future campaign organization, that person can still donate the maximum allowable amount of $1,000 to the PAC sponsor's campaign. Individuals who support a presidential aspirant/PAC sponsor can therefore contribute up to $21,000 to assist that candidate; individuals who support a candidate who has not established a PAC can only contribute $1,000.

Candidates have eagerly exploited this opportunity to circumvent the contribution limit. In the 1988 election cycle alone, nine candidates accepted donations through their precandidacy PACs that would have been considered illegal if given to their campaign organizations. These candidates received more than 3,300 individual gifts in excess of $1,000, including aggregate donations of $10,000 or more from more than 300 "fat cats." These large contributions generated at least $13.4 million in PAC revenues, or more than half of the total monies reported by these committees. The primary beneficiary of the largesse of these big givers was then-Vice President George Bush, whose PAC solicited contributions of $10,000 or more from over 200 individuals. These large donors were responsible for $5.9 million of Bush's $11.2 million in total PAC receipts. No other candidate came close to matching these sums.

These data clearly demonstrate the inefficacy of the contribution limit in light of the widespread use of PAC operations, but they fail to document the extent to which these committees have been used to avoid the law. An individual can contribute even greater amounts to a candidate if that aspirant's PAC has a state subsidiary (or subsidiaries) or soft money accounts. These devices create opportunities for further giving. Moreover, they also allow a presidential hopeful to solicit funds from sources such as corporations or labor unions that are banned from making direct contributions on the federal level. For example, Mondale's Committee for the Future of America established a number of soft money accounts that took in close to $400,000, including more than $80,000 in donations from individuals who had already given his committee the maximum amount allowed under federal law. The PAC also received approximately $150,000 in contributions from corporations,which are not allowed to participate in federal elections.[1]

The increasing sophistication of PAC fundraising operations has reduced the contribution limits of the Federal Election Campaign Act to little more than a legal fiction. A PAC can be used to accept donations of virtually any size from almost any source; all that is necessary is the appropriate legal structure. By establishing such a structure, especially some form of soft money accounts, a presidential hopeful gains access to the large contributors who can pour significant amounts of money into a fledgling campaign. Or, viewed from another perspective, a candidate can provide supporters with a greater ability to participate financially and thereby to influence the outcome of an election than that enjoyed by the supporters of an opponent who fails to exploit these opportunities to solicit additional funds.

Precandidacy PACs thus facilitate the type of inequities in resources and ability to participate that the Federal Election Campaign Act sought to eliminate. By doing so, they open the door to a possible resurrection of the types of undue and potentially corruptive financial practices that catalyzed the demand for reform in the early 1970s. Although a gift of $10,000 to $20,000 is less significant than the soft money donations of $100,000 or more that are made in general elections,[2] it is nonetheless a sizable contribution, especially when contrasted with the $1,000 limit imposed on contributions to political campaigns. These large PAC donations may prove to be particularly meaningful to a presidential aspirant because they are received in the earliest stage of an individual's bid for office and often provide the seed money needed to launch a candidacy. Their relative importance therefore transcends their absolute dollar value. In addition, there is no guarantee that the high water mark for individual contributions to a PAC will remain at $20,000. If a candidate wishes to solicit even larger amounts from wealthy supporters, this can be facilitated by establishing a PAC state subsidiary or soft money accounts. This would allow that candidate to accept even larger gifts, possibly including donations of $100,000 or more. It would also allow an aspirant to accept these exorbitantly large contributions from sources such as corporations and labor unions that are not permitted to make direct contributions to federal candidates.

Finally, the Federal Election Campaign Act established aggregate and state expenditure limits to restrict campaign spending and improve the competitiveness of presidential elections. These ceilings, which apply to candidates accepting public matching funds, were adopted to reduce the role of wealth in elections and create a level playing field for presidential contests. By ensuring that all challengers are subject to the same restraints, the regulations enhance the fairness of the process and guard against the possibility of a wealthy candidate winning an election by simply exploiting superior resources and greatly outspending opponents. The limits also reduce the possibility of the costs of campaigning serving as a barrier to entry for candidates who are not well known or lack substantial financial resources. This latter concern is central to the state spending limits, which were adopted to improve the ability of lesser-known candidates to wage a competitive campaign in individual state contests. The ultimate purpose of the ceilings, therefore, is to ensure that financial demands do not overly restrict the choices available to the electorate.

This effort to control campaign spending and ensure a level playing field has also become relatively meaningless as a result of the proliferation of PACs. The primary reason that presidential hopefuls establish these committees is to avoid the expenditure limits and thereby gain a strategic advantage over their opponents. Although few candidates ever reach these limits, the number who have met or approached these ceilings, especially in the crucial early contests that are the key to the nomination, has increased in recent elections. Every candidate must therefore be concerned about the spending caps and pursue strategies or tactics that mitigate their potential effects. The best strategy is to establish a precandidacy PAC, because this type of committee can operate wholly outside of the spending restrictions.

Candidates have used PACs to shift millions of dollars in campaign expenses off of their campaign committee budgets, thereby increasing the amount they may spend on their individual quests for the nomination. Overall, presidential hopefuls reported PAC expenditures of approximately $40 million in the last three elections, every dollar of which represented an extra dollar that could be spent under the limits. In addition, an undetermined amount was spent by state and local committees or through soft money accounts. PAC operations have thus proven to be an extremely effective technique for financing campaign-related activities outside of the limits imposed by federal law. In essence, by creating a PAC early in an election cycle, a presidential aspirant can spend as much as he or she can raise.

A number of candidates have been able to violate the spending limits without incurring a penalty by channeling funds through a PAC. Reagan in 1980 and 1984, Mondale in 1984, and Bush, Dole, and Robertson in 1988 would have exceeded the overall limit on spending by substantial amounts if they had had to allocate their PAC expenditures against the expenditure ceilings. Robertson would have exceeded the limit by approximately $500,000[3]; the others would have surpassed the limit by millions of dollars.

The most massive violation of the intent of the law to date was perpetrated by Bush. His campaign committee spent $22.9 million of the $23.1 million allowed by the law in the race for the 1988 Republican nomination (his committee spent $30.6 million overall when exempt fundraising and compliance costs are included).[4] His PAC spent approximately $10.8 million for a total of $33.7 million. Bush's total spending therefore exceeded the maximum permissible amount for a candidate accepting public funds by $10.6 million. Yet the Bush campaign received no penalty for breaking the law because his PAC's spending was not considered to be campaign-related under the definitions set forth in the regulations. Instead, he was rewarded for this creative financing scheme since it enabled him to gain a competitive edge that helped him to secure his party's nomination and, ultimately, the presidency.

TABLE 7.1
Spending in Presidential Nomination Campaigns, 1980-1988 (million $)

Election	Campaign Spending[a]	PAC Spending	Total Spending	PAC Percentage
1976	71.8[b]	0.0	71.8	0.0
1980	106.3	7.5	113.8	6.6
1984	105.9[c]	6.9	112.8	6.1
1988	212.0	25.2	237.2	10.6

[a]Includes compliance costs.

[b]Based on the sums reported in Table 5.1 in Alexander, *Financing the 1976 Election,* 209. Figure does not include the amount spent by Ellen McCormack.

[c]Based on the sums reported in Tables 3.4 and 3.5 in Alexander and Haggerty, *Financing the 1984 Election,* 86-87.

Source: Data on spending for 1976 based on the sums reported in Herbert E. Alexander, *Financing the 1976 Election* (Washington, DC: Congressional Quarterly Press, 1979), 209; for 1980, on Table 4.3 and Herbert E. Alexander, *Financing the 1980 Election* (Lexington, MA: Lexington Books, 1983), 111; for 1984, on Table 4.5 and Herbert E. Alexander and Brian A. Haggerty, *Financing the 1984 Election* (Lexington, Massachusetts: Lexington Books, 1987), 85-86; and, for 1988, Table 4.7 and Herbert E. Alexander, "Financing the Presidential Elections, 1988," paper prepared for the Research Committee on Political Finance and Political Corruption, International Political Science Association, Tokyo, Japan, September 8-10, 1989, 4.

The spending ceilings have therefore had a minimal effect on the costs of campaigns. Although they have reduced the spending of some candidates who were forced to cut back on anticipated expenditures in order to remain within the limits, these savings represent but a fraction of the amount that has been spent through PAC operations and other unregulated activities. As a result, spending in presidential nomination campaigns has continued to grow, with a rising proportion of the total amount spent attributable to precandidacy PACs (see Table 7.1).

The candidates in the 1976 race spent a total of $71.8 million, none of which was disbursed through a PAC. In the 1980 and 1984 elections, the candidates spent around $113 million. By 1988, the costs incurred by candidates seeking the nomination had risen to $237 million, more than twice the total of previous races. This increase was largely due to the fact that there were competitive races in both parties. But this total is also the result of an exponential rise in the amount spent through precandidacy PACs. PACs were responsible for at least $25 million, or more than 10 percent of all spending by candidates for the major party nominations. This amount dwarfed the sum spent independently ($4.1 million)[5] exceeding it by at least $21.1 million, making precandidacy PACs the most important source of unregulated spending in the 1988 presidential nomination contests. Moreover, these estimates of the proportion of funds credited to PACs represent the minimum for the amounts spent by these committees because they do not include undisclosed soft money accounts or the sums spent by the state-level PAC used by Republican Pete du Pont to advance his presidential ambitions.

PACs AND THE
PRESIDENTIAL SELECTION PROCESS

The rise of candidate-sponsored PACs has also had a significant impact on the presidential selection process. These committees help candidates achieve important strategic objectives that can influence electoral prospects. Lesser-known candidates establish PACs in an effort to improve their public recognition and begin to develop a broad base of potential campaign supporters. Well-known candidates form such organizations in order to capitalize on their public recognition and broad bases of support. In recent elections, certain well-known aspirants have taken full advantage of the opportunities afforded by a PAC and have thus built an insurmountable early lead that propelled them to their party's nomination.

PACs have also changed the organizational strategies employed by candidates, stimulating a more formal, systematic, and extensive type of precandidacy campaigning. This development has made the strategic calculus involved in deciding whether to seek office more complex and, in many instances, has made the road to the White House more arduous. Consequently, this shift in organizational strategies may be influencing the quality of candidates who compete for our nation's highest office.

One of the most significant effects of candidate PACs on the presidential selection process is the strategic advantage it provides to well-known candidates. Individuals who are perceived to be potential frontrunners or to enjoy extensive public recognition in the early years of a presidential election cycle tend to realize the greatest benefits from a PAC. These politicians usually have a well-established base of financial support and a greater ability to solicit large contributions. They therefore have access to financial resources that lesser-known candidates can rarely, if ever, match.

The campaign finance laws recognize that financial disparities will always exist between candidates and try to level the playing field by limiting the extent to which one candidate may outspend another. This attempt to equalize the resource gap between candidates, like the attempt to limit contributions, runs counter to the realities of modern presidential politics. Given the stakes in a nomination contest, well-known candidates are not going to be satisfied with a level playing field and may even be uncomfortable with the financial edge they can achieve within the parameters of the law. They will therefore seek out ways to capitalize on their superior resources and thus maximize their potential competitive advantage. And this is exactly what they have done through precandidacy PACs.

PACs have allowed well-known candidates, particularly those recognized by the media as early frontrunners or serious contenders, to gain a substantial head start in the presidential sweepstakes. Instead of acceding to a contest staged on a level playing field, they have shifted the contest to a new arena, the realm of PAC activity, where they can freely exploit their public name recognition and broader bases of financial support. Well-known aspirants consequently enter the race with a substantial financial and organizational lead, which makes the task of lesser-known challengers even more daunting than it would be under the established rules of the game.

Reagan in 1980, Mondale in 1984, and Bush in 1988 achieved a substantial financial advantage over lesser-known, and even some well-known, competitors as a result of their PAC operations, even though many of these prospective opponents had organized PACs of their own. Reagan achieved a net advantage of close to $6 million over his closest prospective opponent; Mondale, $2.2 million; and Bush, approximately $5 million. This sizable head start is undoubtedly an important factor in explaining why Reagan, Mondale, and Bush won their respective party's nomination. These, and other well-known PAC sponsors, had the resources needed to conduct an extensive precampaign campaign. They were able to hire staff, develop an organizational network, build lists of thousands of prospective campaign donors, travel throughout the country, and identify and recruit potential supporters. These activities allowed them to "hit the ground running" once they decided to form their authorized campaign committees and thus maintain their early lead. As a result, they raised more money than their opponents in the year before the election, accrued a greater amount of matching funds, and developed more extensive campaign organizations. They were thus better prepared to meet the financial and organizational demands of the front-loaded delegate selection process, which meant that they were in the best position to capture the nomination.

PACs have also become a popular organizational alternative because they provide aspirants with a means of accommodating the longer campaign period encouraged by modern reforms. Many observers of presidential elections have noted that in the late 1970s and throughout the 1980s the presidential campaign period apparently grew longer in each successive election.[6] This lengthening of the selection process is primarily due to the provisions of the Federal Election Campaign Act and the front-loading of the delegate selection. Instead of reducing the length of presidential campaigns, the reforms, especially the "window" for scheduling primaries, have had the opposite effect. These changes have increased the financial and organizational demands imposed on candidates. In order to meet these demands, candidates usually must engage in an extensive amount of early campaigning beginning at least a year before the election. This is particularly true in hotly contested, multicandidate races because contenders who fail to make an early start risk forsaking a lead to an opponent or may lack the funds and organization needed to mount a competitive campaign in the crucial initial stage of the delegate selection process. Consequently, as Rhodes Cook has observed, "early-starting, long-running campaigns are no longer an exception in presidential politics; they have become the norm."[7]

The problem, however, is that presidential candidates find it difficult, if not impossible, to conduct the early campaigning required by the process within the structural framework of their authorized campaign committees. Candidates who attempt to do so incur the risk of having to reduce their activities later in the process in order to avoid violations of the state or overall expenditure limits. Accordingly, candidates cannot simply fulfill their desire to begin early by beginning their formal campaigns at an early date. Rather, candidates are beginning their informal or preformal campaigns, their PAC operations, at an early point in the cycle and delaying the formation of their authorized campaign committees. It is the development of precandidacy PAC operations, therefore, that has allowed candidates to increase their level of early campaigning in recent elections.

Early campaigning is certainly not a phenomenon unique to recent elections. For example, Nixon in 1965-1966 and Carter in 1973-1974 actively assisted fellow party members and party organizations in order to prepare the way for their presidential bids.[8] What has changed in recent contests is the scope and intensity of this type of activity. Precandidacy politicking has become more structured, extensive, and systematic. In many respects, it has become indistinguishable from a formal campaign operation, entailing structured organizations, large staffs, nationwide fundraising operations, extensive and regular travel and politicking, computerized list-development programs, and state and local volunteer recruitment efforts. Indeed, an increasing number of candidates in recent elections have, for all intents and purposes, initiated a full-fledged campaign operation well before the midterm elections. Political operations on this scale were certainly not common prior to the adoption of the reforms.

That PACs are the primary vehicle by which candidates have extended their campaigns is evidenced by the data in Table 7.2. This table presents an analysis of the length of presidential nomination campaigns from 1976 to 1988. Table 7.2 lists the average number of days of a presidential nomination campaign in each of the last four elections as determined by counting the number of days between the day on which each candidate established a campaign organization and the opening day of the party's national nominating convention. For each election year, three sets of data are presented. The first set of data concerns the length of the "formal" campaign, which is defined as the period between the formation of an authorized campaign committee subject to federal regulations and the opening day of the party convention. The second set concerns the "formal" campaign including any exploratory committees used by the candidates. Candidates often formally or informally establish an exploratory committee to test the waters or engage in early campaigning before registering an authorized campaign committee.[9] Such committees are considered to be part of the formal campaign because any receipts or disbursements made by these groups must be reported on a campaign committee's first disclosure report if the potential candidate decides to run. The third set concerns the "overall campaign," which includes the dates on which candidates began their PAC operations.

Three general conclusions can be deduced from the data in Table 7.2. First, despite the changes in the strategic environment of presidential contests, candidates in recent elections have not established their authorized campaign committees earlier in the election cycle. Although a few candidates have established their campaign committees at an early point in the race (for example, 1976 Democratic candidate Terry Sanford formed his campaign committee on June 21, 1974; 1980 Republican candidate Philip Crane on July 31, 1978; and 1988 Republican candidate Pierre du Pont on June 3, 1986), most candidates have not adopted this approach. In fact, the average length of this component of a presidential campaign has been remarkably consistent from election to election. In 1976, candidates established their authorized campaign committees an average of 478 days before the convention. In 1988, the average was 473 days. The 1976 figure,

TABLE 7.2
Average Length of Presidential Nomination Campaigns, 1976-1988

Period of Analysis	1976 Election		1980 Election		1984 Election		1988 Election	
	No. of Candidates	No. of Days	No. of Candidates	No. of Days	No. of Candidates	No. of Days	No. of Candidates	No. of Days
Formal Campaign (Only Campaign Comm.)	14	478[a]	10	486	9	470	14	473
Democrats	12	491[a]	3	395	8	490	8	458
Republicans	2	406	7	524	1	308	6	492
Formal Campaign (With Exploratory Comm.)	14	504[b,c]	10	507	9	607	14	561
Democrats	12	521[b,c]	3	395	8	644	8	506
Republicans	2	406	7	555	1	308	6	633
Overall Campaign (Including PACs)	—	—	10	712	9	792	14	941
Democrats	—	—	3	395	8	852	8	813
Republicans	—	—	7	848	1	1333[d]	6	1112[e]

[a]Edmund Brown entered the 1976 Democratic nomination contest on March 22, 1976, almost two months after the Iowa precinct caucuses and a month after the New Hampshire Primary. If his late entry is excluded from the calculations, the average for the 1976 campaign is 507 days and the average for Democratic candidates, 525 days.

[b]Although no candidate had a formal exploratory committee in 1976, the Bentsen Committee Fund, a political committee established to raise money for Senator Lloyd Bentsen's reelection campaign, is regarded as an exploratory committee for the purposes of this analysis. The Bentsen Dinner Committee Fund, later renamed the Bentsen Committee Fund, was established on February 15, 1974, with Jack S. Blanton as treasurer. In a letter dated February 10, 1975, Blanton informed the General Accounting Office's Office of Federal Elections that the Bentsen Committee Fund had changed its name to the Bentsen in '76 Committee and would solely support Bentsen's candidacy for the presidential nomination (see Federal Election Commission, Microfilm Series 1976, Roll 22 at 5217, 5221, and 5226). In addition, according to Herbert Alexander, monies from the Bentsen Committee Fund were used by Bentsen to advance his presidential candidacy (*Financing the 1976 Election* [Washington, DC: Congressional Quarterly, 1979], 220-223).

[c]If Edmund Brown is excluded from the calculations, the 1976 average for this period of the campaign is 534 days and the average for Democratic candidates, 558 days.

[d]Reagan's political action committee, Citizens for the Republic, was established in 1977. For the purposes of this analysis, the length of the campaign was calculated on the assumption that the start date for this committee in the 1984 election cycle was January 1, 1981.

[e]Robert Dole and Jack Kemp established political action committees before the beginning of the 1988 election cycle. For the purposes of this analysis, the length of the campaign was calculated on the assumption that the start date for these committees in the 1988 election cycle was January 1, 1985.

Source: Based on the author's calculations of average length of each organizational component of presidential campaign. Length of a campaign was determined by calculating number of days between date on which a candidate established or authorized campaign committee, exploratory committee, or political action committee and first day of presidential nominating convention. Dates were obtained from documents filed with the FEC.

however, is slightly distorted by Edmund "Jerry" Brown's late entry in that year's presidential contest. Brown did not decide to enter the race until mid-March and did not register an authorized campaign committee until March 22, more than two months after the Iowa caucuses and a month after the New Hampshire primary. If his campaign is excluded from the 1976 calculations, the average length of a presidential campaign in 1976 was 507 days. So, if anything, the average period of a presidential campaign, when measured from the dates on which candidates formed their authorized campaign committees, has declined over the last four elections from 507 days to 473 days.

Candidates have not felt compelled to create their campaign committees earlier in the calendar because they have in part adapted to the growing demands of the process by making greater use of exploratory committees. Although these committees (or comparable structures) were relatively unimportant in 1976 and 1980 (increasing the average length of the campaign by only 20-30 days), they were a prominent feature of the 1984 and 1988 elections. In these more recent contests, many of the candidates decided to test the waters before authorizing a campaign committee or simply chose to operate through an exploratory committee for a time, perhaps to take advantage of the less stringent filing requirements applicable to this type of committee. Whatever the reason, the data in Table 7.2 demonstrate that this use of exploratory committees significantly increased the length of presidential campaigns. When these committees are included in the analysis of the timing of presidential campaigns, the average length of a campaign in the 1984 election cycle expands from 470 days to 607 days and of a campaign in the 1988 cycle from 473 days to 561 days.

The most important conclusion to be drawn from Table 7.2 is that the recent growth in the length of presidential campaigns has primarily been facilitated by the use of precandidacy PACs. Although the use of exploratory committees has extended the campaign period, their utility as vehicles for early campaigning is restricted because the financial activities of such committees are governed by the ceilings imposed on presidential campaigns. Precandidacy PACs are not subject to this limitation. Accordingly, candidates have relied on PAC operations to begin campaigning earlier and earlier in each subsequent election.

Overall, the average length of a presidential campaign has nearly doubled over the last four elections, expanding from approximately 500 days in 1976 to 941 days in 1988. This expansion is largely a result of precandidacy PAC operations. In the 1980 election cycle, the average length of a presidential campaign, including PACs, was 712 days; in 1984, 792 days; and in 1988, 941 days. And these figures represent only the average length of a modern campaign. The past four elections have also been characterized by a significant increase in the number of extraordinarily long campaigns. In the 1976 election cycle, none of the candidates began a structured operation designed to advance a prospective presidential candidacy three years before the convention. In the 1980 cycle, only Reagan began this early. But in 1988, six candidates (Bush, Dole, Kemp, Robertson, Gephardt, and Simon) initiated their campaigns at least three years before the convention and Babbitt began only one month short of this benchmark.

The race for the presidency has come to display more of the characteristics of an endurance contest than an electoral one. Individuals considering a presidential candidacy have begun campaigning at least two or three years in advance of an election in order to remain competitive or at least to not concede a substantial head start to a prospective opponent. The system, therefore, is not necessarily conducive to the promotion of the best or the most qualified candidates. It does not function in a way that discriminates in favor of those individuals who have broad government and administrative experience, can build coalitions, are innovative legislators, or can manage crises. Instead, it favors candidates who have the desire, time, and stamina to endure at least two or three years of virtually nonstop fundraising, travel, and politicking. As David Broder has noted, the determinants of success in the long, drawn-out nominating process are not necessarily "the qualities that make an effective president." Rather, they are "the size of the candidate's ambitions, the extent of his leisure time, and the tolerance of his family, his budget and his job for almost unlimited travel."[10] Those candidates who have been willing to submit to this ordeal and suffer the physical, emotional, and psychological strains of a long and arduous national campaign have been in the best position to secure their party's nomination.

Besides influencing the types of candidates who seek the presidency, the lengthy nominating process may actually deter well-qualified candidates from seeking the office. The need to begin campaigning early forces each presidential aspirant to confront a number of difficult choices three years before the election takes place. Every presidential hopeful must decide whether he or she is willing to endure the rigors of the process. Each must also decide when and how to initiate a campaign. Those currently holding public office face additional decisions. First, they must determine whether they can fulfill their public responsibilities and still meet the increasingly time-consuming financial and organizational demands of a presidential campaign. Second, those facing midterm elections must often decide whether to forsake a current office and devote their time to a presidential candidacy or seek reelection and place their presidential aspirations on hold. These considerations are particularly important for an incumbent who faces the prospect of running against one or more opponents who do not hold an office and can thus campaign full time. An aspirant who decides to delay an entry into the presidential fray to fulfill public responsibilities or pursue a midterm bid for reelection must recognize the risk involved in this decision, because delay may allow other candidates to gain a substantial head start in pursuit of the nomination.

These types of decisions, which many candidates would be forced to confront even if there had not been a dramatic rise in the level of early campaigning, are brought into high relief with the advent of precandidacy PACs. The decisions by some challengers to pursue the PAC option force other possible contenders to consider this factor in making their own decisions regarding a candidacy. By failing to respond in kind, a potential challenger faces the prospect of granting a substantial lead to the opposition. PAC campaigning thus intensifies the pressure to make an early decision regarding a candidacy or at least an early decision to increase one's level of political activity. Some candidates resist these pressures and decide to follow their own timetables and strategies. Throughout the 1980s, these contenders rarely succeeded in waging a serious campaign for the nomination. The general outcome of these strategic considerations has thus been a pattern of longer campaigns or more intensive political activity at an early point in the process.

Some insights into the types of early decisions aspirants are now forced to make as a result of the lengthening of the process can be gleaned from the 1988 experience. Gary Hart chose to devote his full attention to the presidential race and thus decided not to seek reelection to the U.S. Senate in 1986. Senator Robert Dole chose to run for reelection and thereby reduced the time, which was already taxed by his role as leader of the Senate Republicans, he could spend in pursuit of the nomination. Congresswoman Pat Schroeder ran for reelection and then explored a candidacy, only to discover that she was too far behind to launch a viable effort. Governor Mario Cuomo decided to put off any presidential ambitions he harbored until after his 1986 reelection campaign and then decided against a presidential bid. Governor Michael Dukakis, however, used his midterm reelection campaign to jump-start his nomination campaign by rolling up a huge margin of victory and amassing a sizable surplus of funds and a donor list that could be transferred to his campaign committee.

The cumulative effect of the changes in the presidential selection process and the decisions they impose on potential candidates is that some qualified or viable candidates are deciding not to seek the office.

As Herbert Asher has observed, the process may be "so dispiriting that distinguished citizens opt out."[11]   In recent elections, a number of prominent politicians widely recognized as possible candidates, such as Walter Mondale (in 1976), Congressman Morris Udall (1980), Senator Edward Kennedy (1984), Senator Dale Bumpers, Senator Sam Nunn, Governor Mario Cuomo, Congresswoman Patricia Schroeder, and former Senate Majority Leader Howard Baker have decided not to contest the nomination. In announcing their decisions not to run, many of these candidates noted that they did not wish to endure the rigors of the process or that they felt the lead achieved by prospective opponents who began earlier could not be overcome. For example, Governor Cuomo cited "the demands on [my] family, the burdens of heading the state government, and the grueling full time effort that a White House campaign would entail" as some of the major factors that had swayed his decision not to run in 1988.[12] Senator Nunn highlighted the problem of splitting time between the campaign and the responsibilites of office, explaining that he "did not fancy the impact of the enterprise on either his family or his Senate responsibilities." He went on to say in a letter sent to supporters that "I have concluded that if I attempted to run for president and also carry out my Senate duties, I would end up doing neither well."[13] Former senator Paul Laxalt, a prospective candidate for the Republican nomination, cited the cost of a presidential bid as his reason for remaining on the sidelines, maintaining that "he foresaw an expensive campaign and did not want to spend his family into a 'financial black hole.'"[14]   Finally, Congresswoman Schroeder, after a three-month exploration of a candidacy, noted that, although the Iowa caucuses were still more than four months away, "it is already too late to get in and . . . catch up with other Democrats."[15]

The political and financial reforms of the 1970s and the consequent rise of precandidacy PACs have thus combined to create a lengthy and demanding selection process that may discourage individuals from pursuing our nation's highest office. The process may also reduce the quality of candidates who seek the presidency by inducing only the most ambitious or determined to run. Such a system was certainly not the intention of those who sought to restructure the process in the 1970s. Yet it is the system the reforms have produced.

The first election in the 1990s, of course, has not followed the pattern established in the 1980s. In the months after the 1988 election, it seemed that the strategies employed in the 1992 race would mimic those of previous contests. By the end of 1989 at least four prominent potential Democratic candidates (Richard Gephardt, Jesse Jackson, Mario Cuomo, and Patricia Schroeder) had active PAC operations and another (Bill Bradley) had an affiliation with a tax-exempt nonprofit foundation.[16] These possible candidates were thus poised to engage in the types of early campaigning that had been practiced by their predecessors in prior elections.

The unusual political situation that arose early in the election cycle, however, thwarted this development. President Bush's enormous popularity, the dramatic events surrounding the invasion of Kuwait and the Gulf War, and the particular political concerns of many of the leading Democratic aspirants combined to produce a chilling effect on early campaigning. As a result, PAC activities did not play a significant role in the politics of the 1992 race. The prospective 1992 candidates also failed to engage in an extensive amount of early campaigning through formal campaign committees. Indeed, as of June 30, 1991, only one Democratic hopeful, former senator Paul Tsongas of Massachusetts, had formed a principal campaign committee.[17] By contrast more than half of the candidates in the four most recent presidential elections had established a campaign committee by this point in the election cycle, including twelve of the fourteen candidates in the 1988 race (see Table 7.3). The two 1988 candidates who had not established a campaign committee by June 30, 1987, Robert Dole and Jesse Jackson, had formed exploratory committees. In 1992, however, only Senator Tom Harkin of Iowa and Governor L. Douglas Wilder of Virginia, both Democrats, had taken even this preliminary step.[18] No Republican had stepped forward by this point in the election cycle to challenge President Bush.

The lack of an extensive 1992 precampaign campaign does not mean that the system is improving or that fundamental reform is no longer necessary. Instead, the 1992 experience highlights another side of the problems posed by the campaign finance laws. Having failed to exploit the opportunity to begin campaigning early, those who will run in the 1992 election must face the problem of how to raise the funds needed to mount a viable national campaign in a limited period of time. Given the $1,000 limit on an individual gift, this will be an enormously challenging task. This job will be made even more burdensome by the fact that most candidates will have less than six months to raise money before the start of the delegate selection process, which does not provide the time needed to develop a mature and profitable direct mail fundraising program that extends beyond the borders of their home states (presumably each candidate will have a well-developed list of in-state donors).

The financial difficulties that can accompany a late start are clearly demonstrated by the initial fundraising efforts of the 1992 candidates. By November 1, 1991, five Democrats had joined Tsongas in

TABLE 7.3
Early Starts in the Presidential Campaign, 1976-1992

Election Year	Total No. of Candidates	Principal Campaign Committee Established	
		Before January of Preelection Year	Between Jan. 1 & June 30 of Preelection Year
1976	14	5	4
1980	10	1	7
1984	9	1	5
1988	14	1	11
1992	—a	0	1

aNot available.

Source: Based on Statements of Organization (FEC Form 1) filed by each candidate with the Federal Election Commission.

the race: Harkin, Wilder, Senator Bob Kerrey of Nebraska, Governor Bill Clinton of Arkansas, and Jerry Brown, a former governor of California and two-time presidential candidate. All of these candidates essentially began their campaigns without the benefit of a PAC-sponsored fundraising effort or the benefit of some other precampaign organization that would have allowed them to develop a large potential donor base and evade the $1,000 limit on contributions. These contenders thus did not "hit the ground running." Instead they faced the prospect of having to raise the large sums needed to finance a competitive campaign from a standing start. As a result, these candidates had raised a combined total of approximately $2.2 million by September 30, 1991, with Tsongas leading the field with total receipts of $792,000.[19] At this point in the 1988 election, Michael Dukakis alone had raised $8.1 million and Richard Gephardt had raised $3.5 million.[20]

The campaign finance laws thus encourage candidates who begin late to place financial concerns at the forefront of their campaign decision-making. In determining whether to run, candidates must give a hard look at whether they can raise even the minimal sums needed to meet the demands of the delegate selection process given the time restraints and contribution limits. This is especially true for lesser-known candidates who lack widespread public name recognition and a broad base of support. Financial considerations may therefore lead some candidates to decide not to run. In these instances, the campaign finance regulations serve to undermine one of their central purposes because their effect is to discourage candidate participation and party competition.

Candidates who decide to enter a presidential contest late in the election cycle will in all probability have to devote a substantial amount of time to fundraising. This outcome is also contrary to the purposes of the reforms. Although fundraising is a time-consuming task in every election, the burden this responsibility imposes on late entrants is particularly acute. No such candidate, except perhaps one who is very well-known and has a large preestablished donor base, will be able to amass a large surplus of private and public funds by the end of the preelection year, which was a common tactic of leading contenders throughout the 1980s. Consequently, these challengers may lack a reservoir of funds that can be used to finance the purchase of such essential items as television time (which cannot be purchased on credit) in the aftermath of the initial contests. They may also lack the capacity to finance their campaigns by accruing large debt obligations because they may lack substantial sums of accrued matching revenues to use as collateral for bank loans. Candidates who survive the initial contests may therefore have to devote a substantial portion of their time to fundraising throughout the early months of the selection process, trying to raise donations while campaigning in a number of states, which will detract from their efforts to present their respective platforms and recruit electoral support.

Even if a candidate is able to overcome the financial hurdle, it is likely that the campaign will be waged on a limited budget (except perhaps in the case of a candidate who has a rare ability to raise large sums with relative ease). This lack of adequate funds will force some challengers to place greater emphasis on free media coverage to compensate for a dearth of paid advertising and organizational resources. Heavy reliance will thus be placed on photo opportunities, "tarmac" campaigning, and other techniques designed to produce sound bites for the national and local news broadcasts. Underfinanced campaigns also increase the strategic value of negative advertising. A challenger who adopts this negative approach may have a significant advantage over the opponent who is the target of the advertisements because that person may lack the resources needed for an effective response. These practices reduce the quality of campaigns because they detract from the substantive aspects of a candidacy and lower the level of political debate, which result in a less informed electorate.

So the lack of extensive PAC activity in the 1992 election cycle, although a welcome reprieve for those who had become disenchanted with seemingly constant campaigning, does not represent compelling evidence that can be used to support the current campaign finance regulations. The 1992 experience simply highlights another aspect of the strategic complications that arise from the unrealistically low limits that have been placed on political donations. More importantly, there is no reason to believe that truncated campaigns will be the model of the future. In the 1996 election cycle, prospective candidates will again have a strong incentive to indulge in early campaigning. Unless a Democrat captures the White House in 1992, there are likely to be strongly contested races in both parties, as was the case in 1988. An "open" race of this sort is likely to encourage some aspirants to begin campaigning early. A lesser-known challenger is apt to begin campaigning early in order to build a base of political and financial support and to increase his or her public name recognition. A well-known challenger is apt to begin campaigning early in order to capitalize on a broad base of support and achieve a head start that may earn him or her perceived "frontrunner" status. An early start by a few potential candidates may lead others to follow suit, generating the sort of "keep-up-with-the-Joneses" mentality that was most evident in the Democratic race in 1984 and in both parties in 1988.

The strategic pressures generated by the campaign finance laws and the demands of the delegate selection system will also induce 1996 hopefuls to start early and will encourage these aspirants to find ways to evade the financial restraints imposed on their campaigns. The conflicting pressures generated by the limit on contributions, the matching funds program, and the indexed expenditure ceilings will continue to present candidates with strategic choices that are difficult to resolve and yet remain within the parameters of the law. Unlike in previous elections, however, the leading contenders will be well prepared to take advantage of the technicalities of the law that offer a solution to their strategic dilemma. Having witnessed the efforts of the 1980s, potential challengers are now well aware of the advantages that a PAC or tax-exempt foundation can offer. Moreover, the number of federal officials who are already affiliated with a PAC or tax-exempt foundation is greater than ever before, largely due to the rise of so-called leadership PACs and a "dramatic increase in the number of tax-exempt organizations created by politicians or individuals aspiring to political office"[21] in the 1980s. Converting these organizations into precampaign operations will be a simple task. That such organizations will again play a prominent role in presidential electoral politics is thus very likely. Congress should therefore attend to this problem before candidates once again have a chance, now armed with better knowledge and in some instances more established organizations, to exploit the opportunity to circumvent the law.

PACs AND THE REGULATION OF
PRESIDENTIAL CAMPAIGN FINANCE

The proliferation of candidate-sponsored PACs also highlights the limited effectiveness of the Federal Election Commission in administering and enforcing the Federal Election Campaign Act. Unlike other forms of unregulated campaign financing, which have developed as a result of court decisions or legislative action, the precandidacy PAC phenomenon is solely a creation of the regulatory decisions made by the commission. Instead of restricting the establishment of PACs by presidential aspirants, the commission has allowed potential candidates to sponsor these committees and has expanded the range of activities they may perform. Given this permissive interpretation of the law, presidential aspirants have had little difficulty converting PACs into shadow campaign organizations.

The commission essentially sanctioned the role of precandidacy PACs in the presidential selection process through a number of advisory opinions that were decided between 1981 and 1986. These rulings concerned the definition and application of the testing-the-waters provisions of the federal campaign finance regulations. The provisions were adopted in order to ensure that the campaign finance regulations did not serve as a barrier to political participation. Under the original statutory definitions of the Federal Election Campaign Act, any individual who received or spent more than $5,000 on activities associated with a particular federal office was legally considered to be an authorized candidate subject to all of the act's reporting requirements and restrictions. In practice, this meant that any individual considering a bid for the presidential nomination would be forced to comply with all of the burdensome regulations imposed on candidates because the threshold for qualifying as a candidate was set so low. For example, the cost of one public opinion survey conducted by a professional pollster in an effort to determine the feasibility of a candidacy would easily surpass the $5,000 limit. This raised concerns that the law might discourage potential candidates from considering a run for office since the regulations essentially made this a black or white decision: practically speaking, an individual was either a candidate or not.

Responding to this concern, the commission changed the regulations to ease the requirements imposed on individuals who want to explore the possibility of running for office. In their original form, these testing-the-waters provisions exempted the monies spent by an individual on activities designed to assess the desirability and feasibility of a possible candidacy from the legal limits on contributions and expenditures and from the reporting requirements established for political committees. They also identified the types of activities that could be performed under this exemption. These included, but were not limited to, conducting a poll, making telephone calls, and engaging in some travel. This reform made it easier for an individual to study the feasibility of a candidacy. It also created a gray area in the law that prospective candidates quickly began to exploit.

The vague and open-ended nature of the testing-the-waters regulations and the desire to exploit the potential benefits of a PAC operation led a number of presidential hopefuls, beginning with Reubin Askew in 1981 and Alan Cranston in 1982, to seek clarification of the types of activities that might be included under the exemptions. In deciding these cases, the commission advanced a broad interpretation of the law and permitted a wide range of activities despite Commissioner Harris's objections that the regulations only intended a narrow exemption and that the commission's rulings reduced the possibility of distinguishing testing-the-waters activities from "campaign activities." The commission's stance encouraged other candidates, such as Howard Baker and George Bush, to test the limits of the law further by requesting rulings in advance of the 1988 election on the extent to which a possible, but unannounced, candidate could participate in political activities conducted by a PAC. In these decisions, the commission maintained its permissive interpretative approach, although it refined its stance by defining the conditions under which a PAC's finances would be subject to the limits established for presidential candidates.

The commission's rulings significantly undermined the effectiveness of the Federal Election Campaign Act by opening the door to a new form of unregulated presidential campaign financing. The agency allowed undeclared candidates to establish PACs and use these organizations to perform the basic tasks essential to a campaign such as hiring a staff, forming state steering committees, recruiting volunteers, engaging in direct mail fundraising, conducting polls, sponsoring issues forums, developing policy papers, hosting political events, promoting public appearances, and subsidizing travel throughout the country. Moreover, these decisions clarified how an ambitious aspirant with a bit of artful deception and an eye for legal technicalities could conduct all of these activities without being subject to the financial limits imposed on political campaigns. To do so, a prospective candidate simply has to avoid the five specific activities the commission uses to determine a sponsor's formal candidacy. The law has therefore been implemented in a way that essentially allows presidential aspirants to spend as much as they can raise in the early years of an election cycle. It has significantly weakened the contribution and spending limits established by the Federal Election Campaign Act and has thus created a regulatory environment in which it is virtually impossible to realize the principal goals of these reforms.

Yet, paradoxically, the commission's rulings on permissible testing-the-waters activities and precandidacy PACs have also fulfilled some of the basic objectives of the campaign finance regulations as well as the broader purposes of our political system. By expanding the sphere of activities included in the testing-the-waters exemption, the commission guaranteed that individuals interested in exploring the feasibility of a candidacy could employ a number of means to accomplish this end. Presidential aspirants can therefore develop much more realistic measures of the potential for a candidacy than those that could be achieved through a poll, some telephone calls, and limited travel. The array of activities permitted by the regulations thus allows candidates to make more informed decisions. These provisions also encourage the highest form of political participation, running for office, by setting forth less restrictive reporting requirements for individuals or committees involved in exploratory activities. This helps to ensure that reporting and filing requirements do not unnecessarily stifle potential candidacies.

The commission's decisions also promoted increased political participation by reinforcing the right of any individual, including prominent politicians who may seek the presidency, to establish a PAC or other political organization or to be associated with such a committee. The agency thus affirmed the rights of freedom of association and freedom of expression guaranteed by the First Amendment. To the extent that these committees activate citizens and encourage political involvement through their activities, they fulfill a basic purpose of a democratic polity.

Finally, the rulings foster the generally accepted goal of strengthening political parties. For years, supporters of electoral reform have decried the decline of party organizations and advocated the strengthening of parties and the development of a more responsible party system. Indeed, one of the common criticisms of the campaign finance reforms in the late 1970s was that the new regulations had reduced the role of parties in presidential elections. This criticism was the primary reason that Congress in 1979 revised the law to exempt funds for party-building activities from the act's contribution and spending limits (and thus sanctioned the use of soft money in presidential general elections). In allowing prospective candidates to establish PACs, the commission has therefore facilitated one of the central objectives of the law. After all, these committees are established for the avowed purpose of helping candidates and building the party, which are legitimate objectives under the law. And they do engage in some activities that enhance party organizations such as grass-roots organizing, making contributions to candidates, staging issues forums, and assisting with party events. To prohibit or restrict such committees would be contrary to the law and its purpose.

The experience with precandidacy PACs thus reveals one of the fundamental obstacles to effective enforcement of the campaign finance laws: the conflicting policy demands that the reforms impose on the Federal Election Commission. Under the current campaign finance regulations, the commission is responsible for ensuring compliance with the law, controlling political spending, limiting the influence of money in federal elections, equalizing financial participation, and preserving the integrity of the campaign finance system. But it is also supposed to ensure that the regulations are not unduly burdensome, to encourage participation in the political process, to promote the development of party organizations, and to recognize essential First Amendment rights such as the freedom of speech and freedom of association.

These diverse goals are often incompatible. In order to ensure full compliance with the limits established by the law and control political spending, the commission would have to implement the regulations stringently and narrowly interpret the law's provisions. This is the approach advocated by many of the commission's most strident critics, who condemn the agency for failing to enforce the law in this manner. Strict enforcement, however, may serve to discourage political participation, place an undue regulatory burden on candidates, limit the funds available for party-building activities, and encourage aspirants to pursue organizational alternatives such as PACs that facilitate unregulated campaigning. The commission cannot prevent possible candidates from establishing PACs, because this prohibition would violate rights guaranteed by the First Amendment. But by allowing the formation of these committees, the agency is sanctioning an activity that may serve to undermine the financial constraints intended by the law. Federal regulators could attempt to foreclose this possibility by narrowly defining the activities a PAC may conduct under the rubric of party-building or by advancing a broader understanding of the actions that indicate a formal candidacy. This might reduce the resources available to party organizations and inhibit their development. It would also increase the incentives for prospective candidates to pursue other organizational alternatives, such as tax-exempt foundations, which would allow them to conduct some campaign-related activities wholly outside of the purview of the Federal Election Campaign Act.

In administering and enforcing the campaign finance regulations, the Federal Election Commission is basically responsible for making relative choices among competing goals. This is an extremely difficult task, particularly given the dynamic nature of electoral behavior. The agency is constantly trying to adapt the regulations to new campaign technologies, innovative financial and accounting practices, and increasingly sophisticated political operations. In addressing these changing realities, the commission is often asked to render ex post facto decisions, to judge disputes that have highly partisan implications, or to determine the legality of anticipated actions that involve consequences that are not readily discernible. Further, it must fulfill these responsibilities in an institutional environment that is not conducive to effective regulation. This environment is determined by the agency's lack of institutional resources (budget, staff, and enforcement authority); the piecemeal approach to rulemaking required by the advisory opinion process and the law's enforcement procedures; its unique relationship to Congress (the commission regulates the activities of individuals, some of whom determine its budget and authority); and the legal constraints of the First Amendment.

To date, the commission has attempted to resolve these competing objectives by pursuing a path of least resistance. It has adopted a regulatory posture that places minimal restraints on political activity yet recognizes the limits and restrictions mandated by the law. Individuals who want to explore a candidacy may do so but are limited to accepting individual contributions of up to $1,000 and must duly report all contributions and expenditures associated with exploratory activities upon becoming a formal candidate. Individuals may establish PACs and use these committees to finance a range of activities but may not perform certain actions that are defined as "campaign-related" without triggering the restrictions imposed on candidates and authorized campaign committees. The commission has therefore emphasized the goals of participation, party-building, and freedom of association while trying to maintain the objectives of the contribution and spending limits.

Yet, even this minimalist regulatory approach has failed to produce a realistic or workable campaign finance system. Despite the laxity of the commission's decisions, presidential aspirants still believe that the parameters of the law are unrealistic. They have therefore continued to pursue strategies that allow them to circumvent the law. As a result, the campaign finance reforms have failed to ensure an accountable and rational system of political finance that protects the integrity of the electoral process. With each new election, candidates have proven more willing to take advantage of the law and have engaged in increasingly transparent acts of subterfuge. These blatant violations of the intent of the law have undermined the integrity of the system and pose a future threat to the legitimacy of the electoral process.

CONCLUSION

The current campaign finance laws are incapable of solving the ills that now plague the financing of presidential elections, because the problems are a product of these reforms. The regulations fail to reflect the strategic and operational imperatives of the modern presidential selection process. These statutes have therefore created a strategic environment that has encouraged presidential hopefuls to evade the law by conducting campaign activities through precandidacy PACs and tax-exempt organizations. As a result, the purposes of the Federal Election Campaign Act and its subsequent amendments are not being achieved. Candidates continue to raise and spend millions of dollars that are not disclosed on their campaign finance reports. They continue to use bank accounts and other funds that are not strictly accountable under federal or state law. They continue to conduct increasingly systematic and extensive campaign operations prior to establishing formal campaign committees. The Federal Election Commission has tried to address these problems, but due to the competing statutory objectives that frame the agency's decision-making process, its rulings have failed to limit these innovative methods of campaign financing.

Candidates will therefore continue to abuse the law until the laws are revised to accommodate the realities of the nomination contests. The experience with precandidacy PACs thus provides important insights into not only the failure of previous efforts but also the direction of future reform. To improve the law, federal policymakers must reduce the artificial restraints and pressures imposed on candidates and pursue a regulatory approach with clear goals. That is, the campaign finance system must be fundamentally revised in order to ensure the effective regulation of political money.

8

Reforming the Reforms

Recent electoral experience demonstrates that the current campaign finance laws are incapable of controlling the flow of money in presidential contests. In each of the elections during the 1980s, candidates easily circumvented the regulations and channeled increasingly large sums of unaccountable funds into their campaigns. Yet, despite this growing abuse of the law, federal lawmakers have taken no action to restructure the system since adopting the Federal Election Campaign Act Amendments of 1979. Absent reform, presidential aspirants will continue to subvert the contribution and spending limits in the future, thus making the regulations meaningless.

Although the role of money in presidential elections has been a continuing source of legislative concern, the reform debate over the past decade has been dominated by the issues associated with the financing of congressional elections. The growing reliance on PAC contributions as a source of campaign revenue, rising public perceptions of favoritism toward campaign donors, increasing anxiety over the skyrocketing costs of campaigns, and the widening resource gap between incumbents and challengers have focused public and legislative attention on the funding of congressional contests and produced a new wave of support for campaign finance reform. Congress has responded to this renewed demand for more stringent regulation by producing a number of major legislative packages. Few of these bills, however, have progressed to a floor vote and not one has managed to overcome the deep partisan divisions that have produced a legislative stalemate on the issue of campaign finance reform.[1]

Although most of the bills advanced in recent congresses are primarily devoted to improving the financing of congressional elections, many of these proposals contain provisions designed to correct the flaws in the presidential system. None of the reforms advanced to date, however, offer a viable solution to the problems that plague the financing of presidential nomination contests. Instead of rethinking the goals of campaign finance legislation, Congress seems determined to follow the regulatory approach adopted in the 1970s. Almost all of the changes that have received strong support seek to reinforce the current limits on contributions and spending by plugging regulatory gaps and further restricting the flow of money in presidential campaigns. Such measures will not improve compliance with the law or otherwise enhance the efficacy of the regulations. For the limits are the source of the system's continuing decline. If an effective campaign finance system is to be achieved, Congress must fundamentally alter its approach and craft regulations that recognize the realities of modern presidential contests and the limits of statutory remedies for political problems.

ASSESSING RECENT REFORM PROPOSALS

Advocates of reform have tried to enhance the efficacy of the Federal Election Campaign Act's contribution and spending ceilings by suggesting changes that would control the unregulated sources of funds that serve to undermine these limits. In this regard, legislators on both sides of the aisle have emphasized the need to control the use of independent expenditures and soft money in federal elections. Dozens of proposals have been submitted in recent years to address these problems. Most of the bills seek to limit the influence of these monies by requiring more stringent disclosure and reporting procedures for these activities. Others go further and attempt to eliminate the role of soft money altogether by repealing the statutory exemption for financing party activities that serves as the conduit for channeling soft money funds into presidential general election campaigns.[2]

In comparison, the operations of candidate-sponsored PACs and their role in the financing of nomination campaigns have received relatively little attention in legislative and public debates. There has been no public outcry over this major source of unregulated campaign monies, and only a handful of proposals have been advanced to address this problem. Why the activities of these organizations have engendered so little interest may be due to a number of factors. One reason is clearly the decision of congressional lawmakers to concentrate on the problems that have emerged in their own elections. Reform of the presidential system will not be the focal point of legislative concern until the two parties can reach a consensus on how to address the issues associated with congressional campaign financing.

Another reason may be that these committees operate in the deepest shadows of a presidential campaign. The bulk of the activities conducted through a PAC occur during the early year of a presidential election cycle or more than a year before the fi   primary contest.

Unlike independent spending or soft money, this form of campaign financing takes place months before the presidential campaign becomes a major topic of media coverage and public interest. Consequently, precandidacy PACs have not received the intensive scrutiny given these other types of financing, which usually occur in the midst of a heated campaign.

Further, candidate-sponsored PACs perform the types of activities that rarely capture the public's imagination. The funds raised by these committees are not used to finance negative television advertisements or vicious direct mail campaigns. They are used to pay for the more mundane initial organizational tasks that are essential to the success of a campaign. These sorts of activity fall under the rubric of what is commonly referred to as "inside baseball" and tend to attract the interest of none but the most zealous political observers and a few dedicated journalists. As a result, the public has little knowledge of the extent to which these organizations have been used to conduct campaigns outside of the law.

The few bills that have recognized the problem of candidate-sponsored PACs have primarily been advanced in response to the growth of "leadership PACs," which are PACs established by members of Congress to expand their legislative influence. These bills are also designed to resolve the problems posed by the PACs maintained by presidential contenders.[3] The proposals seek to curb the formation of such committees by prohibiting federal candidates or officeholders from sponsoring PACs or by attempting to place a PAC's finances within the purview of the contribution and spending limits imposed on presidential candidates. These approaches, however, will not solve the problem, because they fail to address the factors that have induced candidates to circumvent the law.

For example, in the 101st Congress, the House and Senate each passed a major campaign finance reform package. The Senate bill, S. 137, which was sponsored by the Democrats, was passed by a vote of 59-40 on August 1, 1990. It included a provision that would curb the use of PACs by federal candidates by prohibiting the sponsorship of such committees. Section 401 of the bill stated that "an incumbent in or candidate for Federal office may not establish, maintain, or control a political committee, other than an authorized committee of the candidate or a committee of a political party." The legislation also included a regulation that sought to restrict the use of tax-exempt organizations by federal candidates. Section 217 mandated that any federal officeholder or candidate who "established, maintains, or controls" such an organization "may not solicit contributions to, or accept contributions on behalf of, such organization from any person . . .

which, in the aggregate, exceed $5,000." Further, if "a significant portion of the activities of such organization include voter registration or get-out-the-vote campaigns," a candidate or officeholder may not raise any contributions for the group.[4]

The Senate thus sought to solve the problem of unregulated funding through alternative organizations by prohibiting the sponsorship of PACs by candidates or officeholders and by restricting the activities that could be conducted through a tax-exempt foundation. Whether these provisions would have withstood court scrutiny if challenged as an infringement on the freedom of association, particularly if the candidate or officeholder had not received any public subsidies, is questionable. Even so, had the law been enacted, it would have done little to resolve the problems that persist in the financing of nomination campaigns. For the Senate's bill is based on a regulatory approach that is characteristic of many recent efforts to "improve" the campaign finance system: it treats the symptom rather than the disease.

The Senate's proposal would not ease the pressures placed on candidates by the unrealistic contribution and spending limits established by the current law. Instead, it seeks to reassert these restraints by closing off the alternatives that candidates have developed in response to the law. With each new election, the aggregate spending limit would be adjusted upward to account for inflation and the contribution limit would remain static, intensifying the pressure to begin fundraising early. The adjustments in state and aggregate expenditure ceilings would continue to lag behind the rising costs of basic campaign technologies, thus fueling candidate concerns about violating the ceilings. Candidates would thus continue to experience the strategic pressures that induce them to seek out alternative methods of funding their campaigns. And given the provisions of the bill, aspirants would still be able to subvert the law. For example, the statute would not deter a presidential aspirant who is not a federal officeholder or who is not a legally qualified candidate from taking advantage of the opportunities for unregulated campaigning afforded by a PAC or tax-exempt foundation. So prospective candidates who hold no federal office, such as Reagan in 1980 and Mondale in 1984, could fully exploit the financial benefits of these organizations. An aspirant who holds federal office would still be able to derive substantial benefits from a PAC or tax-exempt foundation because that person could participate in some PAC activities such as making public appearances on the committee's behalf, participating in issues forums, or raising funds (so long as the amounts were within the federal limits) for other candidates. The bill also contains no provision that would prevent an aspirant's supporters from creating an alternative organization and using it to finance the basic tasks needed to launch a campaign.

The Senate proposal would not eliminate the use of alternative organizations to circumvent the campaign finance regulations. The primary consequence of this legislation would be, at best, to reduce the amount of unaccountable funding in presidential campaigns and alter the extent to which prospective candidates use PACs. It is as likely, however, that such a statute would simply encourage aspirants to find new, more ingenious methods of circumventing the reforms because the strategic environment of the nominating process would remain unchanged. Simply plugging the holes in the dike will not resolve the problems created by the increasing pressure behind the dam.

The campaign finance legislation passed by the House in the 101st Congress offers an approach similar to that adopted by the Senate in addressing the issue of precandidacy PACs. The House, however, did include a reform that would reduce the incentive to avoid the law. This bill, H.R. 5400, which was also sponsored by the Democrats, was adopted by a vote of 255-155 on August 3, 1990. Like the Senate legislation, H.R. 5400 sought to put an end to the use of PACs by presidential aspirants by prohibiting "a candidate for Federal office" from "establishing, maintaining, or controlling a political committee other than an authorized campaign committee or committee of a political party."[5] The House proposal differed from the Senate bill in that it did not include federal officeholders among those who could not sponsor a PAC. Nor did it contain a corresponding regulation designed to restrict the use of tax-exempt organizations. Indeed, Section 105 stated that a candidate's PAC could continue to make contributions to other candidates for one year after the act became law and that any remaining funds must be disbursed by donating them to federal candidates, the U.S. Treasury, a party committee, or a tax-exempt foundation.

Had it been enacted, the House package might have been even less effective than the Senate's in restraining the use of alternative organizations by presidential contenders. Like the Senate bill, it would not have eliminated the use of PACs by individuals who were not formal candidates for the presidential nomination. Because it did not prohibit the establishment or maintenance of a PAC by a federal officeholder, it seems that it would have also failed to control the creation of PACs by prospective candidates like Howard Baker, Gary Hart, or George Bush in the 1988 election, who formed alternative organizations while holding office and who were not formal candidates for federal office since they had announced their decision not to seek reelection (Baker and Hart) or were constitutionally prohibited from seeking reelection (Bush). Moreover, the bill would have undoubtedly encouraged aspirants to make greater use of tax-exempt foundations. There was no prohibition against the creation of these committees and, under the provisions of the act, an aspirant with a PAC could transfer any monies raised through the PAC to the foundation after the one-year phase-out period.

The House did, however, attempt to extend the scope of the campaign finance regulations beyond the limits established by the Senate by specifically incorporating some of the financial activities associated with prospective candidates under the limits of the law. Whereas the Senate made no specific proviso for individuals who were not formal candidates, the House mandated that any contribution or expenditure made "by any person for the purpose of encouraging any specific individual who is not a candidate to become a candidate" is subject to the limits of the act and further noted that any such contribution "donated to prospective candidates for Federal office" would be treated as a legally qualified contribution under the terms of the act "whether or not [the aspirant] becomes a candidate."[6] This provision would ensure that the only contributions that could be accepted by an exploratory committee or a candidate draft committee are those that would meet the campaign limits. Depending on its interpretation by the Federal Election Commission, the provision might also be used to restrict contributions to other precampaign organizations including a PAC if the contributions were judged to be gifts that helped finance activities that serve to "encourage" an individual to become a candidate.

Another important difference between the House and Senate proposals was that the House supported the elimination of state spending limits in presidential nomination contests. H.R. 5400 thus sought to remove one of the major restraints in the current law that encourage candidates to subvert the regulations. In this regard, the House bill presented a better alternative than that offered by the Senate because it at least recognized the need to ease some of the restraints in the current system. The bill made no change, however, in the aggregate ceilings or in the contribution limit, which are key factors in inducing candidates to begin campaigning early.

This review of the most recent efforts to reform the campaign finance system indicates that Congress is generally abiding by the same approach it has followed for the past two decades with respect to the regulation of political finance. Instead of rethinking the law and devising a workable and realistic system for governing the financing of presidential campaigns, members of Congress continue to pursue regulatory solutions designed to control political behavior and restrict the flow of money in presidential elections. Rather than admit the limits of reform, policymakers have attempted to reform the limits by simply "improving" the current law. The basic thrust of these efforts is to maintain the integrity of the original design adopted in the mid-1970s and to reassert its value by adjusting the law's provisions to encompass changing practices and technologies. Given the dynamic nature of political campaigns and the ingenuity of political professionals, this is an extremely difficult task.

This task is further complicated by the apparent willingness of federal regulators to acknowledge some changes in the financing of presidential elections while refusing to acknowledge others. Congress has demonstrated a desire to adopt more restrictive regulations to prohibit unintended practices or outcomes but has displayed little support for changes that recognize the financial and strategic pressures that have been generated by changes in the selection process and the conduct of presidential campaigns. Although the regulations have maintained the limits on the amount of money a candidate may raise and spend, other factors have sharply increased the cost of a bid for the presidential nomination. Campaigns have become more sophisticated with each passing election. In addition to relying on television and other forms of media advertising, candidates now rely on advanced polling techniques, computerized targeting and mailing programs, satellite teleconferencing, and other new technologies to help spread their message to the voters. Changes in the selection process, such as the growth in the number of primaries and the trend toward early contests that has produced a front-loaded delegate selection calendar, have exacerbated the resource demands placed on a presidential campaign, especially in the earliest stage of the formal process. The growth in the cost of campaigns that has resulted from these changes has exceeded the rate of inflation, the only adjustment in the spending ceilings that the law allows. And increased costs have highlighted the inadequacy of the static $1,000 limit on individual donations, which now represents a real donation of approximately $400.

No action has been taken in more than a decade to restructure the law to accommodate these developments. As a result, the regulations are becoming increasingly counterproductive. Rather than ensuring compliance, they encourage defiance. They induce candidates to engage in unaccountable methods of funding their campaigns, to solicit contributions in excess of the legal limit, and to spend money through unregulated mechanisms. The current system therefore does not ensure strict accountability and disclosure of campaign monies, which is the key to preventing corruption or the appearance of corruption—the primary goal of any system of campaign finance regulation. It does not ensure compliance with the law, which is a crucial factor in protecting the integrity of the process. Nor does it ensure public faith in the selection process, which is needed to maintain the legitimacy of electoral outcomes.

RETHINKING REGULATORY REFORM

If a workable and effective presidential campaign finance system is to be achieved, federal lawmakers must recognize the limits of their ability to legislate political behavior and reconsider the purposes of regulation. What is needed is a campaign finance system that acknowledges the realities of modern presidential politics and does not impose unrealistic constraints on candidates. Such a system would allow candidates to raise and spend the sums needed to mount a viable or even winning campaign without having to rely on legal shenanigans or subversive actions. It would thus eliminate the incentives to circumvent the law that have rendered the current regulations ineffective. Candidates would no longer be induced to pursue methods of financing their campaigns that were not intended by the authors of the Federal Election Campaign Act. This approach would therefore promote compliance with the law and rid the process of actions that serve to undermine the integrity and legitimacy of the electoral system.

A workable and effective system will also require a realistic sense of the goals of campaign finance legislation. The current system attempts to cure almost all of the perceived ills of the electoral process. It is designed to eliminate the possibility of corruption or the appearance of corruption, create a more informed electorate, encourage participation, promote the development of parties, ensure greater equality among citizens and between candidates, and enhance the representative character of presidential elections. These diverse and, in some cases, contradictory objectives are not being achieved, and the prospects for attaining them will not be enhanced by simply passing additional regulations designed to reinforce these purposes. What is needed is to rethink these objectives and determine which are most essential for an effective regulatory scheme.

The primary goal of campaign finance regulation is and must continue to be "the prevention of corruption and the appearance of corruption spawned by the real or imagined coercive influence of large financial contributions on candidates' positions and on their actions if elected to office."[7] The law must eliminate the possibility of bribery or political or legislative favoritism in exchange for campaign contributions. Such outright acts of real corruption, actions that are blatantly illegal or rely on quid pro quo relationships that result in a betrayal of the public trust, especially the use of public office for private gain, must be prevented and strictly prosecuted. These actions should be the focal point of any regulatory effort because they pose a grave threat to democratic self-government: they debase public service, severely damage the integrity of the electoral process, and promote public cynicism and alienation.[8]

Equally important is the need to eliminate the possibility of actions that appear to be corrupt. These practices, which political scientist Larry Sabato describes as "quasi corruption," normally consist of practices that are legal but are perceived to be improper or illegal by members of the public. For example, members of Congress may legally accept honoraria and free trips from organized interest groups. These gifts, however, are perceived to be means by which special interests provide private benefits to individuals and "buy influence" in the legislature. Similarly, in presidential elections, large individual contributions to state and local party organizations for voter registration and mobilization activities, or soft money contributions, are perfectly legal but are considered to be improper because the public financing provisions of the campaign finance laws sought to eliminate large private donations in the financing of presidential election contests. Such practices tend to have effects similar to those of acts of real corruption: they promote negative public attitudes toward the electoral process that serve to undermine the perceived integrity and legitimacy of electoral outcomes. Accordingly, they, too, should be subject to strict regulation.

Comprehensive public disclosure requirements in conjunction with severe criminal penalties constitute the most effective regulatory means of eliminating corruption and guarding against the appearance of corruption. As Larry Sabato has noted, "Disclosure is the single greatest check on the excesses of campaign finance, for it encourages corrective action, whether judicial or political."[9] Disclosure provides public access to information concerning contributors and the amount spent by candidates so that citizens or members of the press can determine the sources of a candidate's funds, the role played by particular donors or groups in the financing of a campaign, and other matters such as whether a candidate is excessively spending funds in an attempt to win an election. Information of this type allows a voter to know whether a candidate may be beholden to particular interests. It also aids enforcement of the law by revealing large donations or expenditures that violate federal regulations. Further, it can be used to identify potential connections between a candidate's official actions and campaign contributions. Disclosure therefore discourages candidates from engaging in corrupt or controversial financial activities because such practices would entail the risk of exposure, which could result in a loss of political support or cause an individual to face some sort of enforcement proceeding.

Disclosure also facilitates another major objective of campaign finance regulation: the creation of an informed electorate. The information made available through disclosure reports concerning the groups and individuals that are financially backing a candidate can be used by voters in deciding whom to support. These reports thus provide the electorate with a unique knowledge of those seeking office. This knowledge can only be achieved, however, if the reports are filed in a timely and efficient manner. Information filed just before or after an election or documents with incomplete or vague descriptions of the interests or occupations of donors do little to promote an informed electorate. The documents should contain all required information and be available far enough in advance of an election to allow time for journalists and opponents to review the material and publicize any irregularities or questionable gifts. In addition, the reports should be organized in a way that allows an individual reviewing them to comprehend and summarize the information easily without having to engage in an extensive amount of deciphering or rearrangement of the data.

Some scholars of campaign finance have viewed the educative value of disclosure with skepticism, arguing that such laws produce more information than the voters, politicians, or media can master in the relatively short period of a campaign and that, even when information is presented to the public, it does not necessarily affect a voter's perception of a candidate.[10] Yet there is evidence that financial information can have an impact on a campaign.[11] It has certainly played a role in the last two presidential elections. In the 1984 Democratic nomination contest Gary Hart relied on disclosure reports to expose Mondale's use of delegate committees, independent committees established to help individuals win election as delegates. These committees supplemented the activities of Mondale's campaign organization and were primarily employed to circumvent contribution and spending limits and receive PAC donations (which Mondale publicly declared he would not accept in his campaign). When Hart revealed this practice, the role of these committees quickly became a campaign issue. Mondale admitted that these groups were affiliated with his campaign and agreed to pay $398,140 in fines and repayments to the U.S. Treasury.[12] In 1988, Michael Dukakis used public reports to develop negative campaign advertisements on the PAC contributions accepted by Richard Gephardt. These commercials, which were aired the week before Super Tuesday, played a role in reducing support for Gephardt at this crucial point in the race.[13]

Although disclosure may not have met reformers' expectations with respect to its effect on voting decisions, it is an important source of voter information that can be used to influence public support for a candidate. This is especially true in the context of the lengthy presidential nominating process because the monthly filings required by the law help to ensure that information is available before the race is over, although problems remain with respect to the release of data before the date of particular primaries. Even in these instances, disclosure continues to serve a number of valuable purposes. It is an effective instrument for identifying violations of the law; it facilitates postelection scrutiny of an elected official's actions; and it provides a basis for developing proposals for reform.

Another major objective of campaign finance regulation should be to encourage a choice among qualified candidates. By fulfilling this goal, the law provides the electorate with a meaningful decision in the exercise of the franchise and increases the competitiveness of elections. Fostering electoral competition helps promote many of the essential qualities of a free electoral system: it enhances the representativeness of the process, stimulates political debate, expands public interest in electoral outcomes, and improves individuals' perceptions of the importance of participating.

The best means of achieving this objective is by ensuring that the law does not erect regulatory provisions that prove to be so burdensome as to discourage qualified individuals from running. The regulations must be stringent enough to prevent corruption and guarantee full and meaningful public disclosure yet not be so rigorous as to pose a possible barrier to candidate participation. That is, they must provide safeguards against the possible corrupting influence of extremely large donations and ensure strict accountability of all campaign monies yet not impose limits on contributions and spending or disclosure requirements that are so severe that they fail to reflect the realities of modern campaigning or place unnecessary constraints on candidates. As this study has shown, regulations of the latter sort simply complicate an individual's decision regarding a candidacy and, in some instances, may have discouraged the candidacies of otherwise qualified persons. More importantly, they encourage aspirants to seek out methods of circumventing the law, which can only lead to a loss of integrity in the process and a weakening of public faith in the electoral system.

Any regulatory scheme for political finance should include contribution limits and expenditure ceilings in order to eliminate the potentially corruptive influence of unlimited donations and to prevent exorbitant spending in presidential campaigns. The contribution limits, however, should be set high enough to allow candidates to raise the seed money needed to initiate a competitive campaign and to generate the sums needed to meet the financial demands of the modern nominating process without having to spend an inordinate amount of time raising funds. The expenditure ceilings should be set at a level reflective of the real costs of presidential nomination contests and should allow candidates a substantial amount of freedom to determine how and where to spend their money. Deciding how to allocate campaign resources is a crucial strategic component of a political campaign. Candidates should have the latitude to make these decisions with a minimum of regulatory constraint. At least they should not be subjected to regulations that force them to engage in accounting gimmicks or other unintended practices in order to spend the funds considered necessary to contest a particular state election. The law should impose realistic and enforceable ceilings on candidates and play a less prominent role in a candidate's strategic decision-making.

The campaign finance laws should not seek to enhance the representativeness and competitiveness of the presidential selection process by mandating a system of regulation based on an overly strict notion of equality. The law should ensure an equal opportunity to run to all prospective candidates, but it should do so by establishing rules that provide aspirants with a reasonable opportunity to raise the funds needed to mount a viable campaign. It should not seek to achieve this purpose by trying to force candidates to compete on a narrowly constrained playing field, as does the current law. This approach is unrealistic and its goal will not be achieved.

Candidates will always have access to unequal resources. Those who are better known by the public or enjoy a broad base of financial support will usually have access to greater resources than those available to relatively unknown or less well-established aspirants. Recent experience demonstrates that attempts to equalize this inherent inequality through statutory provisions, such as state-by-state spending limits, which are designed to create a relatively level playing field and thus improve the opportunities for lesser-known candidates to be competitive in individual state primaries, do not achieve their intended goals. Instead of encouraging compliance with the law and enhancing the equity of the process, the primary effect of these provisions has been to induce some of the best contenders to shift playing fields and compete under different rules. As a result, the major objectives of the reforms have not been achieved.

PROPOSALS FOR REFORM

Federal legislators must recognize the limits of their ability to control political behavior if they hope to improve the presidential campaign finance system. Instead of pursuing minor changes that seek to reinforce the provisions of the Federal Election Campaign Act, Congress should acknowledge that the current regulations are part of the problem, not part of the solution, and consider comprehensive reforms to correct the flaws in the present system. Patchwork revisions designed to plug loopholes and improve enforcement of the law will not eliminate the financial abuses found in the presidential nominating process. Nor will they produce a regulatory system capable of fulfilling its legislative mandate. These objectives can only be achieved by addressing the factors that encourage candidates to circumvent the law.

Two fundamental changes will be necessary if the presidential campaign finance system is to be significantly improved. First, the financial restraints imposed on candidates must be reduced to allow aspirants to meet the actual costs of a presidential campaign without having to engage in extraordinary practices. Second, the disclosure requirements must be strengthened to ensure the strict accountability of all campaign-related receipts and expenditures.

The primary thrust of any future reform package should be to loosen the financial restrictions that have been placed on presidential campaigns. This can best be accomplished by restructuring the limits on contributions and expenditures. Easing these limits will allow candidates to raise and spend the sums required by the modern nominating process while remaining within the parameters of the law. This change will thus alter the incentive structure that has developed under the current guidelines and significantly reduce the financial and strategic pressures that encourage candidates to subvert the law. Easing the contribution and spending limits will therefore improve compliance with the law by allowing candidates greater freedom in the conduct of their financial affairs.

Raising Money

Raising the limit on individual contributions will allow candidates to solicit the funds needed to finance a competitive campaign without having to devote excessive amounts of time to fundraising. At a minimum, the limit should be increased to account for the effects of inflation since the adoption of the 1974 reforms. This simple change would have increased the maximum donation from $1,000 to approximately $2,400 in 1988. A more appropriate level, however, would be $5,000 per donor with the ceiling adjusted annually for inflation, rounded to the nearest $100 increment.

An adjusted $5,000 ceiling on contributions would have a number of beneficial effects. The fundraising burden candidates currently face would be significantly lightened, reducing the need to begin soliciting funds a year or more in advance of the election. Aspirants, especially less prominent challengers, would find it less difficult to raise the seed money needed to launch a viable campaign because they could generate a substantial sum from a relatively small base of donors. This higher limit would also lessen the comparative advantage offered by a precandidacy PAC since individuals willing to donate up to $5,000 to a candidate could do so within the legal framework of a campaign organization.

A $5,000 cap would also fulfill the policy goals that led to the adoption of a cap on individual donations in the early 1970s. The primary objective of this provision was to eliminate the role of large donors in the financing of campaigns and thus prevent corruption or the appearance of corruption in federal elections. A higher limit, in all likelihood, would not undermine this purpose, particularly given the relative insignificance of a $5,000 gift in the context of a presidential campaign that may spend as much as $10 million to $20 million or more. Indeed, one would be hard pressed to advance a serious argument claiming that an even larger donation, perhaps $10,000, would have a corrupting or undue influence when compared to the costs of modern campaigns. A higher limit would also serve the function of equalizing the relative influence of citizens on electoral outcomes. Although a higher limit would not maintain the strict notion of equity advanced by the current law, there is no substantive reason such a low contribution threshold is needed to guarantee a representative system of elections. The $5,000 ceiling would eliminate massive disparities in political giving, which is the crucial concern with respect to the relative influence of individuals in the electoral process, and would strike a better balance than the current law between the desire to limit participation by the wealthiest members of society and the realities of modern politics.

An increase in the contribution limit should be accompanied by a proportionate increase in the total amount an individual may give to federal candidates. The aggregate individual contribution of $25,000 per calendar year should be adjusted to $50,000 or more. It should also be indexed to reflect changes in the Consumer Price Index and rounded to the nearest $100 increment. This higher aggregate limit would ensure that the higher ceiling on individual gifts did not reduce the funds available to other candidates or party organizations. A donor would be allowed to give the maximum gift to one or more presidential hopefuls and still contribute a substantial amount to other candidates or party committees.

The fundraising demands of the presidential selection process can also be reduced by revising the regulations that govern the public matching funds program. The current eligibility threshold to qualify for subsidies should be retained, but the amount of a donation eligible for matching should be doubled from the first $250 given by an individual to the first $500. Eligible contributions would continue to be matched on a dollar-for-dollar basis with each candidate limited to aggregate receipts equal to 50 percent of the national expenditure limit.

This proposal essentially adjusts the public subsidy program to account for the effects of inflation since its adoption. Although the change might at first appear to be rather modest, it should have a significant effect on campaign fundraising. The higher eligibility level would reduce the amount of money a candidate must personally solicit because it would increase the amount that could be received in the form of public subsidies. For example, an aggregate donation of $1,000 would yield $500 in matching funds, or $250 more than the present system. A candidate would therefore have to solicit fewer contributions to generate the sums needed to mount a competitive campaign.

A higher eligibility limit might also reduce the financial demands of a presidential campaign by lowering fundraising expenses. The public subsidies program now encourages candidates to solicit donations through direct mail appeals because this is the most efficient mechanism for raising the tens of thousands of small gifts needed to produce substantial revenues under the current matching funds limit. This type of fundraising, however, is very expensive, especially during its initial stages, and usually consumes a substantial portion of a campaign's fundraising budget. This is true even in those instances when a candidate uses a PAC or alternative organization to finance the development of a direct mail program.[14]

Increasing the amount of a matchable donation may induce candidates to move away from direct mail in favor of less costly alternatives. Specifically, candidates might place greater emphasis on fundraising events and the personal solicitations and networking of campaign fundraisers. In addition to being less expensive than direct mail, these alternatives are a more effective and efficient means of soliciting larger donations that would be matchable under the suggested limit. Placing less emphasis on direct mail fundraising would thus constitute a rational response to the proposed reform.[15] This tactic would allow a candidate to raise larger amounts with greater matching revenue at a lower cost. Although some candidates might still use direct mail, the regulations would no longer provide a major incentive to pursue this approach.

If the higher matching funds limit did result in a decline in the role of direct mail fundraising in presidential campaigns, it might yield the additional benefit of enhancing the quality of the dialogue in presidential contests. As many observers of the political process have noted, direct mail fundraising lowers the caliber of argument that takes place in electoral campaigns.[16] These solicitations are designed to produce an emotional response in the reader that will spur the individual to contribute. They are therefore often based on negative messages that present distorted information couched in threatening or heightened rhetoric. Such appeals fail to provide meaningful discussions of policy issues and do little to promote the creation of a well-informed electorate. Any reduction in the use of this technique would thus be a welcome development to those concerned with the quality of debate in presidential elections.

An expanded public subsidy would be most valuable to candidates if the funds were available to help defray the start-up costs of a campaign and meet the early expenses required by the front-loaded delegate selection process. Changing the initial date for the commencement of matching fund payments from the Treasury from January 1 of the election year to July 1 of the year before the election would fulfill this need. Beginning July 1 the Treasury should issue subsidy checks on a bi-weekly basis. The Federal Election Commission should continue its current practice of certifying eligible contributions on a continuing basis from January 1 of the year before the election, which is the initial date set forth in the statutes for receiving eligible contributions. Candidates who qualify for the subsidy will thus be assured a regular flow of public money in the early stages of the process. In addition, these changes will eliminate the absurd practice of having to arrange a bank loan with matching certifications posted as collateral to gain access to funds to which a candidate is rightfully entitled.

Finally, the higher matching funds amount will require an increase in the matching fund program's revenues to meet the anticipated rise in costs. To finance this expansion the amount that may be checked off on federal income tax forms for the Presidential Election Campaign Fund should be increased from $1 to $3 on individual returns and $3 to $6 on joint returns. This amount should also be indexed to changes in the Consumer Price Index and rounded to the next dollar increment.

To ensure the efficacy of the Presidential Election Campaign Fund, measures designed to promote taxpayer participation should also be adopted. Between 1980 and 1989, the percentage of eligible taxpayers participating in the program has dropped from 28.7 percent to 19.9 percent. The consequent decline in checkoff contributions poses a serious threat to the future availability of public funds to candidates for the party nominations.[17] In anticipation of a shortfall in the amount available in the fund for the 1992 election, the Treasury Department adopted revised regulations that would require the distribution of pro rata shares of matching monies to candidates during the presidential primaries with the balance to be paid after the election if the funds were not available to provide dollar-for-dollar subsidies during the delegate selection process.[18] This solution, however, will in all likelihood be reconsidered prior to the 1996 election because the FEC estimates that the fund will fall $75 to $100 million short of the $250 million needed for that election.[19]

The primary cause of the fund's financial problems, according to Federal Election Commission Chairman John Warren McGarry, is a "fatal flaw" in the public financing system—that payments are indexed for inflation but receipts are not. Consequently, in each subsequent election, the amount that is withdrawn from the fund increases without a proportionate increase in the amount received through the checkoff. This problem should be alleviated by the change in the amount of the checkoff suggested previously. Indeed, McGarry has stated that the fund's financial difficulties would not exist if the checkoff had been indexed in the original legislation.[20]

The long-term health of the matching funds program, however, can only be protected by addressing the drop in participation rates. This is a more complicated task. Although many hypotheses have been offered by knowledgeable observers, the factors that have led to the sharp decline of the 1980s have not been fully determined. Indeed, a sound first step toward correcting this problem may be to require the Treasury Department and Internal Revenue Service to conduct a comprehensive review of the tax checkoff program and report their findings to Congress so that legislators might gain a better understanding of the causes of decline.

One 1990 survey sponsored by the Federal Election Commission found that the public lacks a clear understanding of the operation of the Presidential Election Campaign Fund and its purposes and that this lack of information may be affecting checkoff participation. For example, the report estimated that 13 percent of noncontributors fail to participate because they do not want to *spend* a dollar, when in fact the checkoff results in no additional tax liability.[21] This suggests that taxpayer education may be needed to improve contributions. Accordingly, in 1991, the Federal Election Commission began a limited outreach program to increase public understanding of the program.[22] One reform, therefore, that merits serious attention is to expand this program to promote widespread public knowledge of the fund and its purposes. To supplement the print materials that are currently available, the commission should be given the resources needed to prepare and produce public service announcements for distribution to broadcasters. These ads, which should be developed in 30- and 60-second formats, could be aired each year during the February to April "tax season" when public awareness of federal tax filings is highest.

Spending Money

Simply addressing the problems that have developed with respect to fundraising will not substantially improve compliance with the law or produce a more reasonable regulatory system. These ends will only be achieved if the strategic difficulties created by the campaign spending limits are also resolved. Reforms designed to enhance a candidate's ability to raise funds will have little salutary effect on the process if the limits on spending fail to reflect the actual costs of campaigns. If these limits are not changed, candidates will still be forced to find ways to spend money outside of the law, especially in those states with crucial early contests. To improve the campaign finance system, reforms must be adopted to resolve the strategic problems on both sides of the tactical equation; that is, the problems encountered in spending money, as well as those in raising money, must be addressed.

The first change to be made in the expenditure ceilings is to abolish the state limits. These caps serve no significant purpose in the modern nominating process. The Federal Election Commission has declared that these "limitations have little impact on campaign spending in a given state, with the exception of Iowa and New Hampshire." In the other states, they are essentially meaningless because candidates are "unable or do not wish to expend an amount equal to the limitation."[23] Even if a candidate receiving public funds did wish to spend the allowable amount in each state, this would not be possible under the current regulations. For, as Herbert Alexander has noted, the "ultimate absurdity" of the present situation is that the sum of the fifty state ceilings in 1988 was $70 million, three times the amount a candidate could legally spend under the national limit.[24]

The state expenditures, in effect, are therefore administered solely to check expenditures in Iowa and New Hampshire. The law thus imposes a significant administrative burden on candidates as well as the commission in an effort to check spending in only two states. And in these contests they have been, at best, only partially successful. Candidates who wish to exceed the limit can easily do so. They can establish a PAC or tax-exempt foundation before becoming a candidate and essentially spend an unlimited amount in these states. They can make use of an array of accounting gimmicks and legal technicalities to avoid the cap. Or they can just violate the law and pay any fine assessed by the commission as a result of its postelection audit, which occurs long after the election is over.

Experience has also shown that these limitations are no longer needed to address the primary concerns that led to their adoption. State ceilings were established in part to discourage candidates from placing heavy reliance on the outcome of large state primaries. Legislators were concerned that candidates would concentrate their spending in the large delegate-rich states as a way of securing their party's nomination.[25] At that time, big states were considered the key to the nomination due to the size of their delegations and rules that awarded most or all of a state's delegates to the primary winner. Large-state spending, however, has not been an issue since the 1974 finance law was adopted. Moreover, party rules reforms that have been adopted since then make it highly unlikely that a candidate could secure the nomination by pursuing a large-state strategy barring some extraordinary circumstance. This is especially true in the Democratic nomination contest since the party, which banned the use of winner-take-all primaries in the 1970s, eliminated the use of loophole primaries and bonus delegate systems in favor of strict proportional representation after the 1988 election. Although large states are still important, the early contests now play the key role in the nominating process.

The state ceilings were also established for the broader purpose of providing lesser-known candidates a more equitable opportunity to compete against better-known or better-financed opponents.[26] Limits on spending in each state were accepted as a way of promoting competitive contests because they prevented a candidate from winning a primary by massively outspending other challengers. The law is thus predicated on the assumption that the best way to improve competition is to restrict the spending of front-running candidates, even though there is no clear evidence that state spending determines primary outcomes.[27]

In practice, the limits are so porous that they have not significantly restricted spending and appear to have had a minimal effect on the competitiveness of presidential contests. An analysis of the effects of these limitations by political scientist L. Sandy Maisel, for example, concluded that the state ceilings may have played a role in improving the prospects of only one candidate since their adoption: Democrat Gary Hart in the 1984 Iowa caucuses.[28] Even this instance is questionable given that Mondale, the frontrunner, spent close to $370,000 more than Hart and defeated him by a 3-1 margin.[29]

The experience with state limits suggests that a more effective and practical way to improve competition may be to ensure that all candidates have a fair opportunity to raise the funds needed to wage a viable campaign. Instead of narrowly restricting the expenditures of wealthier candidates in an attempt to impose a level playing field on an inherently unequal game, the law should allow relatively unknown challengers to generate the sums needed to launch a campaign and contest the early primaries. This can be accomplished by adopting the proposed changes in the contribution limits and in the public subsidy program. The law should, however, continue to guard against inordinate spending by a wealthy candidate. State limits are not needed for this purpose; that is the role of the national spending limit.

Although the removal of state limitations will obviously increase spending in some of the early primaries, the national cap on aggregate expenditures will serve as a restraint on state spending. The delegate selection rules in both parties guarantee that no candidate can secure the nomination simply by winning the initial contests; this requires extensive campaigning in a large number of states. With a growing number of states vying for a campaign's limited resources in the front-loaded selection process, a candidate could not spend lavishly in the initial contests and be assured of having the resources needed to finance the later primaries and a convention operation. Thus, the national limit will act as a control on state spending even in the earliest primaries. At the same time, candidates will have broader discretion in allocating their resources.

The national spending limit should be retained, but two changes are necessary. First, the separate limit for exempt fundraising expenses should be eliminated and one overall ceiling established. The fundraising limit, which is set at 20 percent of the aggregate expenditure limit with adjustments for inflation, was created in recognition of the higher costs that would accompany the small-donor fundraising required by the 1974 reforms. In practice, this limit has little effect on spending. The ceiling is meaningless for those campaigns that do not come close to reaching the overall expenditure limit, and many smaller campaigns do not even use the exemption except to help reduce their allocable spending in Iowa and New Hampshire.[30] Campaigns that have the funds to approach the overall limit usually allocate their expenditures in such a way that they come close to spending the maximum allowed by both the overall limit and the fundraising limit. The exemption thus affects the accounting practices of these campaigns more than their actual spending.

Incorporating the fundraising exemption into a single national cap will not have a significant impact on campaign spending patterns. It will, however, greatly reduce accounting burdens and simplify campaign reporting requirements, which in turn will reduce the Federal Election Commission's auditing workload. In addition to eliminating the need to enforce the fundraising exemption, candidates and the commission will also no longer have to worry about complying with rules related to the exemption. For example, the commission will no longer have to ensure compliance with the twenty-eight-day rule, which is the regulation that prohibits candidates from allocating disbursements as exempt fundraising expenditures within twenty-eight days of the primary in the state where the expenditure was made.[31] This change might also decrease the incentive to inititate precandidacy fundraising efforts because the amount spent on fundraising will not be viewed as an additional sum to be maximized beyond the aggregate limit.

The second change to be made in the national spending limit is to increase it. The estimated amount a candidate may legally spend on a presidential nomination campaign in 1992 is $33.6 million including fundraising costs.[32] This amount should be increased to a 1992 base of at least $40 million with future adjustments to reflect changes in the Consumer Price Index. This higher national spending limit should provide candidates with sufficient spending authority to meet the actual costs of a presidential campaign. It will thus ensure that the national cap does not encourage circumvention of the law. At the same time, it will guard against inordinate spending in the absence of a more acceptable alternative.

Improving Disclosure

Reforming contribution and spending limits will allow candidates to raise and spend the funds needed to meet the actual costs of a presidential nomination campaign and remain within the parameters of the law. Yet these reforms will not wholly eliminate the advantages that have led candidates to establish PACs and other alternative organizations. Candidates eager to capitalize on every possible funding source in order to maximize their resources could still accrue benefits from a PAC or tax-exempt foundation. These organizations could continue to be used to solicit individual contributions and soft money donations in excess of $5,000. They could also be used to spend sums beyond the more generous expenditure ceilings that have been proposed. Accordingly, future reform initiatives must go beyond changes designed to reduce the negative consequences of contribution and spending limits. Although these revisions will significantly reduce the incentive to circumvent the law, they do not guarantee compliance. Measures designed to promote the full accountability of all campaign-related funds must also be adopted.

One of the primary benefits of a precandidacy PAC is that it allows an aspirant to conduct financial activities outside of the candidate disclosure requirements. Candidates who sponsor PACs are not required to file reports of their PAC activities with their campaign committee filings, which complicates the tracking of funds and blurs the distinction between campaign and noncampaign monies. Although federal law requires that PACs organized at the federal level report all financial activities associated with federal elections, these committees are not required to report monies used solely to influence state or local elections or to assist state and local party organizations. PACs formed at the state or local level are not subject to federal reporting regulations and are required to provide information on their financial activities only in those states with disclosure laws. This ability to avoid strict disclosure must be eliminated if the law is to promote a well-informed citizenry and provide an effective safeguard against the possibility of financial abuse or corruption in the presidential selection process. The law must therefore be revised to ensure that all funds received and disbursed by precampaign organizations are subject to full public disclosure.

A presidential candidate should be required to file complete disclosure reports with the Federal Election Commission of the financial activities of any PAC that he or she establishes, maintains, sponsors, or controls. This would include any PAC with which a candidate has a significant affiliation by virtue of serving as an organizer of the PAC, an honorary official or committee officer, a public spokesperson, or a major participant in the committee's fundraising or political activities. The operative definition of participation for the purposes of this requirement should include such activities as drafting or signing a fundraising appeal, soliciting total contributions in excess of $10,000 per congressional election cycle, or regularly traveling or making public appearances on the PAC's behalf or under the committee's sponsorship. This reporting requirement would apply to any such PAC organized at the federal or nonfederal level with which a candidate was affiliated either at the time of becoming a candidate or during the four-year period prior to that time.

The candidate's PAC disclosure reports should include all of the information currently required under federal law. For example, the reports should include a statement of organization; a list of principal officers and bank depositories; the name, address, and occupation of donors; the date and amount of contributions; detailed listings of expenditures with the purpose, date, and amount of each payment; and debts and other obligations. In addition, the reports should include a separate filing noting similar information for all soft money accounts and any soft money funds raised or spent at the federal level or at the state and local level. This will ensure that monies not currently subject to federal disclosure will be filed with the Federal Election Commission and made available to the public. These reports should not preempt any relevant state reporting requirements that may also apply to a PAC's financial activities. All committees would still have to comply with applicable state disclosure laws.

A candidate should also be required to file complete disclosure reports with the Federal Election Commission on the financial activities of any tax-exempt organization that he or she establishes, maintains, sponsors, or controls. Under current law, these organizations, which can be used to finance precampaign activities, are required to provide very limited information to the public concerning their finances. They are responsible for filing tax returns with the Internal Revenue Service and disclosing basic organizational information such as a statement of the group's purpose, the names and salaries of principal officers, and a summary of annual receipts and expenditures. They are not required to provide a full summary of their contributions or expenditures. Consequently, a candidate can use a tax-exempt organization to raise and spend funds free of intensive public scrutiny. To eliminate this possibility, candidates should be required to release detailed information on the financial activities of any such group with which he or she has an affiliation. The reports should include the type of information on contributions and expenditures required for PAC reports. The operative definition of affiliation for the purposes of this requirement should be based on criteria similar to those suggested above for PAC operations.

To ensure that these separate reports are filed in a timely and efficient manner, candidates should have to file soon after becoming a candidate. The reports for any such organization that is no longer active at the time of an individual's filing for candidacy should be included with the candidate's early campaign committee filings. That is, the reports should be filed at least by the time of the candidate's second campaign disclosure filing with the Federal Election Commission. In the preelection year, this means that the information would be available by the time of the candidate's second quarterly filing. If an individual waits until the election year to become a candidate, the reports would be due by the time of the second monthly filing. If the organization is still active after an individual becomes a candidate, reports on its financial activities should be filed with campaign disclosure documents during the period of candidacy.

These disclosure requirements will bring the financial operations of candidate PACs and tax-exempt foundations into public view and facilitate detailed analysis of the sources of funds and expenditures of these organizations. This will allow journalists and others to determine a candidate's sources of support and report on the possible precampaign spending of presidential aspirants. It may also provide information to challengers that could be used to develop particular campaign strategies. Interested members of the public will thus be more fully informed on the financial activities of particular candidates. These prospective voters can then decide for themselves whether a candidate is spending too much money on the election, attempting to circumvent campaign finance laws, or receiving funds from interests that may influence an individual's voting choice. These revised reporting requirements will thus significantly strengthen the political and legal checks on illegal or improper financing, which is the fundamental purpose of disclosure legislation.

The advantages of a PAC or other form of precandidacy organization can also be substantially reduced by modifying the criteria used by the Federal Election Commission to determine whether funds spent by such organizations are campaign-related and thus subject to regulation. The five basic guidelines now used by the commission to determine a formal candidacy are so narrow in their application that they are easily circumvented and have little effect on precampaign spending. The scope of these criteria should be expanded to provide a more practical and realistic conception of the types of expenditures that should be subject to the regulations governing presidential campaigns. In other words, the funds spent by a PAC or other precandidacy political organization that are clearly campaign-related or of direct benefit to a campaign should be considered campaign expenses subject to the limits imposed on candidates.

For example, the direct mail fundraising conducted by PACs affiliated with a potential candidate should be regarded as an activity that may indicate a formal candidacy on the part of the PAC's sponsor. Although in some cases the use of this fundraising technique may bear no relation to the potential future candidacy of a PAC's sponsor, the commission should adopt a realistic attitude toward this practice and acknowledge that it can be of direct value to a prospective campaign. As such, it should be subjected to appropriate scrutiny. If a candidate's campaign committee uses the lists developed by a PAC that is established, maintained, sponsored, or controlled by that candidate, at least a portion of the costs incurred for list development should be regarded as a campaign expense. Similarly, any list that is developed through a fundraising appeal that is signed by the candidate or otherwise highlights the candidate should be reviewed to determine whether the costs of the appeal should be allocated as a campaign expenditure.

Expanding the scope of the criteria used to determine whether a precampaign expenditure is indicative of an individual's formal candidacy will limit an individual's ability to employ a PAC or alternative organization to avoid campaign spending limits. Aspirants will no longer be able to use PACs as vehicles for open-ended spending on most of the activities needed to launch a presidential bid. This reform will thus alter the incentive structure that has encouraged the proliferation of PACs and help to discourage the kinds of systematic, wide-scale campaign operations that developed prior to the 1988 election. While these types of operations may still exist, candidates will at least have to allocate some or all of a PAC's expenditures as campaign-related disbursements subject to limitation. As a result, the accountability of campaign-related monies will be dramatically improved.

One final way to improve the law is to grant the Federal Election Commission the staff and resources needed to secure full compliance from candidates and their committees. The Federal Election Commission currently has one of the smallest budgets of any federal agency.[33] Its resources should be increased to provide the funds needed to improve the enforcement of the law and implement the broader disclosure requirements that have been suggested. With regard to the former purpose, the commission should receive the funds needed to expand the number of investigators and auditors it employs and pay for the travel associated with their work. In addition, as Brooks Jackson has suggested, the commission should reestablish a field staff trained to conduct financial investigations.[34] These changes will provide the staffing needed to conduct full and timely investigations and audits. It will also free the commission lawyers from the passive approach to enforcement now practiced wherein investigators and auditors administer the law from their desks in Washington, evaluating statements submitted by complainants and others involved in the process. Instead, commission staff will be able to conduct detailed investigations and engage in independent fact-finding activities, which should speed up the regulatory process and improve enforcement.

The time has also come to consider changes in the commission's structure. The bipartisan six-person format has been severely criticized since its inception. Recently, there has been growing support among scholars and advocates of reform for changing the law to create a less partisan organization with greater decision-making authority.[35] The details of the reform proposals differ, but all call for an odd number of commissioners (usually five or seven) to avoid bipartisan deadlocks and a limit on terms to avoid the influence of partisan or political considerations in regulatory decision-making. Because Congress is more likely to add a position than cut one, the more feasible alternative may be to increase the number of commissioners from six to seven. The seventh commissioner, again following a proposal advocated by Jackson, would be a "public" commissioner who would represent the interests of neither party and "whose essential qualification would be a strong reputation for integrity, civic involvement and political independence."[36] This public representative could thus serve as the swing vote on issues that provoke strong partisan feelings.

Congress should also end the practice of confirming commissioners in pairs, which encourages partisan selections and minimizes the scrutiny given to appointees. Commissioners should be selected for a single seven-year term, with the terms staggered so that one member is appointed each year. Appointments should reflect the party preference of the commissioner whose term is expiring, excepting the "public" member, in order to maintain a fair partisan representation. This will eliminate the possibility of a member deciding an issue with an eye toward reappointment. As one former commissioner has noted, "There are those who would suggest that actual decisions have been affected by [reappointment] considerations. . . . The mere perception that a commissioner might, consciously or subconsciously, tailor his or her views as reappointment time approaches is cause for concern."[37]

CONCLUSION

The reforms proposed herein are essentially designed to streamline the regulatory system and reduce the administrative burdens imposed on candidates. The elimination of the limits on state spending and exempt fundraising expenditures, as well as the regulations that correspond to these ceilings, will substantially reduce the administrative demands of the law and simplify the auditing process. The effect of these changes, however, will be partially offset by other reforms, such as the reporting requirements for precandidacy organizations and the revised criteria for determining campaign-related spending, which will increase the administrative demands on candidates and the commission's workload. On balance, the recommended changes should produce a regulatory structure that is less burdensome and bureaucratic than the current system. This will make it easier for candidates to comply with the law, especially because they should no longer need to campaign through precandidacy organizations, which is the circumstance that triggers the additional disclosure requirements. The revisions will also make it easier for the Federal Election Commission to enforce the law, because there will be fewer regulations to administer and fewer potential violations to review in the auditing process. Moreover, it will free commission resources to pursue more important matters than the allocation of a campaign worker's travel expenses in Iowa or the accounting formula used by a candidate to apportion media monies spent in the Boston television market.

Convincing a majority in Congress to support these reforms may prove to be a difficult task. Most of the proposals are based on the assumption that the way to improve the system is to loosen regulatory restraints, an approach that has not been embraced by Congress in recent years. The renewed interest in campaign finance reform, however, has created a political climate conducive to fundamental change. With the 1996 election still on the horizon, federal lawmakers will have a chance to restructure the system before the next campaign. If they fail to take advantage of this opportunity, the goals of the campaign finance statutes will remain unfulfilled. Candidates will continue to pursue creative financing schemes to accommodate the conflicting pressures of the law, and the only real limits on campaign money will be the limits of ingenuity.

Acronyms and Abbreviations Used in the Notes

ADA	Americans for Democratic Action
AEI	American Enterprise Institute
AO	Advisory Opinion
AOR	Advisory Opinion Request
CC	Common Cause
C.F.R.	Code of Federal Regulations
CRP	Center for Responsive Politics
CQP	Congressional Quarterly Press
CQWR	*Congressional Quarterly Weekly Report*
CRSR	Congressional Research Service Report
DAO	Draft Advisory Opinion
FEC	Federal Election Commission
FECA	Federal Election Campaign Act
FECFG	*Federal Election Campaign Financing Guide*
GPO	Government Printing Office
H.R.	House of Representatives
U.S.C.	United States Code
LC	Library of Congress
SC	Statement of Candidacy
SO	Statement of Organization
Stat.	United States Statutes at Large

Notes

For an explanation of abbreviations used in the Notes and Selected Bibliography, please refer to the List of Acronyms and Abbreviations on page 227.

Chapter 1

1. SO for the Fund for America's Future (FEC Form 1). A copy of this form is on file at the FEC. Federal regulations require a political committee to register with the FEC by filing an SO (FEC Form 1) no later than ten days after its establishment (11 C.F.R. 102.1). For an unconnected political committee, that is, a political committee not established by a corporation or labor union, "establishment" is considered to have occurred when the committee meets the requirements set forth in 11 C.F.R. 100.5(a); for example, when a committee raises or expends more than $1,000 in a year. The SO contains the following information: (i) the name, address, and type of committee; (ii) the name, address, relationship, and type of any connected organization; (iii) the name, address, and committee position of the custodian of records; (iv) the name and address of the treasurer; and (v) a listing of the financial depositories used by the committee (at least one must be designated). See 2 U.S.C. 433(b) and (c); and 11 C.F.R. 102.2(a).

Although the term "political action committee" is commonly used to denote the legal entity established by a labor union, corporation, or other group to raise and spend money in conjunction with federal elections, this term does not appear in federal statutes. Rather, the law recognizes three legally distinct types of committees, all of which are included in the common usage of the term "political action committee." The first type of committee is a "political committee," which is defined as "any committee, club, association, or other group of persons which receives contributions aggregating in excess of $1,000 during a calendar year" (2 U.S.C. 431[4][A]). The second type of committee is a "separate segregated fund," which is essentially a separate bank account established by a labor union, corporation, membership organization, cooperative, or corporation without capital stock for the purpose of collecting and distributing voluntary political contributions from their members without involving union treasury monies or corporate funds (2 U.S.C. 431[4][B] and 441b[b]). The third type of committee is a "multicandidate political committee," which is defined as "a political committee which has been registered . . . [with the FEC] for a period of not less than 6 months, which has received contributions from more than 50 persons, and . . . has made contributions to 5 or more candidates for Federal office" (2 U.S.C. 441[a][4]). Almost all political committees and separate segregated funds qualify as multicandidate political committees under the law. For a discussion of the different types of political action committees, see Joseph E. Cantor, *Political Action Committees: Their Evolution, Growth and Implications for the Political System,* CRSR No. 84-78 (Washington, DC: LC, November 6, 1981; updated April 30, 1984), 1-6.

All of the committees considered in this study qualify as multicandidate political committees under federal law. So the term "political action committee" is used to denote multicandidate political committees unless otherwise noted. Because all of the committees considered herein are established by prospective candidates or other individuals, they are also categorized as "nonconnected" committees by the FEC. See FEC, *Campaign Guide for Nonconnected Committees* (Washington, DC: FEC, June 1985), 3.

2. SO for Citizens for the Republic (FEC Form 1), FEC Microfilm, Series 1977, Roll 46 at 4034.

3. "Reaganites to Back G.O.P. Conservatives," *New York Times,* February 1, 1977, A12. Herbert Alexander and Brian Haggerty note that Reagan's approach was based on Richard Nixon's strategy prior to the 1968 campaign. Nixon prepared the way for his 1968 candidacy by campaigning on behalf of Republican candidates in the 1966 midterm elections (Herbert E. Alexander, *Financing the 1980 Election* [Lexington, MA: Lexington Books, 1983], 146).

4. FEC, Committee Index of Disclosure Documents (C Index), 1977-1978 and 1979-1980, computer printouts, n.d.; and Maxwell Glen, "Starting a PAC May Be Candidates' First Step Down Long Road to 1988," *National Journal,* February 16, 1985, 376.

5. The activities considered to be indicative of a formal candidacy are noted at 11 C.F.R. 100.7(b)(1)(ii).

6. The FECA of 1971 (Public Law 92-225) was signed into law by President Nixon on February 7, 1972, and went into effect sixty days later. The text of the act is at 86 Stat. 3. For the 1974 amendments (Public Law 93-443), see 88 Stat. 1263; for the 1976 amendments (Public Law 94-283), 90 Stat. 475; and for the 1979 amendments (Public Law 96-187), 93 Stat. 1339.

7. The original provisions of the law also included spending ceilings for Senate and House campaigns and limits on independent spending and on the amount a federal candidate could personally contribute to his or her own campaign. The Supreme Court ruled these provisions unconstitutional in its decision in *Buckley* v. *Valeo* (424 U.S. 1 [1976]), with the exception of the limit on personal contributions by a candidate, which was retained for presidential candidates accepting public subsidies.

8. The literature assessing the effects of the FECA and its subsequent amendments is extensive. A thorough, ongoing effort to monitor the implementation of these reforms and their effect on the presidential campaign finance system is provided by Herbert E. Alexander in his quadrennial series of

studies on presidential campaign finance. See Alexander, *Financing the 1972 Election* (Lexington, MA: Lexington Books, 1976); Alexander, *Financing the 1976 Election* (Washington, DC: CQP, 1979); Alexander, *Financing the 1980 Election* (Lexington, MA: Lexington Books, 1983); and Alexander and Haggerty, *Financing the 1984 Election* (Lexington, MA: Lexington Books, 1987). See also, Herbert E. Alexander and Brian A. Haggerty, *The Federal Election Campaign Act: After a Decade of Political Reform* (Los Angeles, CA: Citizens Research Foundation, 1981). Two major studies of the act have been conducted by the Harvard Campaign Finance Study Group: *An Analysis of the Impact of the Federal Election Campaign Act, 1972-1978*, Final Report to the Committee on House Administration of the U.S. House of Representatives, 96th Cong., 1st sess. (Washington, DC: GPO, 1979); and *Financing Presidential Campaigns: An Examination of the Ongoing Effects of the Federal Election Campaign Laws upon the Conduct of Presidential Campaigns* (Cambridge, MA: Institute of Politics, Harvard University, 1982). Among others, see David Ifshin, "An Analysis of the Impact of the Federal Election Campaign Act on the 1976 Democratic Presidential Primary," *Santa Clara Law Review* 18(1978), 1-72; Gary R. Orren, "Presidential Campaign Finance: Its Impact and Future," *Commonsense* 4:2(1981), 50-66; Xandra Kayden, "Regulating Campaign Finance: Consequences for Interests and Institutions," in Alexander Heard and Michael Nelson, eds., *Presidential Selection* (Durham, NC: Duke University Press, 1987), 247-282; Robert J. Samuelson, "The Campaign Finance Reform Failure," *New Republic*, September 5, 1983, 28-36; and Carol Matlack, "Frayed Finance Law," *National Journal*, March 5, 1988, 591-594.

9. These loopholes include the use of accounting gimmicks to avoid state spending ceilings, the creation of compliance funds to evade the contribution limits, the formation of delegate committees, the establishment of precandidacy PACs and tax-exempt foundations, the ability to make independent expenditures, and the use of "soft money" in general election campaigns. Many of these loopholes are reviewed in the studies cited in note 8. See also Michael S. Berman, "Living with the FECA: Confessions of a Sometime Campaign Treasurer," in Lloyd N. Cutler et al., eds., *Regulating Campaign Finance, The Annals of the American Academy of Political and Social Science* 486(July 1986), 121-131; and Brooks Jackson, "Loopholes Allow Flood of Campaign Giving by Businesses, Fat Cats," *Wall Street Journal*, July 5, 1984, 1 and 16.

10. An independent expenditure is legally defined as "an expenditure by a person expressly advocating the election or defeat of a clearly defined candidate which is made without cooperation or consultation with any candidate, or any authorized committee or agent of such candidate" (2 U.S.C. 431[17]). For a discussion of these expenditures and their role in the financing of federal campaigns, see Joseph E. Cantor, *The Evolution of and Issues Surrounding Independent Expenditures in Elections Campaigns*, CRSR No. 82-87 (Washington, DC: LC, May 5, 1982); Susan G. Sendrow, "The Federal Election Campaign Act and Presidential Election Campaign Fund Act: Problems in Defining and Regulating Independent Expenditures," *Arizona State Law Journal*, Fall 1981, 977-1005; Xandra Kayden, "Independent

Spending," in Harvard Campaign Finance Study Group, *Financing Presidential Campaigns*, Chap. 7; Thomas M. Durbin, *Independent Expenditures in Presidential Elections* (Washington, DC: LC, July 17, 1985); Maxwell Glen, "Spending Independently," *National Journal*, June 21, 1986, 1533-1537; and Richard E. Cohen, "Spending Independently," *National Journal*, December 6, 1986, 2932-2934. The available data on independent expenditures are compiled by the FEC and disclosed in its *Index of Independent Expenditures*.

11. In recent elections, "soft money" and its role in financing presidential campaigns has received a substantial amount of attention. See, among others, John F. Noble, "Soft Money," *Campaigns & Elections* 5(Summer 1984), 44-45; Center for Responsive Politics, *Soft Money—A Loophole for the '80s* (Washington, DC: CRP, 1985); Herbert E. Alexander, *"Soft Money" and Campaign Financing* (Washington, DC: Public Affairs Council, 1986); David Earl Frulla, "Soft Money: The Outlook for Reform," *Journal of Law and Politics* 3(Spring 1987), 769-809; Thomas M. Durbin, *"Soft Money" in Federal Elections: A Legal Analysis*, CRSR No. 88-492A (Washington, DC: LC, July 14, 1988); and CRP, *Soft Money '88* (Washington, DC: CRP, 1989).

12. Kayden, "Independent Spending," 7-1 to 7-5. Kayden bases this estimate on her analysis of independent spending in the 1980 presidential election.

13. Based on the figures in Kayden, "Independent Spending," Table 1, 7-5.

14. According to Alexander and Haggerty, the FEC reported $17.4 million in independent expenditures in the 1984 presidential election. Of this amount, at least $8.4 million was disbursed in the general election ($7.2 million in support of Reagan, $228,000 against Reagan, $657,000 for Mondale, and $344,000 against Mondale). An additional $8.6 million was spent in support of Reagan on or before August 22, the date of his renomination. Because Reagan was unopposed for the nomination, these funds were in effect spent in support of his reelection. If this $8.6 million is added to the $8.4 million previously identified, then $17.0 million of the $17.4 million total represents general election spending. See Alexander and Haggerty, *Financing the 1984 Election*, 358-361 and 367-368.

15. For an analysis of the use of "soft money" in the 1980 and 1984 elections, see Alexander, *"Soft Money" and Campaign Financing*, 14-25. For the 1988 election, see CRP, *Soft Money '88*, 15-19, and Fred Wertheimer, "Bush and Dukakis Took Illegal Money," *New York Times*, February 1, 1989, 25.

16. The data in this paragraph are based on the compilation of reform proposals contained in Joseph E. Cantor, *Campaign Finance Reform: A Summary and Analysis of Legislative Proposals in the 98th and 99th Congresses*, CRSR No. 87-1 GOV (Washington, DC: LC, January 5, 1987); and Joseph E. Cantor and Thomas M. Durbin, *Campaign Financing* (Washington, DC: LC, December 15, 1987). These summaries have been supplemented by the author's own compilation of the bills submitted to the 100th Congress.

17. The number of bills noted in discussing particular reforms may be greater than the total number of bills listed in a given area because many proposals advocate more than one change in the laws.

18. One bill, H.R. 5950, was passed into law during this period, but it did not require a fundamental change. This legislation increased the base amount of the public subsidy given to the major political parties for their presidential nominating conventions from $3 million to $4 million, plus an adjustment for inflation. The change was requested by the leaders of both parties, largely to cover increased security costs. The proposal was passed by the House with a vote of 226-169 on June 29, 1984, and by the Senate on a voice vote on the same day. It became Public Law 98-355 on July 11.

19. Brief attention to the activities of candidate-sponsored PACs is provided in Alexander, *Financing the 1980 Election*, 146-148, and Alexander and Haggerty, *Financing the 1984 Election*, 173-177. This practice is also mentioned in Frank J. Sorauf, *Money in American Elections* (Glenview, IL: Scott, Foresman, 1988), 174-181. Thomas M. Durbin examines the legal foundations of these committees in *Legal Analysis of Specialized Multicandidate PACs and Private Tax-Exempt Foundations of Potential Federal Office Candidates*, CRSR No. 86-844A (Washington, DC: LC, August 12, 1986). The results of a Common Cause survey of the PACs established in advance of the 1988 election are provided in Teresa Riordan, "Who's Campaigning?" *Common Cause Magazine* 13(May/June 1987), 14-17. For the view of a former participant in the process, see Berman, "Living with the FECA," 121-131. Many of the most insightful analyses of the role of these committees in the presidential selection process have been written by journalists. See, among others, Maxwell Glen, "Starting a PAC May Be Candidates' First Step," 374-377; Thomas B. Edsall, "'88 Candidates' New Tricks Stretch Federal Election Law," *Washington Post*, October 20, 1985, A18; Paul Taylor, "Hey, Didn't We Just Finish a Presidential Election Campaign?" *Washington Post National Weekly Edition*, October 28, 1985, 11; Ronald Brownstein, "Counting Down to 1988," *National Journal*, December 7, 1985, 2803; Ronald Brownstein and Maxwell Glen, "Money in the Shadows," *National Journal*, March 15, 1986, 632-637; and Thomas B. Edsall, "Bush's Bunch is Leader of the PACs," *Washington Post National Weekly Edition*, February 17, 1986, 12.

20. 424 U.S. 1 (1976).

21. This provision was codified at 18 U.S.C. 608(e)(1) and can be found at 88 Stat. 1265.

22. For the Court's argument, see 424 U.S. 1, 39-59 (1976).

23. The legislative background of the 1979 amendments and the exemption for state and local party-building activities is provided in Durbin, *"Soft Money" in Federal Elections*, 5-15; Alexander, *"Soft Money" and Campaign Financing*, 9-14; and Alexander, *Financing the 1980 Election*, 8-16. For the earliest beginnings of this loophole, see Brooks Jackson's discussion of FEC advisory opinions prior to 1979 in his *Broken Promise: Why the Federal Election Commission Failed* (New York: Priority Press, 1990), 42-44.

24. Jackson, *Broken Promise*, 1-2.

25. For these arguments, see Jackson, *Broken Promise*; Common Cause, *The Failure-to-Enforce Commission* (Washington, DC: CC, 1989); William C. Oldacker, "Of Philosophers, Foxes, and Finances: Can the Federal Election

and Colleen O'Connor, "Who's Afraid of the FEC?" *Washington Monthly* 18(March 1986), 22-26.

26. Money plays an essential role in determining electoral outcomes largely because it is a convertible resource. That is, it can be exchanged for whatever goods and services are needed to wage a campaign. Alexander Heard, in his classic study of political finance, *The Costs of Democracy* (Chapel Hill: University of North Carolina Press, 1960), notes that "regardless of the fluctuating significance of financial and nonfinancial elements from one campaign to another, in virtually all campaigns a basic amount of organizational work, communication through commercial media, and getting-out-the-vote must be accomplished if the candidate expects to compete seriously. These things require money. Unless money to meet these minimum, essential expenses is available—regardless of how large or small the amount—contestants lacking it will be decisively handicapped." For similar arguments, see David Adamany, "PAC's and the Democratic Financing of Politics," *Arizona Law Review* 22(1980), 569; and Herbert E. Alexander, *Financing Politics: Money, Elections and Political Reform,* 3rd ed. (Washington, DC: CQP, 1984), 3-4.

27. David Adamany, *Financing Politics* (Madison: University of Wisconsin Press, 1969), 9. See also Heard, *The Costs of Democracy,* 48-49.

28. FEC, *Legislative History of the Federal Election Campaign Act Amendments of 1974* (Washington, DC: GPO, 1977), 109.

29. See FEC, *Annual Report 1978* (Washington, DC: FEC, 1978), 43-44; and U.S. Senate, Committee on Rules and Administration, *Federal Election Campaign Act Amendments of 1979,* Sen. Rpt. 96-319, 96th Cong., 1st Sess. (Washington, DC: GPO, 1979), 4.

30. See Durbin, *"Soft Money" in Federal Elections,* 5-15.

Chapter 2

1. Seymour Martin Lipset and William Schneider, *The Confidence Gap* (New York: Free Press, 1983), 16.

2. The polling data indicating these trends are summarized in Herbert E. Alexander, *Financing the 1972 Election* (Lexington, MA: Lexington Books, 1976), 559-564.

3. Congressional Quarterly, *Dollar Politics,* 3rd ed. (Washington, DC: CQP, 1982), 8.

4. Figures based on the data in Herbert E. Alexander, *Financing Politics,* 3rd ed. (Washington, DC: CQP, 1984), 7.

5. Figures based on the data in Herbert E. Alexander, *Financing Politics* (Washington, DC: CQP, 1976), 8.

6. See Alexander, *Financing the 1972 Election,* 39-75 and 513-557.

7. For further discussion of the 1971 law and its background, see Alexander, *Financing Politics;* Alexander, *Financing the 1972 Election;* David W. Adamany and George E. Agree, *Political Money* (Baltimore, MD: Johns Hopkins University Press, 1975); and Joseph E. Cantor, *Campaign Financing in Federal*

Elections: A Guide to the Law and Its Operation, CRSR No. 87-469 (Washington, DC: LC, August 8, 1986; revised July 20, 1987).

8. The act also placed a limit of $2 million, to be adjusted for inflation, on the amount a party could spend on its national nominating convention.

9. This provision was instituted in recognition of the added fundraising expenses that would accompany the need to finance a campaign through small donations.

10. FEC, *Legislative History of the Federal Election Campaign Act Amendments of 1974* (Washington, DC: GPO, 1977), 107.

11. For background on the origins of political action committees, see Joseph E. Cantor, *Political Action Committees: Their Evolution, Growth and Implications for the Political System*, CRSR No. 84-78 (Washington, DC: LC, November 6, 1981; updated April 30, 1984), 19-35; Larry Sabato, *PAC Power: Inside the World of Political Action Committees* (New York: Norton, 1984), 3-27; and Edwin M. Epstein, "The Emergence of Political Action Committees," in Herbert E. Alexander, ed., *Political Finance* (Beverly Hills, CA: Sage, 1979), 160-166.

12. The law also provided national party committees with the option of financing their national nominating convention with public funds. Major parties could receive the entire amount authorized by the spending limit established for nominating conventions ($2 million with adjustments for inflation); minor parties were eligible for lesser amounts based on their proportion of the vote in the previous presidential election. The base amount of the subsidy for major parties was increased to $4 million in 1984 under the provisions of Public Law 98-355.

13. The problems encountered in implementing the 1974 amendments are reviewed in Herbert E. Alexander, *Financing the 1976 Election* (Washington, DC: CQP, 1979), 11-38.

14. All of the campaigns, however, found the new law's reporting requirements burdensome, and the level of compliance varied to a considerable degree, particularly due to the lack of definitive and operable interpretations of the regulations available to candidates during the 1976 campaign. These problems are discussed in Alexander, *Financing the 1976 Election*, 208-215.

15. This need to begin raising funds early due to the contribution limit has been noted by, among others, Harvard Campaign Finance Study Group, *Financing Presidential Campaigns* (Cambridge, MA: Institute of Politics, Harvard University, 1982), 1-27 and 5-22; Herbert E. Alexander, *Financing the 1980 Election* (Lexington, MA: Lexington Books, 1983), 139-141; and Xandra Kayden, "Regulating Campaign Finance: Consequences for Interests and Institutions," in Alexander Heard and Michael Nelson, eds., *Presidential Selection* (Durham, NC: Duke University Press, 1987), 259.

16. For a discussion of the costs and lead times characteristic of direct mail fundraising, see R. Kenneth Godwin, *One Billion Dollars of Influence* (Chatham, NJ: Chatham House, 1988); and Larry J. Sabato, *The Rise of Political Consultants* (New York: Basic Books, 1981); 220-263.

17. Maxwell Glen, "Front-Loading the Race," *National Journal*, November 29, 1986, 2884; and Frank J. Sorauf, *Money in American Elections* (Glenview, IL: Scott, Foresman, 1988), 196.

18. See Austin Ranney, *The Federalization of Presidential Primaries* (Washington, DC: AEI, 1978); and Nelson W. Polsby, *Consequences of Party Reform* (New York: Oxford University Press, 1983), especially 55-64.

19. Figures for 1968 and 1980 based on Stephen J. Wayne, *The Road to the White House*, 3rd ed. (New York: St. Martin's Press, 1988), 12. Figures for 1988 based on Rhodes Cook, "The Nominating Process," in Michael Nelson, ed., *The Elections of 1988* (Washington, DC: CQP, 1989), 28.

20. Alexander, *Financing Politics*, 3rd ed., 17-18.

21. FEC, *Disclosure Series, Report No. 7: Presidential Campaign Receipts and Expenditures* (Washington, DC, May 1977) and *Reports on Financial Activity 1987-88, Final Report: Presidential Pre-Nomination Campaigns* (Washington, DC, August 1989).

22. For background, see David E. Price, *Bringing Back the Parties* (Washington, DC: CQP, 1984), 223-230.

23. For background on "Super Tuesday" and the creation of a southern regional primary, see, among others, James I. Lengle, "Democratic Party Reforms: The Past as Prologue to the 1988 Campaign," *Journal of Law and Politics* 4(1987), 261-272; Harold W. Stanley and Charles D. Hadley, "The Southern Presidential Primary: Regional Intentions with National Implications," *Publius* 17(Summer 1987), 83-100; and David S. Castle, "A Southern Regional Presidential Primary in 1988: Will It Work as Planned?" *Election Politics* 4(Summer 1987), 6-10.

24. Lengle, "Democratic Party Reforms," 264.

25. Gerald M. Pomper, *The Election of 1988* (Chatham, NJ: Chatham House, 1989), 42-43 and 62-63.

26. Based on the author's estimates from information contained in Rhodes Cook, *The First Hurrah: A 1992 Guide to the Nomination of the President, Congressional Quarterly Weekly Report Special Report*, September 7, 1991; and an unofficial calendar of the 1992 delegate selection process prepared by the Democratic National Committee.

27. Based on the summary of state filing deadlines in Rhodes Cook, *Race for the Presidency* (Washington, DC: CQP, 1987), 4.

28. Based on Thomas A. Devine, "Delegate Selection Calendar—Dukakis for President," Unpublished campaign memorandum, November 19, 1987, 2. The delegate selection activities noted in this paragraph are listed in the individual state delegate selection plans developed by state parties. For examples of state-by-state provisions, see Joseph B. Gorman, *The 1984 Democratic National Convention: National and State Party Rules and State Legislation Concerning the Election of Delegates and Alternates*, CRSR No. 84-25 GOV (Washington, DC: LC, February 14, 1984), and Americans for Democratic Action, *1984 Democratic Delegate Selection: An Overview* (Washington, DC: ADA, n.d.).

29. Susan B. King, "Living with the Act: The View from the Campaigns," in

Harvard Campaign Finance Study Group, *Financing Presidential Campaigns*, 5-22.

30. Alexander, *Financing Politics*, 3rd ed., 10-18; Sorauf, *Money in American Elections*, 342-343; and Garry R. Orren, "Presidential Campaign Finance: Its Impact and Future," *Commonsense* 4:2(1981), 54-55.

31. Robert E. DiClerico and Eric M. Uslaner, *Few Are Chosen: Problems in Presidential Selection* (New York: McGraw-Hill, 1984), 92.

32. Orren, "Presidential Campaign Finance," 56.

33. Alexander, *Financing the 1976 Election*, 308, 314, 322-323, and 328; Alexander, *Financing the 1980 Election*, 172-174; Alexander and Haggerty, *Financing the 1984 Election* (Lexington, MA: Lexington Books, 1987), 165; and Rita Beamish, "GOP Funds Trips as Bush Near Spending Cap," *Central Maine Morning Sentinel* (AP Release), July 4, 1988, 13.

34. In 1980, the overall spending limit was $14.7 million. The FEC audit of the Reagan for President Committee determined that the committee exceeded this amount by $77,387 (Alexander, *Financing the 1980 Election*, 174). In 1984, the overall limit was $20.2 million. The FEC audit of the Mondale for President Committee determined that the committee exceeded this amount by $578,904 (Alexander and Haggerty, *Financing the 1984 Election*, 165, and Rita Beamish, "Mondale Campaign Fined," *Central Maine Morning Sentinel* [AP Release], January 10, 1987, 13).

35. FEC, *Reports on Financial Activity 1979-80, Final Report: Presidential Pre-Nomination Campaigns* (Washington, DC, October 1981), 7-8; FEC, *Reports on Financial Activity 1983-84, Final Report: Presidential Pre-Nomination Campaigns* (Washington, DC, April 1986), 55; Alexander and Haggerty, *Financing the 1984 Election*, 165; and FEC, *Reports on Financial Activity 1987-88, Final Report: Presidential Pre-Nomination Campaigns* (Washington, DC, August 1989), Appendix 2.

36. A more detailed analysis of the data in Table 2.2 for 1976-1984 is provided in Anthony J. Corrado and L. Sandy Maisel, "Campaigning for Presidential Nominations: The Experience with State Spending Ceilings, 1976-84," Center for American Political Studies, Occasional Paper 88-4 (Cambridge, MA: Harvard University, 1988).

37. For background on the 1976 Wisconsin primary and its role in the campaign for the Democratic nomination, see Jules Witcover, *Marathon: The Pursuit of the Presidency 1972-1976* (New York: Viking, 1977), 274-288; and Elizabeth Drew, *American Journal: The Events of 1976* (New York: Random House, 1977), 137-153. For the 1980 Connecticut primary, see Charles O. Jones, "Nominating 'Carter's Favorite Opponent': The Republicans in 1980" in Austin Ranney, ed., *The American Elections of 1980* (Washington, DC: AEI, 1981), 81-87.

38. FEC, *Record* 15:5(May 1989).

Chapter 3

1. The role of the FECA and recent nomination process reforms in

inducing candidates or potential candidates to establish PACs or exploit other loopholes in the law has been observed by a number of scholars, campaign practitioners, and journalists. See, among others, Thomas M. Durbin, *Legal Analysis of Specialized Multicandidate PACs and Private Tax-Exempt Foundations of Potential Federal Office Candidates*, CRSR No. 86-844A (Washington, DC: LC, August 12, 1986); Gary R. Orren, "Presidential Campaign Finance: Its Impact and Future," *Commonsense* 4:2(1981), 50-66; Michael S. Berman, "Living With the FECA: Confessions of a Sometime Treasurer" and Fred Wertheimer, "Campaign Finance Reform: The Unfinished Agenda" in Lloyd N. Cutler, et al., eds., *Regulating Campaign Finance, The Annals of the American Academy of Political and Social Science* 486(July 1986); Maxwell Glenn, "Starting a PAC May Be Candidates' First Step Down Long Road to 1988," *National Journal,* February 16, 1985, 374-377; Bob Benenson, "In the Struggle for Influence, Members' PACs Gain Ground," *C Q W R*, August 2, 1986, 1751-1754; and Teresa Riordan, "Who's Campaigning?" *Common Cause Magazine* 13(May/June 1987), 14-17.

2. 2 U.S.C. 432(e) and 433(a); 11 C.F.R. 101.l(a) and (b), 102.1(b), and 102.13(a). See also FEC, *Candidate Registration* (Washington, DC: FEC, September 1985), 6. A presidential candidate authorizes a committee by filing an SC (FEC Form 2) or by filing a letter with the same information, that is, the individual's name and address, federal office sought, the name and address of his or her principal campaign committee, and the committee's campaign depository (FEC, *Candidate Registration,* 6).

3. 11 C.F.R. 100.3. Cf. 2 U.S.C. 431(2).

4. 11 C.F.R. 100.7(b)(1)(i) and 100.8(b)(1)(i).

5. In addition to the circumstances listed in the regulations cited in note 4, the law identifies a number of activities that indicate that an individual has decided to become a candidate and is no longer merely exploring this possibility. The testing-the-waters exemption does not apply if an individual (1) uses general public political advertising to publicize his or her intention to campaign for federal office; (2) raises funds in excess of what could reasonably be expected to be used for exploratory activities or amasses funds to be spent after becoming a candidate; (3) makes or authorizes statements that refer to him or her as a candidate for a particular office; (4) conducts activities in close proximity to an election or for a protracted period of time; and (5) takes action to qualify for the ballot. See 11 C.F.R. 100.7(b)(1)(ii) and 100.8(b)(1)(ii).

6. 11 C.F.R. 101.3.

7. 2 U.S.C. 432(e)(3); 11 C.F.R. 102.12(c) and 102.13(c).

8. The other types of political action committees defined in the FECA are political committees and separate segregated funds. See 2 U.S.C. 431. For the differences between and background of these legal entities, see Joseph E. Cantor, *Political Action Committees: Their Evolution, Growth and Implications for the Political System,* CRSR No. 84-78 (Washington, DC: LC, November 6, 1981; updated April 30, 1984), 1-6 and 19-54.

9. 2 U.S.C. 441a(a)(4); 11 C.F.R. 100.5(e)(3).

10. Berman, "Living With the FECA," 124.

11. 2 U.S.C. 431(1)(C) and (D); 11 C.F.R. 100.2(c).

12. The aggregate amount an individual may contribute to federal candidates or committees in any calendar year is limited to $25,000. Any contribution made to a campaign in a year other than that in which the election is held with respect to which the contribution is made, for the purposes of this limit, is included in the aggregate amount for the calendar year in which the election is held (2 U.S.C. 441a[a][3]).

13. For example, the authorized committees of the four nominees in the last two elections (Reagan, Mondale, Bush, and Dukakis) made only one contribution to a candidate or political committee. The Mondale for President Committee contributed $1,000 to Congressman Frank Guarini of New Jersey. See FEC, *Committee Index of Candidates Supported/Opposed* (D Index), 1983-1984 and 1987-1988, computer printout, November 22, 1988.

14. Durbin, *Legal Analysis of Specialized Multicandidate PACs*, 6.

15. Ibid. Here Durbin also notes that an authorized candidate committee can make contributions of up to $20,000 to a national party committee whereas a multicandidate PAC can contribute a maximum of only $15,000. Again, this represents a statutory advantage without practical consequence. As with contributions to other federal candidates or political committees, a contribution of this sort would reduce the resources available to the candidate for his or her election. It is not the type of action likely to be taken by an active candidate in a primary campaign.

16. Herbert E. Alexander, *Financing the 1980 Election* (Lexington, MA: Lexington Books, 1983), 193.

17. Candidates also seek to achieve this end by exploiting technical statutory provisions that allow them to allocate costs to exempted activities or, in the case of state spending limits, to other states or the national headquarters. See, among others, Berman, "Living With the FECA," 128; Herbert E. Alexander, "Election Reform In Its Second Stage: Momentum Passing from Reformers to Powerbrokers," in Herbert E. Alexander, ed., *Political Finance* (Beverly Hills, CA: Sage, 1979), 94-95; "Take It to the Limit— and Beyond," *Time*, February 15, 1988, 19-20; and Charles R. Babcock, "Stretching the Limit in Iowa," *Washington Post*, January 25, 1988, A4.

18. For the statutory provisions and regulations for campaign depositories, see 2 U.S.C. 432(h) and 434: 11 C.F.R. 103 and 104. See also 11 C.F.R. 101.1(a) and 102.2(a)(1)(vi).

19. Riordan, "Who's Campaigning?" 14.

20. An overview of state campaign finance legislation is provided in James A. Palmer and Edward D. Feigenbaum, *Campaign Finance Law 86: A Summary of State Campaign Finance Laws* (Washington, DC: National Clearinghouse on Election Administration, 1986), and Sandra K. Schneider, ed., *Campaign Finance, Ethics and Lobby Law Blue Book 1986-87* (Lexington, KY: Council of State Governments, 1986). See also Frank J. Sorauf, *Money in American Elections* (Glenview, IL: Scott, Foresman, 1988), 284-290; and Herbert E. Alexander, *Financing Politics*, 3rd ed. (Washington, DC: CQP, 1984), 163-184.

21. These data are based on the summaries of state campaign finance legislation in Palmer and Feigenbaum, *Campaign Finance Law 86*. Their

compilation reflects the major provisions of state laws in effect through December 31, 1985.

22. 2 U.S.C. 441b; 11 C.F.R. 114.

23. Sorauf, *Money in American Elections*, 287.

24. This analysis is based on the summaries of state contribution and solicitation limitations (Chart 2-A) in Palmer and Feigenbaum, *Campaign Finance Law 86*. In a similar analysis, Sorauf adds Indiana and Washington to the list of states with no contribution limits and no prohibition against contributions by corporations, unions, or regulated industries (Sorauf, *Money in American Elections*, 288). But according to Palmer and Feigenbaum, Indiana and Washington limit corporate and union contributions. In Indiana, contributions from these sources are limited to an aggregate of $5,000 for statewide candidates; $5,000 for state party central committee members; and $2,000 for other offices. In Washington, the law is less stringent. The one restriction is that corporations and labor unions are not allowed to make aggregate contributions of more than $5,000 to candidates or political committees within 21 days of a general election.

25. State campaign finance report filing requirements are summarized in Palmer and Feigenbaum, *Campaign Finance Law 86*, Chart 1.

26. Sorauf, *Money in American Elections*, 288.

27. Riordan, "Who's Campaigning?" 14.

28. 11 C.F.R 100.7(b)(1), 100.8(b)(1), and 101.3. For an explanation of these regulations, see Durbin, *Legal Analysis of Specialized Multicandidate PACs*, 9-20; FEC, *Record* 7:7(July 1981), 4-5; Ibid. 10:3(March 1984), 3-4; Ibid. 11:4(April 1985), 3-4. An individual is not required to establish an exploratory committee to conduct testing-the-waters activities. But this is the standard approach employed by potential candidates due to the practical problems of undertaking such activities without assistance.

29. FEC, AO 1979-26: Effect of Committee to Determine Candidacy, June 18, 1979, reported in *FECFG, Volume II: New Developments* (Chicago, IL: Commerce Clearinghouse, Inc., 1981), para. 5408. The *FECFG* is a looseleaf reference publication on federal campaign finance law that is regularly updated. All *FECFG* references contained herein are to the second volume.

30. FEC, AO 1981-32: Allowable Activities in Testing the Waters [*sic*], October 2, 1981, *FECFG* (1981), para. 5620. See also AO 1982-3: Permissible Activities in Testing the Water, March 15, 1982, *FECFG* (1982), para. 5647.

31. 11 C.F.R. 100.7(b)(1)(i).

32. 11 C.F.R. 100.8(b)(1)(i).

33. FEC, AO 1981-32, *FECFG* (1981), para. 5620; AO 1982-19: Treatment of Contributions to Testing-the-Waters Committee, May 6, 1982, *FECFG* (1982), para. 5669; and AO 1983-9: Pre-Campaign Loan in Excess of $50,000, May 3, 1983, *FECFG* (1983), para. 5714.

34. See Dissenting Opinion of Commissioner Thomas E. Harris to AO 1982-19, *FECFG* (1982), para. 5669, and the commission's decision in AO 1983-9.

35. 11 C.F.R. 101.3 (1982) and AO 1982-19.

36. FEC, *Annual Report 1985* (Washington, DC: FEC, June 1, 1986), 9; and FEC, *Record* 11:4(April 1985), 3-4. The regulations were published in the

Federal Register on March 13, 1985 (*Federal Register* 50[March 13, 1985], 9992-4) and became effective on July 1, 1985 (*Federal Register* 50 [July 1, 1985], 25698-9).

37. FEC, *Record* 11:7(July 1985), 4.
38. 11 C.F.R. 101.3.
39. 11 C.F.R. 100.7(b)(1)(i) and 100.8(b)(1)(i).
40. This description is based on the discussion of the advisory opinion procedure contained in FEC, *Advisory Opinions* (Washington, DC: FEC, October 1982). The procedure is codified at 2 U.S.C. 437f and 11 C.F.R. 112.
41. Letter from Donald M. Middlebrooks to Charles N. Steele, July 31, 1981, FEC, AOR 1981-32.
42. Ibid., 2-3.
43. FEC, AO 1981-32, passim, and FEC, "Advisory Opinions: Summaries," *Record* 7:11(November 1981), 1.
44. FEC, AO 1981-32. See also 11 C.F.R. 100.7(b)(1)(ii) and 100.8(b)(1)(ii).
45. Letter from Allyn O. Kreps to John Warren McGarry, January 20, 1982, FEC, AOR 1982-3. The full name of the advisory committee was the Committee to Advise Senator Alan Cranston on the Desirability and Feasibility of Seeking the Democratic Nomination in 1984 for the Office of President of the United States.
46. Ibid., 2.
47. Ibid. 3-4.
48. Ibid., 3.
49. FEC, AO 1982-3, *FECFG* (1982), para. 5647.
50. 11 C.F.R. 100.7(b)(1)(ii).
51. 11 C.F.R. 100.8(b)(1)(ii).
52. Dissenting Opinion of Commissioner Thomas E. Harris, AO 1982-3, March 11, 1982, *FECFG* (1982), para. 5647.
53. Ibid.
54. FEC, AO 1985-40: Acceptable Activities in Testing the Waters Discussed, January 24, 1986, *FECFG* (1986), para. 5842. A summary of this opinion is provided in Durbin, *Legal Analysis of Specialized Multicandidate PACs*, 12-15; and FEC, "Advisory Opinions," *Record* 12:3(March 1986), 2-4.
55. FEC, AO 1985-40, *FECFG* (1986), para. 5842.
56. Letter from James M. Cannon to the Office of the General Counsel, FEC, November 25, 1985, FEC, AOR 1985-40.
57. Ibid., 2-6; and Durbin, *Legal Analysis of Specialized Multicandidate PACs*, 14.
58. FEC, AO 1985-40, *FECFG* (1986), para. 5842.
59. Ibid.
60. Ibid.
61. Ibid.; and FEC, *Record* 12:3(March 1986), 4. The requirements for determining whether an event qualifies as a party-building activity are codified at 11 C.F.R. 110.8(e).
62. FEC, *Record* 12:3(March 1986), 4.
63. FEC, AOR 1985-40, 3.
64. FEC, AO 1985-40, *FECFG* (1986), para. 5842.

65. FEC, AOR 1985-40, 4.
66. FEC, *Record* 12:3(March 1986), 3.
67. Dissenting Opinion of Commissioner Thomas E. Harris, Re: AO 1985-40, January 28, 1986, *FECFG* (1986), para. 5842.
68. 11 C.F.R. 100.7(b)(16) and 100.8(b)(17).
69. For example, in his dissenting opinion to AO 1985-40, Commissioner Harris cites the FEC's interpretation of the so-called "coattail exemption" to the definition of "contribution" in the FECA, which pertains to campaign materials of a candidate seeking any public office that refer to someone else who is a candidate for federal office. This exemption is codified at 2 U.S.C. 431(8)(B)(xi). Harris states that in interpreting this provision the FEC equates direct mail with general public communications or political advertising (Dissenting Opinion, Re: AO 1985-40, *FECFG* [1986], para. 5842). He also cites the legislative history of the 1979 amendments which supports this understanding of the law.
70. FEC, AO 1986-6: Expenditures by Committee Organized by a Potential Candidate, March 14, 1986, *FECFG* (1986), para. 5849. A summary of this opinion is provided in Durbin, *Legal Analysis of Specialized Multicandidate PACs*, 15-20; and FEC, *Record* 12: 5(May 1986), 2-3.
71. Letter from Jan W. Baran to Joan D. Aikens, January 22, 1986, FEC, AOR 1986-6, 1.
72. FEC, AO 1986-6, *FECFG* (1986), para. 5849.
73. FEC, AOR 1986-6, 1.
74. FEC, AO 1986-6, *FECFG* (1986), para. 5849.
75. Ibid.
76. The discussion of allowable expenditures and activities that follows is based on the FEC's opinion in AO 1986-6 and the summary provided in FEC, *Record* 12:5(May 1986), 2-3.
77. Thomas Harris, Dissenting Opinion in AO 1986-6.
78. Ibid.
79. Charles N. Steele and N. Bradley Litchfield, DAO 1986-6, February 28, 1986, 19-24. A copy of this document is available from the FEC.
80. Ibid., 24.
81. Dissenting Opinion, Vice Chairman John Warren McGarry, AO 1986-6.
82. FEC, AO 1986-6, *FECFG* (1986), para. 5849.
83. See, among others, Brooks Jackson, *Broken Promise: Why the Federal Election Commission Failed* (New York: Priority Press, 1990); William C. Oldacker, "Of Philosophers, Foxes, and Finances: Can the Federal Election Commission Ever Do an Adequate Job?" *The Annals* 486(July 1986), 132-145; and Colleen O'Connor, "Who's Afraid of the FEC?" *Washington Monthly* 18(March 1986), 22-26.

Chapter 4

1. Herbert Alexander describes the uncertainties and difficulties that

accompanied implementation of the FECA in *Financing the 1976 Election* (Washington, DC: CQP, 1979), 21-38.

2. "Reaganites to Back G.O.P. Conservatives," *New York Times*, February 1, 1977, A12; and Adam Clymer, "New Asset of Reagan: Control of $1 Million," *New York Times*, August 25, 1977, B5. Alexander notes that an FEC audit of Citizens for Reagan determined that the committee had $1,616,461 in surplus funds at the end of the 1976 campaign. Of this amount, $580,857 represented matching funds that the committee was required to repay to the U.S. Treasury. These funds were repaid in November 1977 when the committee returned a total of $611,142 to the Treasury (Herbert E. Alexander, *Financing the 1980 Election* [Lexington, MA: Lexington Books, 1983], 146; and Citizens for the Republic, Year-End Report of Receipts and Expenditures, Schedule B, 44; FEC Microfilm, Series 1978, Roll 65 at 5544).

3. "Reaganites to Back G.O.P. Conservatives," A12; and SO for Citizens for the Republic, FEC Microfilm, Series 1977, Roll 46 at 4034. Reagan resigned from the chairmanship when he became a candidate for the office of president (Maxwell Glen, "Starting a PAC May Be Candidates' First Step Down Long Road to 1988," *National Journal*, February 16, 1985, 376).

4. The ten major presidential candidates in the 1980 presidential nomination campaign were Jimmy Carter, Edmund "Jerry" Brown, and Edward Kennedy, for the Democrats; and John Anderson, Howard Baker, George Bush, John Connally, Philip Crane, Robert Dole, and Ronald Reagan, for the Republicans.

5. Alexander, *Financing the 1980 Election*, 217-218.

6. In AO 1975-72, the FEC ruled that an incumbent president may attend party-building functions without triggering the contribution and expenditure limitations of the FECA, so long as these appearances occur prior to January 1 of the election year. This exemption applies even if the president qualifies as a candidate under the law. Any such travel after January 1 of the election year is considered to be candidate-related and is subject to the relevant portions of the act. See FEC, AO No. 1975-72: Application of Contribution and Spending Limits to Presidential Candidate's Travel for Party Purposes, November 26, 1975, *FECFG* (1976), para. 5152. This exemption is now codified at 11 C.F.R. 110.8(e).

7. Alexander, *Financing the 1980 Election*, 218-220.

8. Kennedy authorized the formation of a principal campaign committee on October 26, 1979, by approving an SO (FEC Form 1) and signing an SC (FEC Form 2). These documents were filed with the FEC on October 29, 1979 (FEC Microfilm, Series 1979, Roll 103 at 237).

9. Alexander, *Financing the 1980 Election*, 143.

10. FEC, AO No. 1979-40: Financial Activities of Unauthorized Committees, in FEC, *Record* 5:10(October 1979), 3.

11. The data in this paragraph on the financial activities of the Kennedy draft committees are based on the summary in Alexander, *Financing the 1980 Election*, 145.

12. The nine major candidates in the 1984 presidential nomination campaign were Reubin Askew, Alan Cranston, John Glenn, Gary Hart, Ernest

Hollings, Jesse Jackson, George McGovern, and Walter Mondale, for the Democrats; and Ronald Reagan for the Republicans.

13. Herbert E. Alexander and Brian A. Haggerty, *Financing the 1984 Election* (Lexington, MA: Lexington Books, 1987), 176-177. See also Walter Schapiro with Howard Fineman, "Reagan's Shadow Campaign," *Newsweek*, August 1, 1983, 26.

14. This description of the transfer is based on the account in Alexander and Haggerty, *Financing the 1984 Election*, 176. See also "Reagan's 1980 Campaign Fund Is History," *PACs and Lobbies*, September 18, 1985, 6-7. The regulation concerning transfers between affiliated committees is found at 11 C.F.R. 102.6(a).

15. SO for the Fund for a Democratic Majority, FEC Microfilm, Series 1981, Roll 191 at 3647.

16. Robert Shrum cited in Adam Clymer, "Mondale and Kennedy Forming Democratic Fund-Raising Units," *New York Times*, February 13, 1981, A16.

17. Clymer, "Mondale and Kennedy," A16.

18. FEC, Committee Index of Disclosure Documents (C Index) for the Fund for a Democratic Majority, 1981-1982, computer printout, n.d.; and Bill Peterson, "Kennedy, Citing Family, Rules Out Campaign for '84," *Washington Post*, December 2, 1982, A1.

19. See FEC, AO No. 1981-32, *FECFG* (1981), para. 5620.

20. On this date Askew filed an amended SO (FEC Form 1) with the FEC changing the name of the Reubin Askew Exploratory Committee to the Askew for President Committee (FEC Microfilm, Series 1983, Roll 215 at 3809).

21. Alexander and Haggerty, *Financing the 1984 Election*, 231. See also Ronald W. Walters, *Black Presidential Politics in America: A Strategic Approach* (Albany, NY: State University of New York Press, 1988), 162-164.

22. The fourteen major candidates in the 1988 presidential nomination campaign were Bruce Babbitt, Joseph Biden, Michael Dukakis, Richard Gephardt, Albert Gore, Gary Hart, Jesse Jackson, and Paul Simon, for the Democrats; and George Bush, Robert Dole, Pierre "Pete" du Pont IV, Alexander Haig, Jack Kemp, and Marion "Pat" Robertson, for the Republicans.

23. SO for the Committee for Economic Strength, FEC Microfilm, Series 1976, Roll 9 at 723; and FEC, Committee Index of Disclosure Documents (C Index), 1977-1978, computer printout, n.d. The committee began to call itself the Campaign for Prosperity on October 14, 1982 (Letter from J. Curtis Herge to the FEC, October 21, 1982, FEC Microfilm, Series 1982, Roll 251 at 1387).

24. Totals based on the amounts reported by the committee and disclosed in the FEC's Committee Index of Disclosure Documents (C Index), 1976-1984, computer printouts, n.d.

25. Glen, "Starting a PAC May Be Candidates' First Step Down Long Road to 1988," 374.

26. Ronald Brownstein, "Counting Down to 1988," *National Journal*, December 7, 1985, 2803.

27. Ibid.

28. Paul Taylor, "Hey, Didn't We Just Finish a Presidential Election Campaign?" *Washington Post National Weekly Edition*, October 28, 1985, 11.

29. Herbert E. Alexander, *"Soft Money" and Campaign Financing* (Washington, DC: Public Affairs Council, 1986), 81. See also "GOPAC Bares Financial Data," *PACs and Lobbies*, October 16, 1985, 5.

30. Alexander, *"Soft Money" and Campaign Financing*, 81.

31. Brownstein, "Counting Down to 1988," 2803.

32. Baker withdrew from the 1980 Republican nomination contest on March 5 (Alexander, *Financing the 1980 Election*, 199). On March 6, an SO was filed with the FEC for the Republican Majority Fund (FEC Microfilm, Series 1980, Roll 149 at 5437).

33. Irvin Molotsky, "Reagan's Request Came as Baker Was on Verge of Presidential Bid," *New York Times*, February 28, 1987, A1.

34. See SO for Citizens for American Values PAC, FEC Microfilm, Series 1985, Roll 393 at 1197; and Phil Gailey, "Laxalt Explores Presidential Bid as Rumsfeld Decides Not to Run," *New York Times*, April 3, 1987, 15. Financial totals based on the amounts reported by the committee and disclosed in the FEC's Committee Index of Disclosure Documents (C Index), 1985-1986; and 1987, computer printouts, n.d.

35. Glen, "Starting a PAC May Be Candidates' First Step," 376.

36. Maxwell Glen, "Kennedy's Early Departure From Race Frees Up Donations for Rest of Field," *National Journal*, January 25, 1986, 208.

37. Ibid.; and "When 'Not Running' Becomes a High Art," *Boston Sunday Globe*, April 12, 1987, 14.

38. Totals based on amounts reported by the committee and disclosed in the FEC's Committee Index of Disclosure Documents (C Index), 1985, computer printout, n.d.

39. Frank Lynn, "Cuomo Forms Action Committee to Pay for His National Agenda," *New York Times*, April 15, 1987.

40. Ibid.; SO for the Empire Leadership Fund, FEC Microfilm, Series 1987, Roll 466 at 2640; Jeffrey Schmalz, "Cuomo Cites Factors in Decision: Family, Job, and a Grueling Race," *New York Times*, February 21, 1987, A1; and Rhodes Cook, "Cuomo's Pullout May Boost Dark Horse Candidates," *CQWR*, February 21, 1987, 332.

41. Total based on the amounts reported by the committee and disclosed in the FEC's Committee Index of Disclosure Documents (C Index), 1987, computer printout, n.d.

42. Bryan Abas, "Hart Has a Better Idea," *Westword*, November 13-19, 1985, 10.

43. This summary of the Center for New Democracy's activities and finances is based on Abas, "Hart Has a Better Idea," 8-10; Ronald Brownstein, "The Lessons of 1984," *National Journal*, July 20, 1985, 1670; and Thomas B. Edsall, "'88 Candidates' New Tricks Stretch Federal Election Law," *Washington Post*, October 20, 1985, A18.

44. Edsall, "'88 Candidates' New Tricks," A18. For example, in 1985 a nonprofit foundation could post a letter at a rate of 6 cents apiece; the cheapest rate a PAC could achieve was 12.5 cents apiece.

45. Michael S. Berman, "Living With the FECA: Confessions of a Sometime Campaign Treasurer," in Lloyd N. Cutler, et al., eds., *Regulating Campaign*

Finance, The Annals of the American Academy of Political and Social Science 486(July 1986), 124. For a summary of the legal background for these foundations, see Thomas M. Durbin, *Legal Analysis of Specialized Multicandidate PACs and Private Tax-Exempt Foundations of Potential Federal Office Candidates,* CRSR No. 86-844A (Washington, DC: LC, August 12, 1986), 20-28; and Perkins Coie, *Non-Profit Organizations, Public Policy, and the Political Process: A Guide to the Internal Revenue Code and Federal Election Campaign Act* (Washington, DC: Citizens Vote, December 1987), 3-40.

46. Edsall, "'88 Candidates' New Tricks Stretch Federal Election Law," A1 and A18; Jean Cobb, "We're Not Campaigning Either!" *Common Cause Magazine* 13(May/June 1987), 16-19; Ronald Brownstein and Maxwell Glen, "Money in the Shadows," *National Journal,* March 15, 1986, 632-637; Maxwell Glen, "Invading Michigan," *National Journal,* May 24, 1986, 1248-1253; and Richard E. Cohen and Carol Matlack, "All-Purpose Loophole," *National Journal,* December 9, 1989, 2980-2987.

47. Center for Responsive Politics, *Public Policy and Foundations: The Role of Politicians in Public Charities* (Washington, DC: CRP, 1987).

48. Ibid. Totals based on the amounts reported for each organization in Appendix 2.

49. Edsall, "'88 Candidates' New Tricks Stretch Federal Election Law," A18; and Glen, "Invading Michigan," 1251. For further discussion of the Fund for an American Renaissance, see Cobb, "We're Not Campaigning Either!" 17-18.

50. Glen, "Invading Michigan," 1251.

51. Ibid.

52. Edsall, "'88 Candidates' New Tricks Stretch Federal Election Law," A18.

53. Brownstein and Glen, "Money in the Shadows," 637; and Cobb, "We're Not Campaigning Either!" 17-18.

54. Statement by Jackson quoted in E. R. Shipp, "Jackson to Put Energies into Political Coalition," *New York Times,* November 10, 1984, 9.

55. Shipp, "Jackson to Put Energies into Political Coalition," 9. See also Sheila D. Collins, *The Rainbow Challenge* (New York: Monthly Review Press, 1986), 306-309; and Tom Sherwood, "Vast Network Keeps Jackson's Hopes Alive," *Washington Post,* October 29, 1989, D11.

56. Collins, *The Rainbow Challenge,* 307.

57. For background on the April 1986 convention, see Paul Taylor, "'88 'Underdog' Jackson Sharpens Political Bite," *Washington Post,* April 16, 1986, A3; and Paul Taylor, "Jackson Declares a 'New Majority,'" *Washington Post,* April 18, 1986, A12. See also Phil Gailey, "Jackson Leads 3 Day Assault on Party's Direction," *New York Times,* April 20, 1986, 31; Rhodes Cook, "Jackson, Democrats: Marriage on the Rocks?," *CQWR,* April 26, 1986, 929-930; and Collins, *The Rainbow Challenge,* 325-329. For the May 1986 convention, see Jacob Weisberg, "Rainbow Warrior," *New Republic,* May 12, 1986, 10-12.

58. Quoted in David S. Broder, "Can Democrats Live With Jesse Jackson . . .," *Washington Post,* April 23, 1986, A23.

59. Cook, "Jackson, Democrats," 930.

60. Sherwood, "Vast Network Keeps Jackson's Hopes Alive," D11.

61. Andrew Kopkind, "The 'New Voters' Find Their Voice," *The Nation*, November 7, 1987, 521.

62. "Jackson Tests Waters with Office in Iowa," *Boston Globe*, March 20, 1987, 4; and James A. Barnes, "Looking for Credibility," *National Journal*, April 25, 1987, 986-987.

63. Wayne King, "Hatcher to Head Study on Jackson Candidacy," *New York Times*, June 6, 1987, 8.

64. Letter from Daniel A. Taylor to the FEC, April 13, 1987, FEC, AOR No. 1987-16, 1.

65. Ibid., 2. The regulations governing transfers between a candidate's previous and current campaign committees are codified at 11 C.F.R. 110.3(a)(2). See also FEC AOs Nos. 1982-52 and 1980-117.

66. Brian Sullam, "The Cash Campaign," *New Republic*, March 14, 1988, 9-10.

67. See U.S. Congress, House Committee on Ways and Means, *Lobbying and Political Activities of Tax-Exempt Organizations: Hearings Before the Subcommittee on Oversight*, H. Rpt. 100-15, 100th Cong., 1st sess., March 12 and 13, 1987.

68. The committee reported no receipts or expenditures in either 1976 or 1977. Financial activity began in 1978.

69. Kemp's PAC raised $389,666 from 1978 to 1982 and $5,418,724 from 1983 to 1986 (FEC, Committee Index of Disclosure Documents for the Campaign for Prosperity [C Index], 1978-1986, computer printouts, n.d.).

70. The Fund for a Limited Government terminated its operations after filing its April 1979 quarterly financial report (FEC, Committee Index of Disclosure Documents [C Index], 1979, computer printout, n.d.). Bush filed an SO for the Bush for President Committee, his principal campaign committee, on January 5, 1979, and publicly announced his candidacy on May 1, 1979 (FEC Microfilm, Series 1979, Roll 101 at 3; and Alexander, *Financing the 1980 Election*, 175).

71. The John Connally Citizens Forum terminated its operations after filing its July 1979 quarterly financial report (FEC, Committee Index of Disclosure Documents [C Index], 1979, computer printout, n.d.). On January 24, 1979, Connally filed an SO for the Connally for President Committee and declared his candidacy (FEC Microfilm, Series 1979, Roll 101 at 150; and Alexander, *Financing the 1980 Election*, 192).

72. FEC, Committee Index of Disclosure Documents (C Index), 1979-1980, computer printout, n.d.

73. The Committee for a Democratic Consensus terminated its operations after filing its 1983 midyear financial report (FEC, Committee Index of Disclosure Documents [C Index], 1983, computer printout, n.d.). Cranston publicly declared his candidacy on February 2, 1983 (Alexander and Haggerty, *Financing the 1984 Election*, 250).

74. FEC, Committee Index of Disclosure Documents (C Index), 1984-1986, computer printouts, n.d.

75. Totals based on amounts reported by each committee and disclosed in

the FEC's Committee Index of Disclosure Documents (C Index), 1985-1986, computer printouts, n.d.

76. Americans for the National Interest terminated its operations as of December 23, 1986 (FEC Microfilm, Series 1987, Roll 452 at 5283). On January 7, 1987, Babbitt filed an SO for the Babbitt for President Committee (FEC Microfilm, Series 1987, Roll 425 at 2622).

77. The Fund for '86 terminated its operations at the end of February 1987 (Fund for '86, Termination Report, FEC Microfilm, Series 1987, Roll 461 at 5182). On March 3, 1987, Biden filed an SO for the Biden for President Committee (FEC Microfilm, Series 1987, Roll 425 at 3360).

78. FEC, Committee Index of Disclosure Documents (C Index), 1987-1988, computer printout, n.d.

79. Ibid.

80. See note 2.

81. Totals based on the amounts reported by the committees and disclosed in the FEC's Committee Index of Disclosure Documents (C Index), 1985-1987, computer printouts, n.d.

82. These figures are based on an analysis of quarterly receipts by candidate-sponsored PACs as disclosed in the FEC's Committee Index of Disclosure Documents (C Index), 1977; 1981; and 1985, computer printouts, n.d.

83. See the summary of public opinion polls in "Opinion Roundup," *Public Opinion* 10:3(September/October 1987), 38-39.

84. Campaign America raised $33,422 more than it spent in 1981-1982 and $417,799 more than it spent in 1983-1984, according to the FEC's Committee Index of Disclosure Documents (C Index) for these years.

85. This discussion of the precandidacy PACs associated with presidential aspirants does not include Independent Action, a PAC that is sometimes associated with Senator Tom Harkin (see, for example, Michael L. Goldstein, *Guide to the 1992 Presidential Election* [Washington, DC: CQP, 1991], Table 2.5; and Ross K. Baker, *The New Fat Cats: Members of Congress as Political Benefactors* [New York: Priority Press, 1989], Table 2). This PAC is not included because it was not established as a personal PAC designed to promote Harkin's presidential aspirations nor is this its primary function. Independent Action was established in 1981 by Congressman Morris Udall and a number of other liberal Democrats to raise money to elect liberal Democrats to Congress; it was not established as a leadership PAC or precandidacy PAC for Tom Harkin (see Edward P. Zuckerman, *Almanac of Federal PACs: 1990* [Washington, DC: Amward, 1990], 584-585). Although Harkin is sometimes listed as one of the principal members of the PAC, his name does not appear on the committee's initial SO or subsequent amendments (see FEC Microfilm, Series 1981, Roll 187 at 5254; Roll 192 at 2470; and Roll 197 at 1847). Moreover, it appears that Harkin did not rely on the PAC as a vehicle for conducting political activities prior to becoming a candidate for the presidency. He also did not initiate his presidential campaign by purchasing or renting lists or equipment from the PAC, which is a common practice of candidates with personal PACs (see FEC, Americans for Harkin, Quarterly Financial Report, October 15, 1991, Schedule B-P).

86. FEC, Committee Index of Disclosure Documents (C Index), 1989-1990, computer printouts, n.d.; and Fund for America's Future, Termination Report, June 4, 1990, Schedule B.

87. *New York Times*, January 30, 1991, A13.

88. Bernard Weintraub, "Jackson Says His PAC Will Have a Wide Impact," *New York Times*, June 21, 1988, A20.

89. Ibid.

90. Tom Sherwood, "PUSHing and Rainbowing and Keeping Hope Alive," *The Washington Post National Weekly Edition*, November 6-12, 1989, 14.

91. Totals based on the amounts reported by the committee and disclosed in the FEC's Committee Index of Disclosure Documents (C Index), 1988-1990, computer printout, n.d.

92. Sherwood, "PUSHing and Rainbowing," 14; and FEC, Committee Index of Candidates Supported/Opposed (D Index), 1989-1990, computer printout, n.d.

93. Sherwood, "PUSHing and Rainbowing," 14.

94. Ibid.

95. David Yepsen, "Iowa Rainbow Forms," *Des Moines Register*, February 26, 1989, 4B.

96. Totals based on the amounts reported and disclosed in the FEC's Committee Index of Disclosure Documents (C Index), 1989-1990, computer printout, n.d.

97. FEC, Committee Index of Candidates Supported/Opposed (D Index), 1989-1990, computer printout, n.d.

98. For the financial activity of the Empire Leadership Fund, see FEC, Committee Index of Disclosure Documents (C Index), 1989-1990, computer printouts, n.d.; and Empire Leadership Fund, Quarterly Financial Report, October 15, 1990, Schedule B, 1. The committee terminated its operations on August 23, 1990. See Letter from Chester Straub, Treasurer, to Donald Averett, FEC, August 23, 1990. A copy of this letter is on file at the FEC.

99. See Frank Lynn, "In a Party Split, Kemp Endorses Conservative's Bid for Governor," *New York Times*, October 6, 1990, 27; "Mr. Cuomo's Fund-Raising Overkill," *New York Times*, November 3, 1990, 24; and Adam Pertman, "Democrats in '92 Field Already Feel a Cuomo Chill," *Boston Globe*, October 24, 1991, 11.

100. FEC, *Record* 17:8(August 1991), 6. In 1988 Schroeder's presidential exploratory committee changed its status to a self-described "organization associated with a public official and certain views on public policy, but no longer with a candidate for any federal office." This "organization," now named the Fund for the Future, incorporated under Colorado state law for liability purposes and filed a 1989 federal tax return as a "political organization." This committee did not qualify as a PAC under federal law, but it did continue to file disclosure reports with the FEC. See FEC, AO 1991-12: Transfer of Funds from Issue Committee to Campaign Committee, June 14, 1991, *FECFG* (1991), para. 6020.

101. Totals based on the amounts reported and disclosed in the FEC,

Committee Index of Disclosure Documents (C Index), 1988-1990, computer printout, n.d.

102. John Aloysius Farrell, "In N.H., Presidential Hopefuls Always Seem to Be in Season," *Boston Globe,* May 21, 1989, 12.

103. See FEC, AO 1991-12.

104. For a summary of the financial activities of this group, see Center for Responsive Politics, *Public Policy and Foundations,* 96-98.

105. Paul Taylor, "The 1992 Campaign is Already Off to a Late Start," *The Washington Post National Weekly Edition,* April 9-15, 1990, 13.

106. George C. Edwards III, "George Bush and the Public Presidency: The Politics of Inclusion," in Colin Campbell and Bert A. Rockman, eds., *The Bush Presidency: First Appraisals* (Chatham, NJ: Chatham House, 1991), 131-132.

107. Ibid., 131.

108. See Paul Taylor, "Democrats, Start Your Engines," *The Washington Post National Weekly Edition,* November 5-11, 1990, 12; Michael Oreskes, "Few Approach Starting Gates for 1992 Presidential Stakes," *New York Times,* August 13, 1990, 1; and David Yepsen, "Gulf Crisis Slows Start of 1992 Campaigns," *Des Moines Register,* November 29, 1990, 1.

109. Edwards, "George Bush and the Public Presidency," 132.

110. 2 U.S.C. 432(e)(3); 11 C.F.R. 102.12(c) and 102.13(c).

Chapter 5

1. The Committee for America registered with the FEC on April 2, 1986, and essentially completed its active solicitation of funds in December 1987. The committee received only $10,600 from December 1987 to October 1988 (FEC, Committee Index of Disclosure Documents [C Index], 1987-88, computer printouts, n.d.).

2. Thomas B. Edsall, "'88 Candidates' New Tricks Stretch Federal Election Law," *Washington Post,* October 20, 1985, A18.

3. Center for Responsive Politics, *Soft Money—A Loophole for the '80s* (Washington, DC: CRP, 1985), 3. The term "soft money" is used in contrast to "hard money," which denotes funds raised, spent, and publicly disclosed in accordance with federal requirements and procedures. The point at which this term entered the political lexicon cannot be precisely determined. For an early use, see Elizabeth Drew, "Politics and Money II," *The New Yorker,* December 13, 1982, 57-111.

4. Herbert E. Alexander, *"Soft Money" and Campaign Financing* (Washington, DC: Public Affairs Council, 1986), 5. For a similar definition, see John F. Noble, "Soft Money," *Campaigns and Elections,* Summer 1984, 44. Common Cause advances a more restrictive definition in FEC, Petition for Rulemaking Filed By Common Cause, November 7, 1984, 1.

5. The following paragraphs are largely based on the regulatory background provided in Alexander, *"Soft Money" and Campaign Financing,* 12-13. See also Elizabeth Drew, *Politics and Money: The New Road to Corruption* (New York: Macmillan, 1983), 14-19.

6. 11 C.F.R. 102.5(a)(1).

7. 11 C.F.R. 106.1(e).

8. Brooks Jackson, *Broken Promise: Why the Federal Election Commission Failed* (New York: Priority Press, 1990), 42-45. See also FEC, AO 1978-10.

9. For the specific activities exempted by the 1979 law, see 11 C.F.R. 100.7(b)(9), 100.7 (b)(15), and 100.7 (b)(17).

10. For a discussion of the use of soft money in the 1980 and 1984 presidential general election campaigns, see Alexander, *"Soft Money" and Campaign Financing*, 14-29. For the 1988 election, see Brooks Jackson, "Democrats, Outflanked in Previous Elections, Rival GOP in Financing of Presidential Race," *Wall Street Journal*, October 3, 1988, A24; Carol Matlack, "Backdoor Spending," *National Journal*, October 8, 1988, 2516-2519; and Center for Responsive Politics, *Soft Money '88* (Washington, DC: CRP, 1989).

11. Alexander, *"Soft Money" and Campaign Financing*, 46. See also Ed Zuckerman, "Opinion Opened 'Soft Money' Spigot for PACs," *PACs and Lobbies*, June 9, 1985, 1-4.

12. Corporations have been prohibited from making contributions to federal election campaigns since the adoption of the Tillman Act in 1907. Labor union contributions to federal candidates were first prohibited by the Smith-Connally Act of 1943. This ban was made permanent by the Taft-Hartley Act of 1947.

13. The difficulties encountered in estimating soft money receipts and expenditures and the laxity of state disclosure laws are noted by Alexander, *"Soft Money" and Campaign Financing*, 18-19; Frank J. Sorauf, *Money in American Elections* (Glenview, IL: Scott, Foresman, 1988), 288; and Teresa Riordan, "Who's Campaigning?" *Common Cause Magazine* 13(May/June 1987), 14.

14. Herbert E. Alexander and Brian A. Haggerty, *Financing the 1984 Election* (Lexington, MA: Lexington Books, 1987), 174.

15. Drew, *Politics and Money*, 128.

16. Ibid., 129.

17. Bill Hogan and Alan Green, "Waltergate," *Regardie's*, July 1984, 26-37.

18. Thomas B. Edsall, "Mondale PAC Reveals Other Contributions," *Washington Post*, July 3, 1984, A7.

19. Ibid.; and Brooks Jackson, "Mondale Staff Issues Details on PAC Funds from Firms and Labor," *Wall Street Journal*, July 3, 1984, 46. The information released by Mondale's PAC is also reviewed in Alexander and Haggerty, *Financing the 1984 Election*, 174-175.

20. Ibid.

21. Jackson, "Mondale Staff Issues Details on PAC Funds," 46.

22. Ibid. and Alexander and Haggerty, *Financing the 1984 Election*, 175.

23. Riordan, "Who's Campaigning?" 12-19.

24. Ibid., 14-15. Riordan also notes that Bush's Fund for America's Future, according to Bush aides she interviewed, did not have a nonfederal account and that Gephardt's Effective Government Committee was encouraged to form

one but, as one campaign staff member admitted, "we felt that was too much" (Ibid., 15).

25. Ibid., 14.

26. Ibid., 15.

27. Ibid.

28. Ibid., 14-15.

29. Ibid., 14.

30. For a description of the statutory provisions governing tax-exempt, nonprofit foundations as compared to those applicable to political committees, see Thomas M. Durbin, *Legal Analysis of Specialized Multicandidate PACs and Private Tax-Exempt Foundations of Potential Federal Office Candidates*, CRSR No. 86-844A (Washington, DC: LC, August 12, 1986), 20-28.

31. Ibid., 23.

32. 2 U.S.C. 441a(a) and 431(1)(A).

33. According to reports filed with the FEC, the authorized committees of the four nominees in the last two presidential elections made only one contribution to a federal candidate. The Mondale for President Committee gave $1,000 to Congressman Frank Guarini of New Jersey in 1984. See FEC, Committee Index of Candidates Supported/Opposed (D Index), 1983-1984 and 1987-1988, computer printouts, November 22, 1988.

34. 2 U.S.C. 431(8), 434(a)(4), and 434(b)(4)(H)(i).

35. The discussion in this paragraph is based on a comparison of the figures in Tables 4.2, 4.4, and 4.6 (PAC receipts) with those in Tables 5.5, 5.6, and 5.7 (PAC contributions).

36. 2 U.S.C. 441a(a)(4); 11 C.F.R. 100.5(e)(3).

37. The legal provisions concerning the establishment of separate segregated funds are codified at 2 U.S.C. 431(7), 441b(b)(2), and 441b(b)(4)(D). For a discussion of this type of PAC and how it differs from a nonconnected PAC, see Joseph E. Cantor, *Political Action Committees: Their Evolution, Growth and Implications for the Political System*, CRSR No. 84-78 (Washington, DC: LC, November 6, 1981; updated April 30, 1984), 1-6 and 22-54.

38. 2 U.S.C. 441b(b)(2)(C) and 441b(b)(4)(D); 11 C.F.R. 114.1(b).

39. Cantor, *Political Action Committees*, 84-89 and 113-117.

Chapter 6

1. 11 C.F.R. 100.7(b)(1)(ii) and FEC, AO 1986-6: Expenditures by Committee Organized by a Potential Candidate, March 14, 1986, in *FECFG, Volume II: New Developments* (Chicago, IL: Commerce Clearinghouse, 1981; updated 1986), para. 5849.

2. Maxwell Glen, "Invading Michigan," *National Journal*, May 24, 1986, 1248.

3. Ibid.; and Thomas B. Edsall, "Bush's Bunch Is the Leader of the PACs," *Washington Post National Weekly Edition*, February 17, 1986, 12.

4. Edsall, "Bush's Bunch Is the Leader of the PACs," 12.

5. Glen, "Invading Michigan," 1248.

6. Edsall, "Bush's Bunch Is the Leader of the PACs," 12.

7. Letter from Jan W. Baran to Joan D.Aikens, January 22, 1986, FEC, AOR 1986-6.

8. Ibid., 3.

9. FEC, AO 1986-6, *FECFG*, para. 5849.

10. Ibid.

11. Paul Taylor, "Hey, Didn't We Just Finish a Presidential Election Campaign?" *Washington Post National Weekly Edition*, October 28, 1985, 11.

12. Ibid.; and Glen, "Invading Michigan," 1252.

13. Jack W. Germond and Jules Witcover, *Whose Broad Stripes and Bright Stars? The Trivial Pursuit of the Presidency 1988* (New York: Warner Brothers, 1989), 88.

14. Paul Taylor, "Bush's PAC Has Nerves of Steal," *Washington Post National Weekly Edition*, February 3, 1986, 13.

15. Edsall, "Bush's Bunch Is the Leader of the PACs," 12.

16. Taylor, "Hey, Didn't We Just Finish a Presidential Election Campaign?" 11.

17. Edsall, "Bush's Bunch Is the Leader of the PACs," 12.

18. Ronald Brownstein, "Sands of Time Move Quickly for Manager of Kemp's PAC," *National Journal,* July 13, 1985, 1627. Congressman Richard Gephardt also focused on Iowa in choosing a PAC director. He selected William Romjue, who ran Carter's 1980 Iowa caucus campaign. See Ronald Brownstein, "Getting an Early Start," *National Journal*, November 29, 1986, 2878.

19. Glen, "Invading Michigan," 1249.

20. Bill Hogan and Alan Green, "Waltergate," *Regardie's*, July 1984, 33.

21. William Phillips, executive director of the Fund for America's Future, once candidly admitted that "this is the first time that an individual who has a multicandidate PAC has this type of operation, or at least one this visible. When they [Congress] set up the laws and regulations, they really didn't take this type of operation into account." Quoted in Edsall, "Bush's Bunch Is the Leader of the PACs," 12.

22. R. Kenneth Godwin, *One Billion Dollars of Influence: The Direct Marketing of Politics* (Chatham, NJ: Chatham House, 1988), 10.

23. Larry J. Sabato, *The Rise of Political Consultants* (New York: Basic Books, 1981), 227.

24. R. Kenneth Godwin notes, for example, that Independent presidential candidate John Anderson mailed a fundraising appeal to his house list every 8 days during his 1980 campaign and the percentage of persons who gave a donation never fell. See "The Structure, Content, and Use of Political Direct Mail," *Polity* 20:3(Spring 1988), 528.

25. Sabato, *The Rise of Political Consultants*, 226.

26. Ibid., 235.

27. Godwin, *One Billion Dollars of Influence*, 11-12.

28. Ibid., 12; and Sabato, *The Rise of Political Consultants*, 252.

29. Sabato, *The Rise of Political Consultants*, 227.

30. Ibid., 252.

31. Ibid., 249.

32. See "Eleven Steps to Raise $2 Million By Direct Mail" in ibid., 228-229.

33. Roger Craver, "The Direct Mailbox: Launching an Effective Fundraising Effort," *Campaigns & Elections*, Spring 1985. Cited in Richard Armstrong, *The Next Hurrah: The Communications Revolution in American Politics* (New York: William Morrow, 1988), 70-73.

34. Ibid.

35. Godwin, *One Billion Dollars of Influence*, 12.

36. Sabato, *The Rise of Political Consultants*, 252.

37. Ibid., 253.

38. Ibid.

39. FEC, AO 1979-18: Receipts from Sale of List of Contributors, June 5, 1979, *FECFG* (1979), para. 5405. The commission's advisory opinion rulings on list purchases are summarized in FEC, *Record*, 11:12(December 1985), 6.

40. See FEC, AO 1981-46: Consequences of Exchanging Mailing Lists, November 16, 1981, *FECFG* (1982), para. 5629; and AO 1982-41: Three Party Exchange of Mailing Lists, June 9, 1982, *FECFG* (1982), para. 5681. The last option mentioned in this paragraph appears to be the way that Mondale's presidential committee obtained a copy of the list created by Mondale's Committee for the Future of America. See Hogan and Green, "Waltergate," 33.

41. The information in this paragraph is from Herbert E. Alexander, *Financing the 1980 Election* (Lexington, MA: Lexington Books, 1983), 147; and Maxwell Glen, "Starting a PAC May Be Candidates' First Step Down Long Road to 1988," *National Journal*, February 16, 1985, 376-377.

42. Hogan and Green, "Waltergate," 33.

43. Glen, "Invading Michigan," 1250.

44. Hogan and Green, "Waltergate," 33-34.

45. George Bush for President Committee, Quarterly Financial Report, April 15, 1987, Line 23, 25. A copy of this report is filed with the FEC.

46. Ibid., Line 23, 88, and Line 25, 8.

47. Maxwell Glen, "Running on a Shoestring," *National Journal*, April 25, 1987, 1002.

48. Ibid.

49. Pete du Pont for President Committee, Quarterly Financial Report, July 15, 1986, Schedule B-P, 7; and Pete du Pont for President Committee, Quarterly Financial Report, April 15, 1987, Schedule B-P, 18, and Schedule B-P: Fundraising, 4. Copies of these reports are filed with the FEC.

50. SO for the Mondale for President Committee, FEC Microfilm, Series 1984, Roll 218 at 6.

51. Dom Bonafede, "Mondale at the End of the Beginning of the Long Road to the Oval Office," *National Journal*, January 22, 1983, 162, and FEC, *Reports on Financial Activity 1983-84, Final Report: Presidential Pre-Nomination Campaigns* (Washington, DC: FEC, April 1986), 41. The FEC certified Mondale's eligibility for matching fund payments on April 14, 1983.

52. FEC, *Reports on Financial Activity 1983-84, Final Report*, 44. Ronald Reagan was not seriously challenged in his bid for renomination and began to submit contributions for matching funds certification later than the

Democratic candidates. He received his first installment of matching funds in March 1984, when the commission determined that his campaign had fulfilled the eligibility requirements.

53. Maxwell Glen, "Front-Loading the Race," *National Journal,* November 29, 1986, 2882.

54. See Gary R. Orren, "The Nomination Process: Vicissitudes of Candidate Selection," in Michael Nelson, ed., *The Elections of 1984* (Washington, DC: CQP, 1985), 55-65.

55. Peter Goldman and Tony Fuller, *The Quest for the Presidency 1984* (New York: Bantam Books, 1985), 55.

56. Dom Bonafede, "Mondale at the End of the Beginning," 164.

57. Hogan and Green, "Waltergate," 30.

58. Ibid., 32.

59. This discussion of Gephardt's travel is based on Ronald Brownstein, "Counting Down to 1988," *National Journal,* December 7, 1985, 2803; and Brownstein, "Getting an Early Start," 2880.

60. Brian Sullam, "The Cash Campaign," *New Republic,* March 14, 1988, 13; and Rhodes Cook, "Race for the White House: Early Is the Norm," *CQWR,* February 28, 1987, 380.

61. Sullam, "The Cash Campaign," 13.

62. Alexander, *Financing the 1980 Election,* 146.

63. Hogan and Green, "Waltergate," 32.

64. Brownstein, "Counting Down to 1988," 2802.

65. Glen, "Invading Michigan," 1250 and 1252.

66. Rule 8A(2) and (3) of the Democratic National Committee's *Delegate Selection Rules for the 1984 Democratic National Convention* (Washington, DC: Democratic National Committee, 1982), 9. For background on the adoption of these provisions, see David E. Price, *Bringing Back the Parties* (Washington, DC: CQP, 1984), 166-174 and 201-205.

67. Rule 8A(1) and (2) of the Democratic National Committee's *Delegate Selection Rules for the 1988 Democratic National Convention* (Washington, DC: Democratic National Committee, n.d. [1987]), 7.

68. The figures for 1980 and 1984 are found in Stephen J. Wayne, *The Road to the White House,* 3rd ed. (New York: St. Martin's Press, 1988), 106. The figures for 1988 are based on the author's calculations.

69. Ibid.

70. Figures based on a comparison of PAC contributions to federal candidates with the official delegate rolls of the 1988 Democratic and Republican national conventions.

Chapter 7

1. Thomas B. Edsall, "Mondale PAC Reveals Other Contributions," *Washington Post,* July 3, 1984, A7; and Brooks Jackson, "Mondale Staff Issues

Details on PAC Funds from Firms and Labor," *Wall Street Journal,* July 3, 1984, 46.

2. For a discussion of the role of large donors in the soft money operations conducted in conjunction with presidential general elections, see, among others, Ed Zuckerman,"'Soft Money': A New Life for Fatcats," *PACs and Lobbies,* January 16, 1985, 1-6; Richard L. Berke, "Prodded by Lobbying Groups, G.O.P. Reveals $100,000 Donors," *New York Times,* January 24, 1989, A16; Xandra Kayden, "Campaign Cash Now Sluicing to State Parties," *Los Angeles Times,* May 14, 1989, V3; and Jean Cobb, et al., "All the President's Donors," *Common Cause Magazine* 16:2(March/April 1990), 21-27 and 38-39.

3. Robertson's 1988 authorized campaign committee spent $22.9 million of the $23.1 million allowed under the spending ceiling (FEC, *Reports on Financial Activity 1987-88, Final Report: Presidential Pre-Nomination Campaigns* [Washington, DC, August 1989], 10). His PAC, the Committee for Freedom, spent approximately $684,000, for a total of approximately $23.6 million.

4. FEC, *Reports on Financial Activity 1987-88,* 10.

5. Herbert E. Alexander, "Financing the Presidential Elections, 1988," paper prepared for the Research Committee on Political Finance and Political Corruption, International Political Science Association, Tokyo, Japan, September 8-10, 1989, 4.

6. See, among others, Robert E. DiClerico and Eric M. Uslaner, *Few Are Chosen: Problems in Presidential Selection* (New York: McGraw-Hill, 1984); William Crotty and John S. Jackson III, *Presidential Primaries and Nominations* (Washington, DC: CQP, 1985); Herbert B. Asher, *Presidential Elections and American Politics,* 4th ed. (Chicago, IL: Dorsey Press, 1988); Maxwell Glen, "Front-Loading the Race," *National Journal,* November 29, 1986, 2882-2886; and Rhodes Cook, "Race for the White House: Early is the Norm," *CQWR,* February 28, 1987, 379-380.

7. Cook, "Race for the White House," 379.

8. Kenneth A. Bode and Carol F. Casey, "Party Reform: Revisionism Revisited," in Robert A. Goldwin, ed., *Political Parties in the Eighties* (Washington, DC, and Gambier, OH: AEI and Kenyon College, 1980), 18; and Martin Schram, *Running for President 1976: The Carter Campaign* (New York: Stein and Day, 1977), 52-71. See also Howard L. Reiter, *Selecting the President* (Philadelphia: University of Pennsylvania Press, 1985), 32-34.

9. Exploratory committees are not required to file complete disclosure reports with the FEC unless the individual whom the committee is assisting decides to become a candidate. In many instances, the date on which such a committee began can be determined from other documents filed with the FEC. In instances where no formal documents were filed with the commission, the date on which an exploratory committee began to operate was determined by reviewing the campaign committee's first disclosure report and identifying the date on which the committee made its first disbursements.

10. David Broder, "Endless Primaries Net Endless Candidacy," *Washington Post,* September 6, 1980, 5.

11. Asher, *Presidential Elections and American Politics,* 12.

12. Jeffrey Schmalz, "Cuomo Cites Factors in Decision," *New York Times,* February 21, 1987, 1.

13. "Sam Nunn's Decision," *Washington Post,* August 28, 1987, 22; and Warren Weaver, "Nunn Rules Out Race for the Presidency," *New York Times,* August 28, 1987, 10.

14. Ronald Elving, "Laxalt, Nunn Won't Run," *CQWR,* August 29, 1987, 2106.

15. T. R. Reid, "Too Late to Seek Presidency Schroeder Decides," *Washington Post,* September 29, 1987, 1.

16. For a discussion of these committees, see Chapter 4.

17. Tsongas signed an SO authorizing the formation of a principal campaign committee on March 7, 1991. This document was filed with the FEC on March 18, 1991.

18. Wilder formed an exploratory committee on March 27, 1991, according to the SO for the Wilder for President Exploratory Committee filed with the FEC. According to the first financial report filed by Harkin's principal campaign committee, an exploratory committee was formed in late May and initiated operations during the first week of June 1991 (Americans for Harkin, Quarterly Financial Report, October 15, 1991, Form 3P, 1).

19. FEC, "1992 Presidential Candidates Raise $2.7 Million by September 30," press release, October 30, 1991, 2. The total figure reported in this release includes funds raised by other candidates, including minor party candidates.

20. Robin Toner, "For Democratic Hopefuls, Race Turns to a Sprint," *New York Times,* October 20, 1991, 14.

21. Ross K. Baker, *The New Fat Cats* (New York: Priority Press, 1990) and Center for Responsive Politics, *Public Policy and Foundations: The Role of Politicians in Public Charities* (Washington, DC: CRP, 1987), 1.

Chapter 8

1. The most recent analyses of the congressional campaign finance reform debate can be found in David B. Magleby and Candice J. Nelson, *The Money Chase* (Washington, DC: Brookings, 1990); and Margaret Latus Nugent and John R. Johannes, eds., *Money, Elections, and Democracy: Reforming Congressional Campaign Finance* (Boulder, CO: Westview Press, 1990).

2. For a review of the campaign finance reform bills submitted in recent congresses, see Joseph E. Cantor, *Campaign Finance Reform: A Summary and Analysis of Legislative Proposals in the 98th and 99th Congresses,* CRSR No. 87-1 GOV (Washington, DC: LC, January 5, 1987) and *Campaign Finance Legislation in the 101st Congress,* CRSR No. 90-113 GOV (Washington, DC: LC, February 20, 1990; updated December 6, 1990).

3. Ross K. Baker discusses the rise of leadership PACs in *The New Fat Cats* (New York: Priority Press, 1989).

4. For the full text of the bill as passed, see *Congressional Record* 136 (August 1, 1990), S11648-S11663. The sections cited are at S11661 and S11658.

5. This provision was included in Section 105 of the bill. For a section-by-

section analysis of H.R. 5400, see *Congressional Record* 136 (August 3, 1990), H6848-H6854.

6. See Sections 102, 103, and 112 of the bill.

7. *Buckley* v. *Valeo*, 424 U.S. 1, 25.

8. The discussion of political corruption here and in the following paragraph is drawn from Larry J. Sabato, *Paying for Elections: The Campaign Finance Thicket* (New York: Priority Press, 1989), 2-5.

9. Larry Sabato, "Real and Imagined Corruption in Campaign Financing," in A. James Reichley, ed., *Elections American Style* (Washington, DC: Brookings, 1987), 172.

10. See David Adamany and George Agree, *Political Money* (Baltimore, MD: Johns Hopkins University Press, 1975), 84-115; and David Adamany, "PAC's and the Democratic Financing of Politics," *Arizona Law Review* 22(1980), 597-598.

11. For example, Herbert Alexander notes that an FEC survey of the 1976 congressional candidates revealed that 7 percent of all candidates thought their financial sources had been a major campaign issue and 11 percent thought they had been a minor issue. Alexander, *Financing the 1976 Election* (Washington, DC: CQP, 1979), 47-48.

12. Herbert Alexander and Brian A. Haggerty, *Financing the 1984 Election* (Lexington, MA: Lexington Books, 1987), 177-180.

13. See Jack W. Germond and Jules Witcover, *Whose Broad Stripes and Bright Stars? The Trivial Pursuit of the Presidency 1988* (New York: Warner Books, 1989), 284-286; and Christine M. Black and Thomas Oliphant, *All By Myself: The Unmaking of a Presidential Campaign* (Chester, CT: Globe Pequot Press, 1989), 109-111.

14. For example, in 1988 Kemp spent $6.2 million on fundraising, a large part of which was incurred in direct mail costs (Herbert E. Alexander and Monica Bauer, *Financing the 1988 Election* [Boulder, CO: Westview Press, 1991], 24).

15. This argument is supported by recent experience, which suggests that candidates are placing less emphasis on direct mail and relying more heavily on other fundraising mechanisms to produce most of their revenues. For example, Alexander and Bauer note that in 1988 Dukakis raised only $2.4 million of the $19.4 million he received in individual contributions through direct mail. Most of the $17 million difference was generated by 1,046 finance committee members who each raised $10,000 and by 203 members of the campaign's board of directors who each raised $25,000. Similarly, Bush based most of his fundraising on the solicitation of large contributions, raising $16.5 million from 16,500 contributors who each gave $1,000. See Alexander and Bauer, *Financing the 1988 Election*, 21-23.

16. See, among others, Larry J. Sabato, *The Rise of Political Consultants* (New York: Basic Books, 1981), 220-258; and R. Kenneth Godwin, *One Billion Dollars of Influence* (Chatham, NJ: Chatham House, 1988).

17. Martin Tolchin, "Cutting Funds for '92 Candidates is Proposed, but to Stiff Resistance," *New York Times*, February 12, 1991, A16; and Glen Craney,

"Public Cash for Presidential Bids Could Be in Jeopardy," *CQWR*, September 9, 1989, 2326-2329.

18. FEC, *Record* 17:7(July 1991), 1-3.

19. Craney, "Public Cash for Presidential Bids," 2327.

20. Rhodes Cook, "Campaign Fund Faces Shortfall As More Taxpayers Check No," *CQWR*, March 2, 1991, 559.

21. FEC, *Presidential Election Campaign Fund Focus Group Research* (Washington, DC, December 1990). This study was conducted by Market Decisions Corporation of Portland, Oregon.

22. FEC, *Record* 17:3(March 1991), 1-4, and 17:4(April 1991), 2.

23. FEC, *Annual Report 1990* (Washington, DC: FEC, 1991), 40.

24. Herbert Alexander, "The Price We Pay for Our Presidents," *Public Opinion* 11:6(March/April 1989), 47.

25. FEC, *Annual Report 1990*, 40.

26. FEC, *Legislative History of the Federal Election Campaign Act Amendments of 1974* (Washington, DC: GPO, 1977), 107.

27. See Michael Robinson, Clyde Wilcox, and Paul Marshall, "The Presidency: Not for Sale," *Public Opinion* 11:6(March/April 1989), 49-53; and David C. Nice, "Campaign Spending and Presidential Election Results," *Polity* 19:3(Spring 1987), 464-476.

28. L. Sandy Maisel, "Spending Patterns in Presidential Nominating Campaigns, 1976-1988," Center for American Political Studies, Occasional Paper 88-6 (Cambridge, MA: Harvard University, 1988), 7.

29. Hart reported expenditures of approximately $460,000 in Iowa. Mondale reported $680,000, but the FEC's postelection audit determined that his allocable spending in Iowa was actually $831,000.

30. FEC, *Annual Report 1990*, 39.

31. Ibid.

32. Tolchin, "Cutting Funds," A16.

33. Brooks Jackson, *Broken Promise: Why the Federal Election Commission Failed* (New York: Priority Press, 1990), 66.

34. Ibid., 66-67.

35. See, among others, Jackson, *Broken Promise*; Magleby and Nelson, *The Money Chase*, 188-192; and Frank P. Reiche, "Weakness of the FEC," in Nugent and Johannes, *Money, Elections, and Democracy*, 237-244.

36. Jackson, *Broken Promise*, 65.

37. Cited in Magleby and Nelson, *The Money Chase*, 189-190.

Selected Bibliography

FEC Documents and Materials

United States. FEC. *Advisory Opinions.* October 1982.

_____ . *Annual Report.* 1975-1990.

_____ . *Campaign Guide for Corporations and Labor Organizations.* September 1986.

_____ . *Campaign Guide for Nonconnected Committees.* June 1985.

_____ . Candidate Index of Supporting Documents (E Index). 1974-1988. Computer printouts, n.d.

_____ . *Candidate Registration.* September 1985.

_____ . Committee Index of Candidates Supported/Opposed (D Index). 1977-1990. Computers printouts, n.d.

_____ . Committee Index of Disclosure Documents (C Index). 1977-1990. Computer printouts, n.d.

_____ . *Disclosure Series No. 1: Presidential Pre-Nomination Receipts and Expenditures—1976 Campaign.* 1976.

_____ . *Disclosure Series No. 7: 1976 Presidential Campaign Receipts and Expenditures.* May 1977.

_____ . "FEC Announces Spending Limits for 1988 Presidential Race." Press release issued by the FEC Press Office, February 5, 1988.

_____ . "FEC Releases Final Report on 1988 Presidential Primary Campaigns." Press release issued by the FEC Press Office, August 25, 1989.

_____ . *The Federal Election Commission: The First 10 Years 1975-1985.* April 1985.

_____ . "Independent Expenditures of $21 Million Reported in '88, FEC Study Shows." Press release issued by the FEC Press Office, May 19, 1989.

_____ . *Index of Independent Expenditures, 1983-1984.* July 1985.

_____ . *Legislative History of Federal Election Campaign Act Amendments of 1974.* Washington, DC: GPO, 1977.

_____ . *Legislative History of Federal Election Campaign Act Amendments of 1976.* Washington, DC: GPO, 1977.

_____ . *Legislative History of Federal Election Campaign Act Amendments of 1979.* Washington, DC: GPO, 1983.

_____ . "1992 Presidential Candidates Raise $2.7 Million by September 30." Press release issued by the FEC Press Office, October 30, 1991.

_____. "PACs Associated with Recognized Individuals." Memorandum prepared by the FEC Press Office, n.d.

_____. *Presidential Election Campaign Fund Focus Group Research.* December 1990.

_____. Presidential Elections Series. Microfilm Collection. 1974-1988.

_____. "Presidential Primary Spending at $200 Million Mark." Press release issued by the FEC Press Office, August 18, 1988.

_____. *Record.* Vols. 4-18 (1978-1991).

_____. *Reports on Financial Activity, 1979-80, Final Report: Presidential Pre-Nomination Campaigns.* October 1981.

_____. *Reports on Financial Activity, 1983-84, Final Report: Presidential Pre-Nomination Campaigns.* April 1986.

_____. *Reports on Financial Activity, 1987-88, Final Report: Presidential Pre-Nomination Campaigns.* August 1989.

_____. Selected List of Receipts and Expenditures (G Index). 1985-1988. Computer printouts, n.d.

Books and Monographs

Adamany, David. *Financing Politics.* Madison: University of Wisconsin Press, 1969.

Adamany, David, and George Agree. *Political Money.* Baltimore, MD: Johns Hopkins University Press, 1975.

Alexander, Herbert E. *The Case for PACs.* Washington, DC: Public Affairs Council, 1983.

_____. *Financing Politics: Money, Elections, and Political Reform.* 3rd ed. Washington, DC: Congressional Quarterly Press, 1984.

_____. *Financing the 1972 Election.* Lexington, MA: Lexington Books, 1976.

_____. *Financing the 1976 Election.* Washington, DC: Congressional Quarterly Press, 1979.

_____. *Financing the 1980 Election.* Lexington, MA: Lexington Books, 1983.

_____. *"Soft Money" and Campaign Financing.* Washington, DC: Public Affairs Council, 1986.

Alexander, Herbert E., ed. *Comparative Political Finance in the 1980s.* Cambridge: Cambridge University Press, 1989.

_____. *Political Finance.* Beverly Hills, CA: Sage Publications, 1979.

Alexander, Herbert E., and Monica Bauer. *Financing the 1988 Election.* Boulder, CO: Westview Press, 1991.

Alexander, Herbert E., and Brian A. Haggerty. *The Federal Election Campaign Act: After a Decade of Political Reform.* Los Angeles, CA: Citizens' Research Foundation, 1981.

_____. *Financing the 1984 Election.* Lexington, MA: Lexington Books, 1987.

Americans for Democratic Action. *1984 Democratic Delegate Selection: An Overview.* Washington, DC: Americans for Democratic Action, n.d.

Armstrong, Richard. *The Next Hurrah: The Communications Revolution in American Politics.* New York: William Morrow, 1988.

Asher, Herbert B. *Presidential Elections and American Politics.* 4th ed. Chicago, IL: Dorsey Press, 1988.

Baker, Ross K. *The New Fat Cats: Members of Congress as Political Benefactors.* New York: Priority Press, 1989.

Black, Christine M., and Thomas Oliphant. *All By Myself: The Unmaking of a Presidential Campaign.* Chester, CT: Globe Pequot Press, 1989.

Buell, Emmett H., and Lee Sigelman, eds. *Nominating the President.* Knoxville: University of Tennessee Press, 1991.

Campbell, Colin, and Bert A. Rockman. *The Bush Presidency: First Appraisals.* Chatham, NJ: Chatham House, 1991.

Cantor, Joseph E. *Campaign Finance Legislation in the 101st Congress.* Congressional Research Service Report No. 90-113. Washington, DC: Library of Congress, February 20, 1990. Updated December 6, 1990.

_____. *Campaign Finance Reform: A Summary and Analysis of Legislative Proposals in the 98th and 99th Congresses.* Congressional Research Service Report No. 87-1.Washington, DC: Library of Congress, January 5, 1987.

_____. *Campaign Financing in Federal Elections: A Guide to the Law and Its Operation.* Congressional Research Service Report No. 87-469. Washington, DC: Library of Congress, August 8, 1986. Revised July 20, 1987.

_____. *The Evolution of and Issues Surrounding Independent Expenditures in Election Campaigns.* Congressional Research Service Report No. 82-87. Washington, DC: Library of Congress, May 5, 1982.

_____. *Political Action Committees: Their Evolution, Growth and Implications for the Political System.* Congressional Research Service Report No. 84-78. Washington, DC: Library of Congress, November 6, 1981. Updated April 30, 1984.

_____. *The Presidential Election Campaign Fund and Tax Checkoff.* Congressional Research Service Report No. 85-180. Washington, DC: Library of Congress, September 17, 1985.

Cantor, Joseph E., and Thomas M. Durbin. *Campaign Financing.* Congressional Research Service Issue Brief. Washington, DC: Library of Congress, December 15, 1987.

Center for Responsive Politics. *Money and Politics: Campaign Spending Out of Control.* Washington, DC: Center for Responsive Politics, 1983.

_____. *Public Policy and Foundations: The Role of Politicians in Public Charities.* Washington, DC: Center for Responsive Politics, 1987.

_____. *Soft Money—A Loophole for the '80s.* Washington, DC: Center for Responsive Politics, 1985.

_____. *Soft Money '88.* Washington, DC: Center for Responsive Politics, 1989.

Collins, Sheila D. *The Rainbow Challenge.* New York: Monthly Review Press, 1986.

Common Cause. *The Failure-to-Enforce Commission.* Washington, DC: Common Cause, 1989.

Congressional Quarterly. *Dollar Politics.* 3rd ed. Washington, DC: Congressional Quarterly Press, 1982.

Cook, Rhodes. *The First Hurrah: A 1992 Guide to the Nomination of the President. Congressional Quarterly Weekly Report Special Report.* September 7, 1991.

_____. *Race for the Presidency.* Washington, DC: Congressional Quarterly Press, 1987.

Crotty, William, and John S. Jackson III. *Presidential Primaries and Nominations.* Washington, DC: Congressional Quarterly Press, 1985.

Cutler, Lloyd N., Louis R. Cohen, and Roger M. Witten, eds. *Regulating Campaign Finance. The Annals of the American Academy of Political and Social Science* 486 (July 1986).

Democratic National Committee. *Delegate Selection Rules for the 1984 Democratic National Convention.* Washington, DC: Democratic National Committee, 1982.

_____. *Delegate Selection Rules for the 1988 Democratic National Convention.* Washington, DC: Democratic National Committee, 1987.

Derthick, Martha, and Paul J. Quirk. *The Politics of Deregulation.* Washington, DC: Brookings, 1985.

DiClerico, Robert E., and Eric M. Uslaner. *Few Are Chosen: Problems in Presidential Selection.* New York: McGraw-Hill, 1984.

Drew, Elizabeth. *American Journal: The Events of 1976.* New York: Random House, 1977.

_____. *Campaign Journal: The Political Events of 1983-1984.* New York: Macmillan, 1985.

_____. *Politics and Money: The New Road to Corruption.* New York: Macmillan, 1983.

Durbin, Thomas M. *Independent Expenditures in Presidential Elections.* Washington, DC: Library of Congress, July 17, 1985.

_____. *Legal Analysis of Specialized Multicandidate PACs and Private Tax-Exempt Foundations of Potential Federal Office Candidates.* Congressional Research Service Report No. 86-844A. Washington, DC: Library of Congress, August 12, 1986.

_____. *"Soft Money" in Federal Elections: A Legal Analysis.* Congressional Research Service Report No. 88-492A. Washington, DC: Library of Congress, July 14, 1988.

Germond, Jack W., and Jules Witcover. *Whose Broad Stripes and Bright Stars? The Trivial Pursuit of the Presidency 1988.* New York: Warner Books, 1989.

Godwin, R. Kenneth. *One Billion Dollars of Influence: The Direct Marketing of Politics.* Chatham, NJ: Chatham House, 1988.

Goldman, Peter, and Tony Fuller. *The Quest for the Presidency 1984.* New York: Bantam Books, 1985.

Goldstein, Michael L. *Guide to the 1988 Presidential Election.* Washington, DC: Congressional Quarterly Press, 1988.

_____. *Guide to the 1992 Presidential Election.* Washington, DC: Congressional Quarterly Press, 1991.

Gorman, Joseph B. *The 1984 Democratic National Convention: National and State Party Rules and State Legislation Concerning the Election of*

Delegates and Alternates. Congressional Research Service Report No. 84-25 GOV. Washington, DC: Library of Congress, 1984.

Harris, Richard A., and Sidney M. Milkis. *The Politics of Regulatory Change.* New York: Oxford University Press, 1989.

Harvard Campaign Finance Study Group. *An Analysis of the Impact of the Federal Election Campaign Act, 1972-1978.* Final Report to the Committee on House Administration of the U.S. House of Representatives. Washington, DC: GPO, 1979.

_____. *Financing Presidential Campaigns: An Examination of the Ongoing Effects of the Federal Election Campaign Laws upon the Conduct of Presidential Campaigns.* Cambridge, MA: Institute of Politics, Harvard University, 1982.

Heard, Alexander. *The Costs of Democracy.* Chapel Hill: University of North Carolina Press, 1960.

Heard, Alexander, and Michael Nelson, eds. *Presidential Selection.* Durham, NC: Duke University Press, 1987.

Hess, Stephen. *The Presidential Campaign.* 3rd ed. Washington, DC: Brookings, 1988.

Hirschfield, Robert S., ed. *Selection/Election: A Forum on the American Presidency.* New York: Aldine, 1982.

Jackson, Brooks. *Broken Promise: Why the Federal Election Commission Failed.* New York: Priority Press, 1990.

_____. *Honest Graft: Big Money and the American Political Process.* New York: Knopf, 1988.

Johnston, Michael. *Political Corruption and Public Policy in America.* Monterey, CA: Brooks/Cole, 1982.

Kessel, John H. *Presidential Campaign Politics.* 2nd ed. Homewood, IL: Dorsey Press, 1984.

Lipset, Seymour Martin, and William Schneider. *The Confidence Gap.* New York: Free Press, 1983.

Magleby, David B., and Candice J. Nelson. *The Money Chase.* Washington, DC: Brookings, 1990.

Malbin, Michael J., ed. *Money and Politics in the United States.* Washington, DC: American Enterprise Institute, 1984.

_____. *Parties, Interest Groups, and Campaign Finance Laws.* Washington, DC: American Enterprise Institute, 1980.

Maisel, L. Sandy. *Parties and Elections in America.* New York: Random House, 1987.

Maisel, L. Sandy, ed. *The Parties Respond: Changes in the American Party System.* Boulder, CO: Westview Press, 1990.

Marshall, Thomas R. *Presidential Nominations in a Reform Age.* New York: Praeger, 1981.

Matasar, Ann B. *Corporate PACs and Federal Campaign Financing Laws.* New York: Quorum Books, 1986.

Mutch, Robert E. *Campaigns, Congress, and Courts: The Making of Federal Campaign Finance Law.* New York: Praeger, 1988.

National Commission on Elections. *Choosing the President.* Washington, DC: National Commission on Elections, 1985.

Nelson, Michael, ed. *The Elections of 1984.* Washington, DC: Congressional Quarterly Press, 1985.

_____. *The Elections of 1988.* Washington, DC: Congressional Quarterly Press, 1989.

Nugent, Margaret Latus, and John R. Johannes, eds. *Money, Elections, and Democracy: Reforming Congressional Campaign Finance.* Boulder, CO: Westview Press, 1990.

Orren, Gary R., and Nelson W. Polsby, eds. *Media and Momentum: The New Hampshire Primary and Nomination Politics.* Chatham, NJ: Chatham House, 1987.

Palmer, James A., and Edward D. Feigenbaum. *Campaign Finance Law 86: A Summary of State Campaign Finance Laws.* Washington, DC: National Clearinghouse on Election Administration, 1986.

Perkins-Coie. *Non-Profit Organizations, Public Policy, and the Political Process: A Guide to the Internal Revenue Code and Federal Election Campaign Act.* Washington, DC: Citizens Vote, December 1987.

Polsby, Nelson W. *Consequences of Party Reform.* New York: Oxford University Press, 1983.

Polsby, Nelson W., and Aaron Wildavsky. *Presidential Elections.* 7th ed. New York: Free Press, 1988.

Pomper, Gerald M., ed. *The Election of 1984.* Chatham, NJ: Chatham House, 1985.

_____. *The Election of 1988.* Chatham House, NJ: Chatham House, 1989.

Price, David E. *Bringing Back the Parties.* Washington, DC: Congressional Quarterly Press, 1984.

Ranney, Austin. *Curing the Mischiefs of Faction: Party Reform in America.* Berkeley and Los Angeles: University of California Press, 1975.

_____. *The Federalization of Presidential Primaries.* Washington, DC: American Enterprise Institute, 1978.

Ranney, Austin, ed. *The American Elections of 1980.* Washington, DC: American Enterprise Institute, 1981.

Reed, Adolph L. *The Jesse Jackson Phenomenon.* New Haven, CT: Yale University Press, 1986.

Reichley, A. James. *Elections American Style.* Washington, DC: Brookings, 1987.

Reiter, Howard L. *Selecting the President.* Philadelphia: University of Pennsylvania Press, 1985.

Sabato, Larry J. *PAC Power: Inside the World of Political Action Committees.* New York: W. W. Norton, 1984.

_____. *Paying for Elections: The Campaign Finance Thicket.* New York: Priority Press, 1989.

_____. *The Rise of Political Consultants.* New York: Basic Books, 1981.

Schlozman, Kay Lehman, ed. *Elections in America.* Boston, MA: Allen and Unwin, 1987.

Schneider, Sandra K., ed. *Campaign Finance, Ethics and Lobby Law Blue Book 1986-87.* Lexington, KY: Council of State Governments, 1986.

Schram, Martin. *Running for President 1976: The Carter Campaign.* New York: Stein and Day, 1977.

Sorauf, Frank J. *Money in American Elections.* Glenview, IL: Scott, Foresman, 1988.

Tolchin, Susan J., and Martin Tolchin. *Dismantling America: The Rush to Deregulate.* New York: Oxford University Press, 1983.

U.S. Congress. House Committee on Ways and Means. *Lobbying and Political Activities of Tax-Exempt Organizations: Hearings before the Subcommittee on Oversight.* H. Rpt. 100-15. 100th Cong., 1st Sess. Washington, DC: GPO, 1987.

_____. Senate Committee on Rules and Administration. *Federal Election Campaign Act Amendments of 1979.* Sen. Rpt. 96-319. 96th Cong., 1st Sess. Washington, DC: GPO, 1979.

Walters, Ronald W. *Black Presidential Politics in America: A Strategic Approach.* Albany: State University of New York Press, 1988.

Wayne, Stephen J. *The Road to the White House.* 3rd ed. New York: St. Martin's Press, 1988.

Whitaker, Paige L. *Federal Election Commission.* Congressional Research Service Issue Brief. Washington, DC: Library of Congress, October 18, 1989.

Winebrenner, Hugh. *The Iowa Precinct Caucuses.* Ames: Iowa State University Press, 1987.

Witcover, Jules. *Marathon: The Pursuit of the Presidency 1972-1976.* New York: Viking Press, 1977.

Zuckerman, Edward P. *Almanac of Federal PACs: 1990.* Washington, DC: Amward, 1990.

Articles

Abas, Brian. "Hart Has a Better Idea." *Westword,* November 13-19, 1985, 8-14.

Adamany, David. "The New Faces of American Politics." *The Annals of the American Academy of Political and Social Science* 486 (July 1986): 12-33.

_____. "PAC's and the Democratic Financing of Politics." *Arizona Law Review* 22 (1980): 569-602.

_____. "Political Finance in Transition." *Polity* 14:2 (Winter 1981): 314-331.

_____. "The Sources of Money: An Overview." *The Annals of the American Academy of Political and Social Science* 425 (May 1976): 17-32.

Adamany, David, and George Agree. "Election Campaign Financing: The 1974 Reforms." *Political Science Quarterly* 90 (Summer 1975): 201-220.

Aikens, Joan. "The Federal Election Commission and Enforcement." *Federal Bar and News Journal* 34 (February 1987): 59-62.

Alexander, Herbert E. "American Presidential Elections Since Public Funding, 1976-1984." In *Comparative Political Finance in the 1980s,* edited by Herbert E. Alexander. Cambridge: Cambridge University Press, 1989.

_____. "Election Reform in Its Second Stage: Momentum Passing from Reformers to Powerbrokers." In *Political Finance,* edited by Herbert E. Alexander. Beverly Hills, CA: Sage Publications, 1979.

_____. "Financing the Presidential Elections, 1988." Paper prepared for the Research Committee on Political Finance and Political Corruption, International Political Science Association. Tokyo, Japan, September 8-10, 1989.

_____. "The Folklore of Buying Elections." *Business and Society Review* 2 (Summer 1972): 48-53.

_____. "The Impact of the Federal Election Campaign Act on the 1976 Presidential Campaign: The Complexities of Compliance." *Emory Law Journal* 29 (Spring 1980): 315-357.

_____. "Making Sense About Dollars in the 1980 Presidential Campaigns." In *Money and Politics in the United States,* edited by Michael J. Malbin. Washington, DC: American Enterprise Institute, 1984.

_____. "The Price We Pay for Our Presidents." *Public Opinion* (American Enterprise Institute) 11 (March/April 1989): 46-48.

Alexander, Herbert E., and Brian A. Haggerty. "Misinformation on Media Money." *Public Opinion* (American Enterprise Institute) 10 (May/June 1988): 5-7, 59.

Baran, Jan W. "The Federal Election Commission: A Guide for Corporate Counsel." *Arizona Law Review* 22 (1980): 519-538.

Barnes, James A. "Hard Questions on Soft Money." *National Journal,* April 8, 1989, 864.

_____. "Looking for Credibility." *National Journal,* April 25, 1989, 986-987.

Benenson, Bob. "In the Struggle for Influence, Members' PACs Gain Ground." *Congressional Quarterly Weekly Report,* August 2, 1986, 1751-1754.

Berman, Michael S. "Living with the FECA: Confessions of a Sometime Treasurer." *The Annals of the American Academy of Political and Social Science* 486 (July 1986): 121-131.

Bibby, John F. "Campaign Finance Reform: Expanding Government's Role or the Parties' Role?" *Commonsense* 6 (December 1983): 1-15.

Bode, Kenneth A., and Carol F. Casey. "Party Reform: Revisionism Revisited." In *Political Parties in the Eighties,* edited by Robert A. Goldwin. Washington, DC, and Gambier, OH: American Enterprise Institute and Kenyon College, 1980.

Bonafede, Dom. "Mondale at the End of the Beginning of the Long Road to the Oval Office." *National Journal,* January 22, 1983, 162-165.

Brownstein, Ronald. "Counting Down to 1988." *National Journal,* December 7, 1985, 2802-2803.

_____. "Getting an Early Start." *National Journal,* November 29, 1986, 2876-2881.

_____. "The Lessons of 1984." *National Journal,* July 20, 1985, 1666-1670.

_____. "The Money Hunt." *National Journal,* June 7, 1986, 1375-1379.

_____. "The Sands of Time Move Quickly for Managers of Kemp's PAC." *National Journal,* July 13, 1985, 1627.

_____. "Soft Money." *National Journal,* December 7, 1985, 2828.

Brownstein, Ronald, and Maxwell Glen. "Money in the Shadows." *National Journal*, March 15, 1986, 632-637.

Budde, Bernadette A. "The Practical Role of Corporate PAC's in the Political Process." *Arizona Law Review* 22 (1980): 555-568.

"Campaign Finance Reform." *Congressional Digest* 69 (October 1990): 228-256.

"Campaign Financing: A Major Issue Forum." *Congressional Research Service Review* 8 (April 1987): 1-24.

Castle, David S. "A Southern Regional Primary in 1988: Will It Work as Planned?" *Election Politics* 4 (Summer 1987): 6-10.

Cobb, Jean. "We're Not Campaigning Either!" *Common Cause Magazine* 13 (May/June 1987): 16-19, 36-37.

Cobb, Jean, Jeff Denny, Vicki Kemper, and Viveca Novak. "All the President's Donors." *Common Cause Magazine* 16 (May/June 1990): 21-27.

Cohen, Richard E. "Spending Independently." *National Journal*, December 6, 1986, 2932-2934.

Cohen, Richard E., and Carol Matlack. "All-Purpose Loophole." *National Journal*, December 9, 1989, 2980-2987.

Colella, Cynthia Cates. "Campaign Finance: The High Cost of Democracy." In *The Transformation in American Politics: Implications for Federalism*. Advisory Commission on Intergovernmental Relations Report No. A-106. Washington, DC: Advisory Commission on Intergovernmental Relations, August 1986.

Cook, Rhodes. "Campaign Fund Faces Shortfall As More Taxpayers Check No." *Congressional Quarterly Weekly Report*, March 2, 1991, 558-559.

_____. "Cuomo's Pullout May Boost Dark Horse Candidates." *Congressional Quarterly Weekly Report*, February 21, 1987, 332.

_____. "In '88 Contest, It's What's Up Front That Counts." *Congressional Quarterly Weekly Report*, August 23, 1986, 1997-2002.

_____. "Jackson, Democrats: Marriage on the Rocks?" *Congressional Quarterly Weekly Report*, April 26, 1986, 929-930.

_____. "The Nominating Process." In *The Elections of 1988*, edited by Michael Nelson. Washington, DC: Congressional Quarterly Press, 1989.

_____. "One Side Is Clearer, the Other Still Murky." *Congressional Quarterly Weekly Report*, March 12, 1988, 636-646.

_____. "Race for the White House: Early Is the Norm." *Congressional Quarterly Weekly Report*, February 28, 1987, 379-380.

Corrado, Anthony J. "An Old Game in a New Arena: PACs as Presidential Campaign Organizations." Paper presented at the 1990 Annual Meeting of the Western Political Science Association, San Francisco, CA, March 22-24, 1990.

_____. "The Pre-Campaign Campaign: The Role of PACs in Presidential Nomination Contests." Paper presented at the 1990 Annual Meeting of the New England Political Science Association, Portland, ME, April 20-21, 1990.

_____. "Presidential Candidate PACs and the Future of Campaign Finance Reform." In *The Quest for National Office*, edited by Stephen J. Wayne and Clyde Wilcox. New York: St. Martin's Press, 1992.

Corrado, Anthony J., and L. Sandy Maisel. "Campaigning for Presidential Nominations: The Experience with State Spending Ceilings, 1976-1984." Center for American Political Studies, Occasional Paper 88-4. Cambridge, MA: Harvard University, 1988.

Cox, Archibald. "Constitutional Issues in the Regulation of the Financing of Election Campaigns." Cleveland State Law Review 31 (Summer 1981): 395-418.

Craney, Glen. "Public Cash for Presidential Bids Could Be in Jeopardy." Congressional Quarterly Weekly Report, September 9, 1989, 2326-2329.

David, Paul T. "The Federal Election Commission: Origins and Early Activities." National Civic Review 65 (June 1976): 278-283.

Drew, Elizabeth. "Politics and Money II." The New Yorker, December 13, 1982, 57-111.

Easterbrook, Gregg. "The Perpetual Campaign." The Atlantic Monthly 251 (January 1983): 27-38.

Edwards, George C. III. "George Bush and the Public Presidency." In The Bush Presidency: First Appraisals, edited by Colin Campbell and Bert A. Rockman. Chatham, NJ: Chatham House, 1991.

Epstein, Edwin M. "The Emergence of Political Action Committees." In Political Finance, edited by Herbert E. Alexander. Beverly Hills, CA: Sage Publications, 1979.

Frulla, David Earl. "Soft Money: The Outlook for Reform." Journal of Law and Politics 3 (1987): 769-809.

Glen, Maxwell. "Front-Loading the Race." National Journal, November 29, 1986, 2882-2886.

_____. "Invading Michigan." National Journal, May 24, 1986, 1248-1253.

_____. "Kennedy's Early Departure from Race Frees Up Donations for Rest of Field." National Journal, January 25, 1986, 208-212.

_____. "Running on a Shoestring." National Journal, April 25, 1987, 998-1002.

_____. "Spending Independently." National Journal, July 21, 1986, 1533-1537.

_____. "Starting a PAC May Be Candidates' First Step Down Long Road to 1988." National Journal, February 16, 1985, 374-377.

Godwin, R. Kenneth. "The Structure, Content, and Use of Political Direct Mail." Polity 20:3 (Spring 1988): 527-538.

"GOPAC Bares Financial Data." PACs and Lobbies, October 16, 1985, 5.

Hogan, Bill, and Alan Green. "Waltergate." Regardie's, July 1984, 26-37.

Ifshin, David. "An Analysis of the Impact of the Federal Election Campaign Act on the 1976 Democratic Presidential Primary." Santa Clara Law Review 18 (1978): 1-72.

Jones, Charles O. "Nominating 'Carter's Favorite Opponent': The Republicans in 1980." In The American Elections of 1980, edited by Austin Ranney. Washington, DC: American Enterprise Institute, 1981.

Kayden, Xandra. "Regulating Campaign Finance: Consequences for Interests and Institutions." In Presidential Selection, edited by Alexander Heard and Michael Nelson. Durham, NC: Duke University Press, 1987.

Kirschten, Dick. "Testing the Waters." National Journal, July 20, 1985, 1671-1674.

Kopkind, Andrew. "The 'New Voters' Find Their Voice." *The Nation,* November 7, 1987, 520-522.

Lengle, James I. "Democratic Party Reforms: The Past as Prologue to the 1988 Campaign." *Journal of Law and Politics* 4 (1987): 261-272.

"Limiting Political Action Committees." *Congressional Digest* 66 (February 1987): 33-64.

Maisel, L. Sandy. "Spending Patterns in Presidential Nominating Campaigns, 1976-1988." Center for American Political Studies, Occasional Paper 88-6. Cambridge, MA: Harvard University, 1988.

Marshall, Thomas R. "Caucuses and Primaries: Measuring Reform in the Presidential Nomination Process." *American Politics Quarterly* 7 (April 1979): 155-174.

Matlack, Carol. "Backdoor Spending." *National Journal,* October 8, 1988, 2516-2519.

_____. "Dukakis's Cash Cow." *National Journal,* April 23, 1988, 1068-1071.

_____. "Frayed Finance Law." *National Journal,* March 5, 1988, 591-594.

Nelson, Candice J. "Campaign Finance in Presidential and Congressional Elections." *The Political Science Teacher* 1 (Summer 1988): 1, 4-6.

Nice, David C. "Campaign Spending and Presidential Election Results." *Polity* 19:3 (Spring 1987): 464-476.

Noble, John F. "Soft Money." *Campaigns and Elections* 5 (Summer 1984): 44.

Norrander, Barbara. "Super Tuesday and Candidate Strategies." Paper presented at the 1990 Annual Meeting of the American Political Science Association, San Francisco, California, August 30-September 2, 1990.

O'Connor, Colleen. "Who's Afraid of the FEC?" *Washington Monthly* 18 (March 1986): 22-26.

Oldacker, William C. "Of Philosophers, Foxes, and Finances: Can the FEC Ever Do an Adequate Job?" *The Annals of the American Academy of Political and Social Science* 486 (July 1986): 132-145.

"Opinion Roundup." *Public Opinion* (American Enterprise Institute) 10 (September/October 1987): 38-39.

Orren, Gary P. "The Nomination Process: Vicissitudes of Candidate Selection." In *The Election of 1984,* edited by Michael Nelson. Washington, D.C.: Congressional Quarterly Press, 1985.

_____. "Presidential Campaign Finance: Its Impact and Future." *Commonsense* 4 (1981): 50-66.

Pomper, Gerald M. "New Rules and New Games in Presidential Nominations." *Journal of Politics* 41 (1979): 784-805.

"Presidential PAC Wars Begin in Anticipation of '88 Primary." *Campaign Practices Reports,* January 27, 1986, 6.

"Reagan's 1980 Campaign Fund is History." *PACs and Lobbies,* September 18, 1985, 6-7.

Reiter, Howard L. "The Limitations of Reform: Changes in the Nominating Process." *British Journal of Political Science* 15 (October 1985): 399-417.

Rice, Tom W. "The Determinants of Candidate Spending in Presidential Primaries: Advice for the States." *Presidential Studies Quarterly* 12 (Fall 1982): 590-597.

Riordan, Teresa. "Who's Campaigning?" *Common Cause Magazine* 13 (May/June 1987): 12-15, 17-19.

Robinson, Michael, Clyde Wilcox, and Paul Marshall. "The Presidency: Not For Sale." *Public Opinion* (American Enterprise Institute) 11 (March/April 1989): 49-53.

Rosenberg, Tina. "Diminishing Returns: The False Promise of Direct Mail." *Washington Monthly* 15 (June 1983): 32-38.

Rosenthal, Albert J. "Campaign Financing and the Constitution." *Harvard Journal on Legislation* 9 (1972): 359-423.

_____. "The Constitution and Campaign Finance Regulation after *Buckley* v. *Valeo*." *The Annals of the American Academy of Political and Social Science* 425 (May 1976): 124-133.

Sabato, Larry J. "Real and Imagined Corruption in Campaign Financing." In *Elections American Style*, edited by A. James Reichley. Washington, DC: Brookings, 1987.

Samuelson, Robert J. "The Campaign Finance Reform Failure." *The New Republic*, September 5, 1983, 28-36.

Schapiro, Walter, with Howard Fineman. "Reagan's Shadow Campaign." Newsweek, August 1, 1983, 26.

Sendrow, Susan G. "The Federal Election Campaign Act and Presidential Election Campaign Fund Act: Problems in Defining and Regulating Independent Expenditures." *Arizona State Law Journal* 1981: 977-1005.

Sorauf, Frank J. "Caught in a Political Thicket: The Supreme Court and Campaign Finance." *Constitutional Commentary* 3 (Winter 1986): 97-121.

Stanley, Harold W., and Charles D. Hadley. "The Southern Presidential Primary: Regional Intentions with National Implications." *Publius* 17 (Summer 1987): 83-100.

Sullam, Brian. "The Cash Campaign." *The New Republic*, March 14, 1988, 9-13.

"Take It to the Limit—And Beyond." *Time*, February 15, 1988, 19-20.

Weisberg, Jacob. "Rainbow Warrior." *New Republic*, May 12, 1986, 10-12.

Wertheimer, Fred. "Campaign Finance Reform: The Unfinished Agenda." *The Annals of the American Academy of Political and Social Science* 486 (July 1986): 86-102.

Wilcox, Clyde. "Organizational Variables and the Contribution Behavior of Large PACs: A Longitudinal Analysis." *Political Behavior* 11 (1989): 157-173.

_____. "Share the Wealth: Contributions by Congressional Incumbents to the Campaigns of Other Candidates." *American Politics Quarterly* 17 (October 1981): 386-408.

Wilcox, Clyde, and Marc Genest. "Member PACs as Strategic Actors." *Polity* 23:3 (Spring 1991): 461-470.

Wright, J. Skelly. "Money and the Pollution of Politics: Is the First Amendment an Obstacle to Political Equality?" *Columbia Law Review* 82 (May 1982): 609-645.

Zuckerman, Ed. "Opinion Opened 'Soft Money' Spigot for PACs." *PACs and Lobbies*, June 9, 1985, 1-4.

_____. "'Soft Money': A New Life for Fatcats." *PACs and Lobbies*, January 16, 1985: 1-6.

About the Book and Author

Ronald Reagan started it, back in 1977. George Bush perfected the art in 1988. In the 1980s and 1990s, Democrats as well as Republicans running for president (or thinking of doing so), have followed Reagan's lead in establishing precandidacy PACs as a way of raising more money faster, without the regulatory rigors laid down by Congress and the Federal Election Commission.

Marshalling years of experience on the campaign trail, Anthony Corrado has documented for the first time the fundraising and spending patterns of presidential candidates who feel forced to circumvent the system in order to amass enough funds to mount a contemporary presidential campaign. He shows how a variety of factors—contribution limits, the delegate selection process, expenditure ceilings, and costly campaign strategies—have combined to push candidates to establish PACs to raise and spend money on campaign activities well in advance of an official declaration to run. These lofty-sounding organizations—such as Bush's "Fund for America's Future" and Gephardt's "Effective Government Committee"—operate as "shadow campaigns" throughout the nomination process and often live on beyond the candidate's formal bid for office.

The year 1992 is a special case in presidential election year history because of the strong Bush incumbency, a reluctant Democratic challenge, and a series of foreign policy crises. Corrado explains why precandidacy PACs persist and how they are likely to grow (in number and clout) if an array of bold new reform measures is not implemented prior to the next open presidential election in 1996. After showing how the Federal Election Campaign Act not only permits but in fact inspires presidential candidates to break the laws governing campaign finance, Corrado points out how, ironically, less regulation may yield greater compliance and a more effective nomination process in the 1990s and beyond.

Anthony Corrado is assistant professor of government at Colby College and author of numerous articles on campaign regulation and finance. He has extensive experience in state and federal elections and served on the campaigns of Carter, Mondale, and Dukakis.

Index